Praise for Forever Herself

"The memoir recounts Stevens' childhood memories, but it's truly about Berthella, with each chapter painting another stroke in a portrait of an exceptional woman. Stevens...has a gift for describing ordinary things in beautiful, artistic ways... Each chapter draws the reader in."

— *Kirkus Reviews*

"The words *maverick* and *mother* are not usually synonymous, but in FOREVER HERSELF, Kerry L Stevens' "love letter" to his mother, ...Stevens beautifully fuses memories of his childhood with Berthella's strength, poetry and essays. The combination inspires the discovery of our individual uniqueness and the courage to be our own person."

— Sylvia Dickey Smith, award-winning author of the *Sidra Smart Mystery Series, A War of Her Own,* and *Original Cyn*

"Forever Herself is a son's stirring tribute to his Indiana mother."

— Philip Gulley, author of the *Harmony series*

FOREVER HERSELF

A Son's Memoir of a
Remarkable Woman

KERRY L STEVENS
with BERTHELLA STEVENS

This is a work of creative nonfiction. The events are portrayed to the
best of the authors' memory and research. While all the stories in this
book are true, some people's names have been changed to preserve
their privacy, and some unknown details have been filled in through
informed imagination.

Published by
Six Points Publishing
www.sixpointspublishing.com

Cover Design by: JD Smith Design, jdsmith-design.com
Editor-in-Chief: Mindy Reed
Interior Design by: Danielle H. Acee, authorsassistant.com

Cataloging-in Publication Data
Stevens, Kerry L w. 1958–
Forever Herself/Kerry L Stevens
p.   cm.

ISBN: 978-1-7324266-0-3
Library of Congress Control Number: 2018909283
1. Berthella Stevens—memoir 2. Family Life—20th Century
3.Mother/Son—relationships 4.American woman—strengths—struggles 5. Rural Life—America

PN 6014 S48 2018   920 ST

FOREVER HERSELF

A Son's Memoir of a
Remarkable Woman

CONTENTS

To my mother, Berthella Stevens

Introduction

My mother, Berthella May (Whitmyer) Stevens, was a remarkable woman, filled with life and ahead of her time. While some women of her era were stifled, she found ways to express herself.

Among her many talents, Mom was a prolific writer. While she wrote out of sheer joy, she dreamed of sharing her words in a published book. Sadly, she died in 2011 without attaining that goal. Her story is so endearing, and her poetry and prose so enchanting, I felt compelled to curate her works with my own remembrances into this book.

Unaware we would one day author a book together, Mom bequeathed to me her personal papers, yellowed with age. These pages were the best gift. Through them, she swept back into my life. I felt her presence in those dry papers she once held in her hands as she scribbled, erased, and revised. As I read her writing, I heard her voice telling me the stories and saw the expressions on her face. Through her tender words, her heart spoke to mine. Each day, as I sat reflecting and writing, she sat beside me, talking, laughing, and crying; I did the same. It's been the most amazing journey to live so closely with someone who has never been so far away.

Mom was in love with books and said they were the greatest things ever invented. With a book, a person can record her thoughts, ideas, and concepts on page after page so they can be passed on from one generation to another. "As long as you have that book," she said, "those thoughts live forever."

My mother's dream is now fulfilled. This is her memoir you hold in your hands. Its pages are filled with stories I experienced, heard, read, or created through informed imagination—told through the seasons of her life. It begins with the promises of her spring then unfurls to the fullness of summer. Shades of autumn reveal the maturation of relationships, finally yielding to the winter we must all face.

Books bring so much to people. They can make us think, laugh, cry, or bring inspiration. I hope you experience some of these emotions as you read.

Books can also be an expression of love and appreciation. For me, this memoir is an everlasting love letter to my mother.

—Kerry L Stevens

SPRING

Spring Prelude

Spring is the dawn of promise. It creates life when a tender shoot emerges from the dormant seed, eager to turn its leaves to the warming sun.

What will become of this seedling? Will she grow strong and healthy? Will the bees and butterflies be drawn to her beauty and fragrance? Will she be fruitful and release many offspring to the winds? Or will weeds and stormy weather choke out her life?

During the unpredictability of her spring, my mother struggled for breath as a child of the Great Depression and its flood of poverty. As a child of divorce and sexism, she withered in the drought of abandonment. But the vitality of spring also nourished her as a child of nature and God. These forces were her seedbed, bending and braiding her into a strong and independent woman.

I love my mother. Spring is the beginning of this love letter to her.

CHAPTER 1

A Leap for Love

"It was the summer of 1943 when most boys were at war, when I met him at the lake on my grandparents' farm in Southern Michigan," reminisced my mother, Berthella Whitmyer. "He was tall, tan, and slender, with a body that showed hard work. His blue eyes smiled in a friendly, mischievous way. I was struck by his unconscious attractiveness of goodness: good health, good looks, and good manners. And he was a farm boy!"

The meeting shook my mother's world. Then twenty-three years old, and a city girl, she'd dreamed of marrying a farm boy since she was a teen. She'd fallen in love with the summers spent on her grandparents' farm and wanted that life for her own. This blue-eyed man named Mick, the same age as her, seemed to have it all. Mom didn't want to miss this opportunity. But as Mick recalled, if he had not taken a dangerous leap, they would never have met.

"My friend, Robert, and I were driving around on a Sunday afternoon two weeks before I met Berthella," Mick said. "We ran across two other guys doing the same thing. They mentioned there were a couple of good-looking girls visiting Helen, a mutual friend. Robert drove by Helen's house but didn't want to stop. I wanted to meet the girls, so I opened the car door and jumped out. I figured that when my feet hit the ground, I'd start running. Instead, I went head-over-heels, rolling down the roadside. When I finally stopped rolling and saw no bones sticking out, I dusted off my clothes and walked up to Helen's house."

Although my mother was not at Helen's house that day, her sister, Joy, was there. When Robert eventually came back to pick up Mick, Robert invited Joy to go roller skating the next weekend. And when Joy and he returned home after their roller skating date, Robert met my mother.

"Do you have any friends I could go out with?" Mom asked. Robert said yes and set up a blind date between Mom and Mick. It was a picnic with a group of friends on Lafferty Lake, my mother's sacred space on her grandparents' farm. But there was a problem. Robert forgot to tell Mick it was a blind date. Mick thought it was just a picnic and an opportunity to meet girls. So he spent all afternoon with another girl.

"I still remember him strolling through the lovely high meadow above the little lake with my sister's really cute girlfriend," Mom recalled. "His shirt was off. He was all brown, mannerly, and innocent-looking. By nightfall, in the woods at the wiener roast, I maneuvered to Mick's side and asked him why he had ignored me all afternoon." After the misunderstanding was cleared up, Mick had a date with Mom for the following weekend.

One date led to two, then three, when Mom's playfulness over-shadowed her tact, as they swayed on her front porch swing one Sunday afternoon.

"Mick, did you hear about the butcher who was grinding ham-burger and suddenly had to go to the hospital?" she asked.

"No, what happened?"

"He got a little behind in his work," replied Mom, with a smirk.

"Uh, okay… But why did he have to go to the hospital?"

"That's a joke. His *behind* got caught in the grinder… Isn't that funny?"

"Not really," Mick said, with a furrowed brow.

"Well, is that because you're a farmer?"

Mom's question hung over the conversation like gathering storm clouds. "I didn't think the joke was very funny," Mick said later. "And

I thought it was even less funny when Berthella insinuated the reason I didn't like it was because I was a hick from the farm. After that, we didn't go out any more."

Mom and her mother, Effie, had seen promise in this relationship and were disappointed when he no longer came around. So Effie took quick action and wrote the young man a letter.

"It was a very complimentary letter," Mick said. "She used terms like 'four square' and 'yard wide,' and said she thought very highly of me and would like to see me return. It had a tremendous impact. I wouldn't have started dating Berthella again without it."

Mick didn't smoke, drink, or swear. He was reliable and steady, and enjoyed fun things. He was so smart, he skipped third grade. He lived on a farm where he grew his own food. Mom's earlier words of jest did not reflect her heart. She felt fortunate that Mick was tied to the farm and had not gone to the battlefield like most men. Their relationship was renewed.

In the summer, Mick took my mom to Lake Michigan where they stretched a blanket atop the sand dunes and listened to waves slap the shore. In fall, they picnicked in the woods on a carpet of crimson leaves, and then, come winter, strapped skates to their feet to glide across the frozen water of Lafferty Lake.

After two years of courtship, they made a covenant of love. It was the summer of 1945, and as WWII approached its end, my parents' married life began. Berthella Whitmyer became Berthella Stevens.

Although she had been a bit homely as a young girl, with unruly hair and a crooked smile, Mom blossomed into a beautiful bride. Soft brown curls framed full lips and hazel eyes, encircled by wire-rimmed glasses. With a 24-inch waist and slender neck and shoulders, she was intellectually and physically "smart."

Mom and Dad honeymooned at the lake where they first met. Dad rigged up a camera on a tripod to take pictures of them by pulling on a string tied to the shutter lever. In my favorite photo, sunbeams burn through the shade of the woods and alight on two lovebirds nestled together in a hammock strung between sturdy trees. Their arms are interlaced around each other's shoulders and again across their waists, as my dad's head lies gently on my mom's shoulder. Their eyes are closed, with their minds seemingly dreaming of a beautiful future.

In the moment, as Dad cradled her in that hammock, neither of them realized this tender embrace which marked their genesis, would one day also mark their exodus. And Dad had no idea he would soon be forced to take another dangerous leap for Mom.

CHAPTER 2

Stolen Dreams

D reams do come true. My father lived his dream on his farmstead near Bremen in Northern Indiana. My mother's dream became real when she married and joined my father, returning to the bucolic life she enjoyed as a child on her grandparents' farm. But without warning, in the light of day, their dream was ripped from their grasp, and their lives were uprooted. You see, nightmares come true, too.

CB

Long before my father's birth, the first settlers to his area tamed the "chaos" they found in the wildness. With strong backs and clever minds, they drained swamps, felled trees, and built roads and farms with their own hands. My father was born on one of those farms, ordained into a life of order.

The roads outlined the conventional lives of these farmers. Some paved and some gravel, they ran perfectly north/south, or east/west, forming precise one-mile squares. The north/south roads were named after trees, and occurred in alphabetical order: Ash, Beech, Cedar, Dogwood, Elm, etc. The east/west roads were named after men, also in alphabetical order. Working backwards were Tyler, Shively, Riley, Quarles, Pierce, etc. Inside each perfect square formed by trees and men was six hundred forty acres of mostly farmland and woods, dotted

11

with the occasional farmhouse and punctuated by the calls of crows. It was an orderly community.

Farming was an orderly business. Farmers planted straight rows, erected straight fences, and hung straight gates and doors. Milking began at 5:00 a.m. and 4:00 p.m. every single day—rain or shine, in sickness or in health. Yards smelled of freshly mowed grass and gardens were well tended. Women, especially those from the Old Country of Belgium like my father's mother, dressed in a crisp linen apron and kept a clean house. Clothes were washed on Monday and ironed on Tuesday, shopping occurred on Wednesday, baking on Friday. There was a time and place for everything. And it ran like clockwork. To keep a farm and family running smoothly, organization and conformity were valued and necessary traits.

This was my father's life. Although my grandfather owned the farmland and buildings, they were promised to my dad, the youngest child, because his older siblings charted other paths for their lives. That certainty of farming was the bedrock on which my parents' relationship was formed. There was no mistaking what the future held.

"Pop, I've got to put in that new gate today in the bean field," said my dad one workday. "Which way do you want it to swing?"

"I don't care," his father replied. He was like his son—tall and strong. "You'll own the farm one day. Do it like you want."

The farmstead was connected to the county road by a straight lane nearly three football fields in length. It was a simple lane bordered by fenced fields on each side, just two tire tracks in the summer, but a sea of mud in the spring and a deep wall of white in winter. The farmhouse, a traditional two-story white clapboard, sat atop a small rise at the far end of the lane. It was conveniently located next to a water-pumping windmill, an outhouse, and a garden of healthy vegetables and tantalizing fruit. Across the grassy yard, beyond the ancient oaks where kids played hide-and-seek, was the heart of the farm, a tawny-red barn with neat white trim around the windows and doors. Perched on its gabled roof, five lightning rods stood silent guard with their little glass balls and sharp points.

Inside, miniature beams of light shined through cracks and illuminated particles of dust that danced with unseen scents of clover, manure, and the wisdom of aged wood. A castle of stacked hay bales filled the upper level with food for Dad's seventeen Guernsey cows below, where they ate, slept, bellowed, and waited patiently to be milked. Tall metal cans stood like sentries in the milk house at one end of the barn, to be filled and chilled until Glen, the one-armed milkman, retrieved them every other day. Massive wooden beams, rough and hewn by hand many years before from trunks of trees, were bound together by wooden pegs, safely securing the life teeming within.

Outside, an earthen embankment protected by turf and gravel allowed my father and grandfather, toiling side-by-side, to move my dad's machinery and hay from the driveway to the upper floor of the barn.

Surrounding the barn were six fields, about twenty acres each. In those fields, Dad knew what would be grown years in advance based on the rotation schedule designed to prevent nutrients from being depleted in the soil. A given field may have towering corn in year one, soybeans in year two, golden wheat and straw the next, followed by sweet alfalfa or clover hay, then open pasture for the cows, concluding with oats and straw in year six. Then the cycle repeated. Farming was an orderly business.

As an adult, my father still lived with his parents when he married my mother. Together, Dad and Mom had the second floor of the farmhouse to themselves, while my grandparents slept on the first floor, which also had a kitchen and living room. Electricity had recently been installed, and a fresh coat of white paint brightened the interior for the new bride. But there was no indoor plumbing or bathroom. Everyone sat on the cold wooden seat in the outhouse just as my mom had done on her grandparents' farm. In these intimate living quarters, my mother and her in-laws began to learn more about each other.

My grandmother and grandfather emigrated from Belgium and brought with them customs unfamiliar to my mother. Men smoked cigars, played cards, and enjoyed whiskey, although my father was a teetotaler. My grandfather enjoyed a stiff drink so much that he distilled his own moonshine in the basement during Prohibition and sold it in nearby Mishawaka when my father was a child. For a Belgian, that was an honorable way to break the law. He transported the quart bottles in a full-length leather coat made from the hide of a cow that had suffocated when a straw pile collapsed on her. Each of the many inner pockets hid a flask of liquid fire. He excelled at this task and caught the eye of professional bootleggers who teamed up with him and dug a secret cave under his barn's earthen embankment.

Early in their marriage, my straight-laced mother tired of these unfamiliar customs. As they sat on the edge of their iron bed on the second floor, I imagine Mom spoke quietly as she shared her growing concerns with Dad.

"Mick, I certainly appreciate your folks letting us live here… but…but the whiskey! Don't they understand drinking is immoral? And then I learn they even made it themselves."

"Berthella, Pop hasn't made moonshine since Prohibition ended…more than a decade ago."

"Well, why didn't you tell me about that before we were married?" she asked, stopping before entertaining what she might have done differently. Then, without waiting for a response from Dad, she continued, "And the cigar smoke. It's difficult to even breathe when I'm downstairs. Who knows what that'll do to any children we have? And I sure as heck don't want the devil in this house playing cards with our kids. Do you know how hard it is to hold my tongue with your folks?" Mom was on a roll and let it all out. "And who do I have to talk with during the day? Sometimes when you're out in the field, I just come up here and cry."

Although living on a farm had been Mom's dream since childhood, the transition from single city life to married farm life was troubling. Before marriage, she had constant companionship with her sisters and mother who talked for hours and shared intimate details of their lives. She was used to walking to the store, to the library, or to visit friends in the city. With no phone and no one around to share her farm life, Mom felt isolated. She hungered for personal conversation.

14

Her mother-in-law struggled with English and seldom spoke. Her father-in-law was a man of few words and seldom smiled. Dad constantly worked hard on the farm that would one day be his.

So Mom did what she knew. She walked the country roads, looking for other farm wives to talk with. Although Dad's brother, Omer, and his wife, Mabel, lived on a farm across the road, the next nearest neighbor was a half-mile away. The dusty road on which she walked was sparsely traveled, used by an occasional tractor or an Amish horse and buggy, but not a woman walking by herself. Loneliness gripped my mother's wandering heart as gravel crunched beneath her feet and a solitary red-winged blackbird scolded her from his fencepost perch. Although no one voiced it in her presence, neighbors and in-laws also passed judgment on her unusual behavior.

After a year of blended living, my father's parents moved into a modest house they bought and transported to the opposite end of the lane near the road. Grandpa still owned the farm and wanted to be close by, but they couldn't continue living in the same house with my mother. They said it was because she had a baby on the way and Dad and she needed more room for their expanding family.

Mom and Dad were in the business of making farmhands. My brother, Mike, arrived first in 1946, followed quickly by my brother, Pat. By the time the cries of Janet, their third child, were heard, Dad and Grandpa remodeled the kitchen and added a nice bathroom. In 1953, my brother, Tom, was born and the family had settled in. Mom made the house her own by painting over her in-laws' staid white walls with Morning Glory Blue in the kitchen and pale yellow and mauve in the living room. When she tired of that, the living room came alive in bold Flamingo Red, which reflected her zest for life. The farmhouse was now hers to steward and soon the entire farm would belong to Dad and her.

My siblings thrived on the farm. As Mike and Pat grew, they worked alongside my dad, eventually taking on man-sized tasks. My father even bought a new tractor for my oldest brother when he was able to work independently. Mom gave all her children freedom to roam, the way she had on her grandparents' farm.

"Queenie, the family collie, was an excellent babysitter," said Mom. "All I had to do was look out my kitchen window or step outside to locate her and I'd know where the children were."

"We'd go wherever we wanted and do whatever we wanted to do," said Janet. "We'd pick fruit, play in the yard, and gather eggs from the chickens."

"We were pretty much released on our own," Pat said. "When we weren't working, we played in the barn's haymow. I got seriously hurt a couple times when I fell down a hay chute and hit my head. It didn't seem to bother Mom too much."

Freedom wasn't limited to the outdoors. "One time, Mike and I were making gunpowder in the kitchen for our rockets," recalled Pat. "For some reason, we had a candle on the table and somehow the whole mixture lit up with huge balls of yellow fire and acrid sulfur smoke in the middle of the kitchen. It melted the Formica on the tabletop and nearly burned the house down before we got the fire put out. I was surprised by Mom's reaction. She didn't get mad because we had done something wrong. Her concern was that we hadn't taken the right precautions in doing it."

Part of Mom's subdued response may have stemmed from the way she kept house. Certainly having a passel of kids would have been a chore in itself, but a clean house had not been a priority when she grew up and it was not a priority in her own home. "Very casual" would be a polite descriptor; nothing was organized. She struggled to find the right balance. "I grew up believing that happiness, good times, culture, and education came before work," she said.

Because children and education came first, there was always something for Mom to put off and she devised shortcuts such as doors shut on rooms with unmade beds, or leftovers shoved to the back of the refrigerator until they were spoiled enough to throw away. "Why have floors which were clean enough to eat off of when we had a table for that purpose?" Mom explained.

Mom had her priorities. There had to be time for books that cried out to be read; time for the neighbor with no one to talk to; time for the lake that needed swimmers, not to mention the ant hill waiting to be studied. As a result, there were days and days when nothing got done around the house—at least not anything her Old World in-laws could see.

My grandparents did take note, not only of Mom's behavior but its contrast with their other daughter-in-law, Mabel, who lived across the road. Mabel washed clothes on Monday, ironed them on Tuesday, and went shopping on Wednesday along with my grandfather and grandmother. They all purchased the same things, at the same stores. Mabel, like my mother, was raising children, but her house was immaculate, and she wore a nice linen apron while she worked.

"While I never heard outright that my in-laws called me shiftless," Mom said, "I certainly had that impression. And I fretted over the fact that I was not perfect in their eyes. But the Old Country idea that a woman must first of all be a perfect housekeeper and lastly a mother, didn't sit well with me. With a farmhouse, chores, and large family, our home was not the beautiful spick-and-span home in the magazines. My firm conviction was that life was for living and not just for keeping house.

"Mick was fond of saying, 'Hard work never hurt anyone.' Although I think that creed started the Stevens' dynasty, I didn't agree that work came first, and my nonconformity caused much trouble in our family."

❧

Although Mom's children came before her housework, so did her own social and intellectual stimulation. Television was new and Mom was aware of a daily quiz show for women called *Cinderella Weekend*. The winner got a trip for two to New York City. She dreamed of winning and taking her first plane ride. When she and my siblings worked outdoors and the sun glinted off the silver wings of a plane overhead she'd look up and say, "There goes Mama. There goes Mama to New York City."

In the summer of 1954, her fantasy came alive when the local TV station approved her contestant application. "The contest consisted of four women a day answering questions of general interest with a stop button that shut out others' responses," Mom recalled. "The daily winners of the first four days of the week came together to compete on Friday of each week, and the four weekly winners met on the last Friday to determine the winner of the month, who won the trip to New York City."

Mom believed she was up against some formidable foes. She clutched an encyclopedia volume even as she cared for her family. She studied hard and scorched a meal or two along the way. "Nobody knew what was going to be asked," she said. "So I just tried to remember as many trivial facts as I could and studied various topics."

She appeared on a Thursday show, and the neighbors with televisions were glued to their sets. She had momentarily transformed herself from a curiosity to a celebrity. My oldest brother, Mike, who attended nearby Madison School, was allowed to go to the office and watch Mom win that daily contest on the live, black-and-white TV program.

She returned the following day to compete against the other daily winners. As the show began, the emcee, Lew Wood, asked the contestants what had happened since they last appeared on the show. Mom volunteered, "During the show yesterday, my neighbor's barn caught fire and he tried to call the fire department, but the telephone exchange operator wouldn't answer his call because she was watching this show. So, he had to drive to a telephone in the neighboring exchange to reach the fire department. In the meantime, his barn burned down."

While her account lingered in the air like smoke, Mom won the weekly contest. When she returned to compete in the monthly game, Mr. Wood pulled her aside before the show began. "The operator of your telephone exchange arrived in my office after your last appearance," he said. "She had her lawyer with her and threatened to sue the station. Please don't share any more stories." Mom kept quiet this time except when it came to answering the quiz questions, trouncing her competition for a third time and winning the coveted trip.

Once in New York, she and Dad stayed on the move. They rode to the ear-popping top of the Empire State Building, climbed the Statue of Liberty, and were mesmerized by the precise dancing and skimpy costumes of the Rockettes at Radio City Music Hall. They enjoyed breakfast overlooking Fifth Avenue and were entertained by the lively music of Xavier Cugat and his orchestra. Mom was bitten by the travel bug and never recovered. The enticement of new places, new people, and new things forever animated her life.

Although she enjoyed her taste of travel, Mom loved children even more, so she and Dad continued to create future farmhands. After a difficult stillbirth, I was conceived and born in 1958, twelve years younger than the firstborn. Although all of us Stevens children were blonde haired and blue-eyed, I arrived with a fuzzy head of black hair, earning the permanent nickname "Fuzz."

Mom's sisters had children as well, and our farm became the gathering place for my mom's side of the family, just as her grandparents' farm had once been. Whether it was holidays, week-long stays in the summer, or just a place to get away from city life, the Stevens' farm was everybody's favorite. "Aunt Berthella was the strength and heart of the family," recalled my cousin, Debby. "That's where we went: to Mick and Berthella's house. It was a place of comfort, especially for the sisters who had gone through so much growing up. The farm was a place for them to renew their bond with each other."

When Mom's mother, Effie, showed up, so did talk of religion. "They would argue for hours about the Bible," recalled my brother, Pat. "Arguments about simple pronouns, like which one was correct and what each meant. Is it 'this is of the Lord', or is it 'from the Lord?' They weren't tearing each other down but enhancing knowledge and trying to figure something out by the end of the day." They were iron sharpening iron, as the Bible says.[1]

Thoughts of Armageddon, the calamitous "end times," were never far away. Mom wrote a letter to Effie about the remodeling her father-in-law planned for their farmhouse:

Pop was up here measuring and figuring out the bathroom and kitchen again. We're drawing plans; we have some good ones, too. He talks like he's going to start pretty soon. Of course, some of the Stevens' are trying to talk him out of it. If we do get it fixed up nice here, I'll be torn between wishing Armageddon would hold off for a while and wishing it would hurry up and get over with.

Mom was thinking of the time of turmoil which she believed the entire world would one day experience during Christ's thousand-year reign, culminating in the resurrection. What she didn't know was that her personal Armageddon would arrive far sooner. She knew she was the family member who colored outside the lines in the Stevens' coloring book—in bold colors like Flamingo Red. However, she was unprepared for the extent to which her father-in-law would go to prevent her picture from being drawn.

⌓

I have an image in my mind of my grandfather walking up the lane, the gravel crunched beneath his feet. The sun was rising above the corncrib and the rooster alerted his flock to the start of a new beginning. His expression was serious, a bit more than usual. My father emerged from the barn after milking, and the two men stood face to face.

"Mick," he said. He turned away momentarily, unable to look my father in the eye. "I know I told you that you would one day own this farm. And I know you've bought all this equipment and your animals…and you've been workin' hard and looking forward to that day…" He glanced at his boots before continuing. "But that isn't going to happen. I've decided to give the farm to your brother and his wife—to Omer and Mabel. I need you to move out in three months."

Then he turned, put his hands in his pockets, and stared at the ground as he ambled slowly back down the lane to his house. The dirty deed was done. There would be no more nonconformity on the Stevens' farm.

My father must have lost his breath, like he'd been kicked in the gut. Maybe for once his tearless eyes streamed with warm, salty water. Maybe he squeezed his weather-worn hands tightly together so he wouldn't pass out. Maybe if he thought no one was looking, he would have stared skyward before collapsing to his knees onto the earth on which his life depended.

The farm was Dad's past, present, and future. It was the very foundation on which he built his family. It shaped the only person he knew how to be. *How could my father steal our dream?*

I don't know the conversation Dad had with Mom when he walked into the house. But she, too, felt the earth shake, while bearing the burden of presumed responsibility.

From their calamity, Mom catapulted into a frantic search for another farm in the neighborhood. She and Dad wanted the kids to remain in Madison School. But families clung to their properties to hand down to their children. Because no farm was for sale or rent, "farmer" would no longer be Dad's title. He arranged to auction off his equipment and animals.

With bold letters of a bold proclamation, the sale bills posted around the community read:

PUBLIC SALE. Having decided to quit farming, I will sell at Public Auction.

But if they had been honest, the sale bills would have declared instead:

PUBLIC SALE. Because my father betrayed me and stole the hopes and dreams of my entire family, I will sell at Public Auction.

The sale took place two days before my first birthday. As friends, neighbors, and strangers loitered on the lawn like vultures, it commenced with the familiar rapid-fire chant of the auctioneer.

"Who'll give me a hundred dollars?
One hundred dollar bid, now two,
now two, will ya' give me two?

"Two hundred dollar bid, now three,
now three hundred, will ya' give me three?

"Two hundred, two and a half, two-fifty,
How about two-fifty? fifty? fifty? fifty? I got it!

"How about two sixty? sixty? sixty?
I've got two sixty, now seventy?
How about seventy? two-seventy?"[2]

By the end of the day, only memories remained.

A brand new 1958 Ford 861 tractor my dad bought because my brother Mike was old enough to work independently was driven away. The three-bottom 16" Ford plow used to till the ground, turned over to a new owner. A corn planter that pressed into the soil seeds that would produce stalks that reached for the sky, moved to another man's earth. A combine, which harvested wheat and oats, was reaped by other farmers.

Twelve gray milk cans that once held white gold until Glen, the one-armed milkman could pick them up, evaporated. The Surge milkers, which rhythmically withdrew the intimate gift from their cows, were sucked up by another dairyman. And the 2,000 bales of scratchy hay and straw, all cut, baled, and stacked by my family's hands, became the pleasures of other animals.

These and other pieces of equipment were tools of the trade. They were mostly just objects, but they were my father's lifeblood. That day, his heart emptied.

CHAPTER 3

Broken Promises

Spring is calling.
> *I hear her in the rippling waters*
>> *Under an ice-covered stream.*
> *I hear her in the fluttering of the birds*
>> *Through leafless trees.*
> *I hear her in the winds that blow*
>> *Over barren fields.*

Spring is calling.

—"Spring is Calling," Berthella Whitmyer, circa 1935

My mother dared to be herself on our family farm and it cost the family dearly. It wasn't the last time such a hefty price was paid. But why was she unable to fill the role expected of her? It began with three powerful forces that shaped her. The first was a virtual winter which refused to release its icy grip from the springtime of her life. It swept into her being by second grade, leaving her fatherless, with the cold winds of the Great Depression howling at her family's door.

ⅎ

Married at the cusp of the Roaring Twenties, my maternal grand-parents' relationship lasted long enough to bring three girls into the world. My mother, Berthella May Whitmyer, firstborn in 1920, was named after her two grandmothers, Bertha and Ella May. Joy and Dorothy, my mother's two sisters, soon followed. In childhood, Mom sported a bobbed hairstyle born from practicality. Her nearly blonde hair was combed forward with bangs cut straight across the forehead, dropping to all one length just below her ears. High cheekbones framed a slightly upturned nose that held round metallic spectacles in place, giving her an air of intelligence. A simple ruffled dress over tights or ankle high socks, and black patent leather Mary Jane shoes completed her tidy and proper ensemble.

"We were living in a converted garage apartment that seemed spacious," recalled Mom. "I had my toy ironing board, table and chairs, and times were happy for me. When Daddy came home from work, he'd pick me up and I'd throw my arms around his neck and say 'a bushel and a peck and a hug around the neck.'" As the family grew, her father, Grant Whitmyer, whose primary job was metalwork at a musical instrument factory, bought a city lot and built a new house. There was a swing set for the kids with a swing and rings. Sunday dinners meant Swiss steak and gravy. "Those were happy days," Mom said, "but I didn't know it."

My mother was a city girl. She lived in the northern Indiana town of Elkhart, formed at the confluence of the St. Joseph and Elkhart rivers, where Ottawa, Chippewa, and Pottawatomie Indian tribes once hunted. The construction of the railroads brought rapid growth. Business flourished and entrepreneurs built lavish homes. Later, the clang-clang-clang of the electric trolleys was replaced by gas fumes and honking horns. Cars and buses shuttled the 30,000 residents to work, to shopping, or to city parks to listen to free band concerts or swim in its rivers, then home again to a tapestry of safe neighborhoods. The shouts of children riding bicycles to school or to the vibrant downtown punctuated the air. The promises of childhood shone brightly.[1]

But as the 1920s drew to a close, Grant's rumored dalliance with another woman ended his marriage as well. Whether his wife threw him out or he abandoned the family on his own, Effie Whitmyer was left with a bottomless well of anger, the weight of intolerable shame from a failed marriage, and the quagmire of raising three young girls alone. The children, all under the age of ten, longed for their father, not understanding why Daddy left them.

"Mama thought she was going to marry again," my mother remembered, "so when the judge asked what she thought she needed to live on for support, she said ten dollars a week." They seldom saw that money, though, and Effie's pride and poisonous resentment left remarriage an impossibility.

Effie had no vocation and her all-female family was as poor as the proverbial church mice. Cleaning houses and businesses brought a trickle of income. She also earned money as a seamstress and used her skills to provide clothes for her girls. Insisting they still dress nicely, Effie once took a lace curtain from the window to make my mother an attractive white frock. But the money Effie brought home from cleaning and sewing didn't meet their needs. Extended family members occasionally helped out, but seldom did she have enough money to pay the rent, even at five dollars per month.

Adrift in a sea of fear and loneliness, the waves of the Great Depression began to hit them broadside, threatening to sink the fragile life to which they clung. Eviction notices were a constant reminder of their fragility, coming every few months when the landlords' patience ran out.

"Once, when a landlord came to collect the rent, Dorothy, who must have been about five years old, answered the door," recalled my mother. "He asked her if our mama was home. 'She's busy taking a douche,' Dorothy replied with innocent honesty. Well, it wasn't long before he returned, offering to, 'take the rent out in trade.' It was such an unsettling experience for Mama that we moved again, pronto."

On another occasion, some men bashed in their door and packed up all their belongings. "I ran home to put some clothes in suitcases before they took it all," Mom exclaimed. "They had a legal paper that said they could do that. It was terrifying."

They lived in some awful places, with paper peeling from the walls like dying petals, and ceilings so low they banged their heads sitting up in bed. Some tiny houses meant the entire family of four slept in one bedroom. With no insulation, the floors in the winter felt like ice to tiny feet. Although the promise of childhood security had been broken, they were thankful for every place that sheltered them from the winds of homelessness.

There were social welfare programs that provided some assistance. Effie was ashamed to go to their offices to beg for handouts and instead sent my mother alone. Head down, towing her squeaky little wagon, she was expected to retrieve basics like sugar, flour, canned beef, or coal for the furnace. Unable to afford even butter—a staple in most families—they were forced to consume hard white margarine. Effie knew my mother felt the pain of their poverty and may have hoped her child didn't understand its shame. But that was not so. "It was a terrible disgrace," my mother recalled. "I died a thousand deaths."

Every morsel of food mattered, as malnutrition crept into their lives and illness hovered like vultures. Nothing went to waste. The sides of an empty cornbread pan were scraped to gather remaining crumbs, followed by a drizzle of milk to loosen the last bits, before it was spooned into waiting mouths.

Mama, what are we going to eat tonight? My stomach is growling like it wants to attack, my mother must have wondered.

Well, let's see what the Lord provides. Indeed, the Lord provided one day when a kindly neighbor, pained by the suffering he witnessed, offered a dead squirrel he shot on their city street.

☙

Throughout childhood, the sisters were inseparable. They clung to my mother, the eldest sibling, for her strength and companionship, while their mother Effie struggled to keep their ship afloat. Despite the depressing worry over the fate of her children, Effie still created bits of spring, which flowed into their lives like water under an ice-covered stream. One of her favorite Bible verses from the book of Matthew enlightened her: "So do not worry about tomorrow, for tomorrow will bring worries of its own."[2]

"Because of this sentiment, happiness and culture came before housework," Mom remembered. "Good work habits were needed, all right, but happiness was so ephemeral that it was grasped for us children as often as possible."

When it was hot, the family dropped their chores and went swimming. When a free band concert played, so did they. Want to have a picnic? Off they marched. My mother learned to draw and to write poetry and prose on scraps of old paper. And from somewhere, money was found for ten-minute piano lessons.

Effie also pushed her children to learn, to absorb their public education, and to understand the world. They walked together to the library where they borrowed books and read voraciously. She taught them that it didn't take money to have brains, and they could be rich in another way—rich in knowledge.

As she'd always done, Mom honored her mother's words and deeds. She excelled academically and finished high school a semester early. Her sister, Joy, claimed my mother got half the brains of the family.

After graduation, Mom found a job making corrugated boxes. She was able to help meet the family's financial needs, boosting them ever-so-slightly from the depths of poverty. With cash from her first paycheck in hand, she proudly walked to the market to purchase real butter—yellow, creamy, sweet butter—casting aside margarine's long held vestige of shame.

Although my mother grew up in a virtual winter of broken childhood promises, she still heard the call of spring and the promise of a verdant tomorrow. The breath of hope still filled her soul. The arc of her life had been permanently bent, but not broken.

CHAPTER 4

Heaven's Borderland

When twilight comes and shadows soften into night,
I love to watch the moon-mist rise across the fading saffron skies
And see the dancing, merry stars come out –
One by one.
The evening breeze blows sweetly across my face
And passes on to breathe upon the waiting trees.

And the lake that once today dimpled so saucily in the sun
Now lies placidly in the stillness,
Reflecting its shadowy shores
Where willows hang and sway so close to the quiet water.
Beneath my feet the frogs sing a song of the night,
And from across the gently rolling hills where cattle lie upon the dewy grass,
Comes a tinkling of a bell that carries far out into the clear, fresh air.

The moon climbs higher and higher in the soft blue sky
And makes a fairy path of shimmering silver gauze
Across the water and into the wood,
Where the fairies are dancing now, I know,
In the columbine patch.

And so I sit in the tall, fragrant grass
And drink in all this loveliness of the peace and beauty of the night.
This is so very lovely that it makes me hurt inside,
And yet drives away the cares and troubles of the day
So that I may go, refreshed, to my sleep,
And dream I am playing with the fairies
In the columbine patch.

—"Nocturne," by Berthella Whitmyer, 1940, reflecting on her
enchantment with Lafferty Lake on her grandparents' farm.

While the Great Depression threatened to end my mother's life, her grandparents' farm helped save it. Though its fields were a washboard of eroded gullies and the buildings run down, the farm became a summer refuge where Grandmother Effie sent her young daughters to escape the economic calamity that thrashed their fragile lives in the city. This was the second force to define my mother's destiny.

Effie's parents, Ella May and William Blyly, owned the farm derisively known as Gully Meadows. William, always on the lookout for a get-rich-quick deal, never failed to make a poor choice. He sold their home in Elkhart, Indiana, and moved ten miles north to Cass County, Michigan, to chase this newest dream. While William may have viewed this property as his promised land, for my mother, it literally was the land of milk and honey. Like a cat drawn to cream, her grandparents' sixty-acre farm fed her body and soul. It was an oasis of joy.

Dairy cows the color of beeswax roamed the fields of Gully Meadows and provided fresh milk and butter. Chickens scratched happily in the yard, leaving gifts of fresh eggs. Baskets of produce: corn, tomatoes, squash, peas, cucumbers, rhubarb, beets, leafy greens all grew just steps from the back door in a large garden. Mom's younger sister, Joy, so enthralled by the cornucopia, plopped herself down on the garden soil, salt shaker in hand, and renewed her spirit with the

29

heavenly taste of sun-ripened tomatoes and Earth's perfume. Healthy food meant healthy lives. The Depression was just a bitter memory when they were at the farm.

But running a family farm meant doing chores, and that's what grandkids were for. Looking back, Mom recalled, "My sweetest childhood memories revolve around the summers I spent on my grandparents' farm. One of my favorite chores was caring for the cows. After the morning milking, they were let out to amble down the well-worn path to pasture. I was responsible for bringing the cows back to the barnyard for the evening milking.

"We kids would trot off, barefoot, carrying sticks and calling to the cows, 'Come boss, come boss, here boss.' We'd often play on the way, swinging on the old wild grapevine, squishing our toes through the mud of bubbling springs, or just watching the birds. Hearing our call, the large white matriarch, named Blossom, started the daily trek back to the barn, the rest of the herd trailing behind. After they were locked in their stanchions to be milked by Grandpa, we'd reward them with hay."

But as the summer sun and hooves took their toll on the meadow, the cows needed a richer food source. That's when Mom was enveloped in her most cherished chore of herding the cows along the roadside.

"It took two or more of us to make the cows leave their familiar path and venture through the early morning dew after milking. There was little traffic on the gravel road and the plentiful grass was lush and sweet," she recalled. "We often found wild berries to pick, or we just talked or read books while the cows spent hours ripping grass with their powerful tongues. When the cows got restless, wanted to lie down, or the noontime dinner bell rang for us kids, Blossom and I herded the cows back to the barn.

"These chores taught me self-discipline, patience, and an appreciation and respect for animals," my mother said. "And the farm influenced my life in other ways, as well. By my mid-teens, I decided I wanted to marry a farmer!"

The cow path of my mother's youth wasn't the only track on the farm. There was also a well-worn people path between the house and their outdoor bathroom called the "path room." As outhouses go, it was comfortable and included a child-sized hole, and two small windows. It was my mother's job to scrub the inside of the little building with hot soapsuds, use a broom to clear out the spiders and dirt, and throw lime into the smelly pit to "sweeten it." The lime must have been effective since it was into this sanctuary the girls escaped the ornery boy cousins, and where William and Ella May sat for quiet evening chats away from the grandchildren.

Cold, fresh water, used for drinking and cooking, came straight from the ground, pumped by a windmill, and carried to the house in buckets. Rainwater, collected from the roof into a cistern, was used to wash clothes and bathe.

The farm was partly on a high bluff and the deep gullies contained spring-fed rivulets that crept into an icy creek. The creek gurgled into a sandy marsh where it slipped silently into Lafferty Lake. Many creatures claimed the lake as home and the rolling hills surrounding it: birds, snakes, sheep, and cows. But people were nowhere to be seen in this paradise. By the age of ten, Mom escorted the younger children to the lake, a half mile away, to swim and play in the boat. With no adult supervision, they were given only one rule: "When we heard the dinner bell we had to go back to the farmhouse," Mom said. "Surely, we must have had a guardian angel, or two. We survived with no problems other than occasional infectious bites from leeches."

It was in this precious lake that Mom communed soulfully with God's creation. Watching a gorgeous sunset on its tranquil waters one evening, a graceful swallow swooped high into the sky and dropped a tiny feather from its beak. As the feather drifted slowly toward the water, the swallow glided down to catch it mid-flight, then up, up, it flew, beyond the treetops to do it again and again, as if it were playing a game for its own enjoyment, and for the inspiration it provided Mom.

At the center of Mom's universe on the farm was her namesake grandmother, Ella May. Soft-spoken, sturdy, and long-suffering, Ella

31

May came from a well-to-do, educated family of teachers. At the age of fifty, when her husband dragged her off to the country, she brought along her silk pongee curtains and hung them in the old farmhouse as a reminder of the refinement now past. "Although Grandpa had also been a teacher, I didn't have to be a grownup to see that my grandmother's family felt she married beneath her," Mom said.

"Grandma toiled in the fields like a man," Mom shared proudly. "She helped with the milking, separated cream from the milk afterward, and washed the separator. She doctored the livestock, cared for the chickens, and butchered and cooked them, as well. The gardens, which bore well and early, were hers, too. She sewed, mended, and helped butcher the pigs, then put up the meat in larded crocks in the cellar. She baked her own bread and daily biscuits. She grew, harvested, and canned strawberries, cherries, wild huckleberries, peaches, plums, and apples. And if she had to, she hitched up the team of horses and a big wagon and drove to where she needed to go."

"I never heard her complain. But had we thought about it then, we would have known she was always tired," Mom lamented. "And yet, she had time to show me how to make hollyhock dolls with broken toothpicks, and how to create a lovely centerpiece for the table with moist sand covered by hollyhock blossoms and how to crochet."

With a strong square jawline, high cheekbones, and dark deep-set eyes, she looked like a Native American squaw, which was reinforced by her harmony with nature. "We tramped together through fields of scratchy grass, woods filled with the pungent smells of decaying trees, and muddy marshes, looking for wild plants to eat or to use for medicine, revealing as we went the secret lessons of nature that only a discerning heart can know," my mother said. "She showed me how to simmer a certain herb in lard to make a healing salve and how to make a marvelous creamy salad from the simple dandelion. And she birthed in me a life-long love affair with flowers!"

While the farm's abundant food may have saved my mother's life, Ella May gave that life meaning and purpose. By the time my mother was grown and moved away, she and Ella May shared more than a name. Mom felt they were kindred spirits.

Although Ella May expressed no physical affection, Mom loved her grandmother and believed her grandmother loved her, too. "Being the way she was, I was surprised one day when I went to visit her in my adulthood," Mom recalled. "I found her not feeling well and she actually let me do a little of her work. Then before I left, without a spoken word she pulled me close and kissed me tenderly on the cheek. It was the first and only kiss, and sweet as honey. But soon after that reassuring moment came the dreadful news that she was dying of cancer. For decades after she left me, at night we were reunited in my dreams."

Ella May had a simple and uncomplicated faith in the Bible. Her favorite hymn, "Beulah Land," sustained her. She often whistled and sang the hopeful song as she went about her day. The beautiful old tune, which moves with purposeful pace, was inspired by a single verse in the Old Testament book of Isaiah.[1] That verse speaks of a land called Beulah, which once was forsaken and void of life until it was blessed by God and fully restored. The song "Beulah Land" describes that restored place as being so blessed with riches that it sat at Heaven's door.

I wonder, as Ella May whistled that tune, if she imagined that Gully Meadows was forsaken, and only the hope of a verdant future kept her going through the endless days of toil? Or, did she feel her farmland had already been blessed by God and filled with riches?

For my mother, Gully Meadows was unquestionably her Beulah Land. Living each summer in bucolic bliss erased the forsaken elements that threatened her life in the city. She was rescued and restored and planted with a forever-yearning for country life.

CHAPTER 5

In the Beginning

A shoot shall come out from the stump of Jesse, and a branch shall grow out of his roots. The spirit of the Lord shall rest on him, the spirit of wisdom and understanding.

—Isaiah 11:1-2a

To understand my mother, we must understand her spiritual journey. It was her most powerful life-shaping force, strong as stone encased with healing hope. Her circuitous journey began long before her grandmother, Ella May, learned to whistle "Beulah Land." It took root when a distant maternal grandfather, Charles Osborn, a Quaker minister and a leader of the Abolitionist movement, planted seeds of righteous resistance. Generations later, the popular ministry of Pastor Charles Russell nourished the seedbed of Mom's life with intellectual certitude and everlasting hope. But it was her own father, also a preacher, who first guided the growth of the tender shoots of my mother's spiritual world.

It was inevitable this lineage would reveal the handprint of God on my mother. Her understanding of life, and the fuel for its living, sprang from her family's "stump of Jesse." But the strength of her convictions would also cast a dark shadow in later seasons.

ﻹﻻ

Charles Osborn became a minister in the Society of Friends in 1806 when this Christian group, often called "Quakers," was throwing off worldly ways. He inherited a vigorous tradition of reform.

He was an outspoken opponent of slavery, like many Quakers, and was referred to as the Father of the Abolitionist Movement, starting *The Philanthropist*, the first abolitionist newspaper in the United States. He also embraced the peculiarly Quaker doctrine of Free Produce, which advocated the boycott of items produced with slave labor as an economic tool of opposition.

Osborn's radical support of abolition conflicted with the conservative temperament of many Indiana Quakers who wanted Friends to eschew politics. In 1842, that conservative faction expelled Osborn. Separated from his former associates, and with his advanced age affecting his health and ministry, Charles later moved to a farm in Michigan. Across the road was a stop on the storied Underground Railroad, which continued to feed his need to make a difference.

Nearly ninety years later, that same farm community also made a difference in my mother's life. It was there, on the farm of her grand-parents, descendants of Charles Osborn, that she discovered utopia. Though Charles had long since passed, he handed down to his family a prophetic call to righteousness, an indelible spirit of resistance to the status quo, a fervent plea to know God, and the belief that education unleashed society's better angels. These traits took root in my mother.[1]

Although many years separated them, my mother held deep admiration for her great-great-great grandfather, Charles Osborn. But others had an even greater influence in the spring of her life.

ﻹﻻ

In 1870, as a zealous young man of eighteen, Charles Taze Russell was perturbed by such traditional teachings as predestination and eternal torment in hellfire. He started a weekly Bible study group with other young men and began to analyze its teachings. They eventually rejected central understandings of many denominations, believing Christian creeds and traditions were harmful. Caught up in the Restoration movement of the era, which sought to correct faults in the established order with a purer form of religion, they wanted to return to the biblical origins of Christianity, similar to the Quakers.

Russell and his Bible students were keenly interested in the biblical prophesies related to Christ's "second coming," the "end of the world," and in the chronology expressed in the Bible. As they analyzed the Greek texts and poured through calculations, they concluded Christ's "second coming" had already occurred in spirit-form in 1874, marking the beginning of a thousand-year transformation from humanity's self-rule to Christ-rule. This period would be marked by wide-spread calamity, known as Armageddon.

At the end of this age, Russell believed, all who had been "resting in death" would be resurrected. They'd be given the opportunity to accept Christ's sovereignty, if they had not done so before they died. This "second chance" would be offered with more evolved thought and understanding not available before death. Those who accepted would live eternally on Earth, restored to the condition of Eden at the beginning of Creation. Those who did not, succumbed to a second death—not torment in Hell.

For Russell, the clock was ticking. At the age of twenty-five, he launched into the new occupation of preacher, telling his followers, "Our object as truth-seekers should be to obtain the complete, harmonious whole of God's revealed plan…since it is promised that the spirit of truth shall guide us into all truth."

His foundational text came from one of his many books, *The Divine Plan for the Ages*, which provided a topical framework for understanding the entire Bible and God's plan for humanity. Some of his books became overnight bestsellers, selling millions of copies. His weekly sermons appeared in as many as 4,000 newspapers with a combined circulation of fifteen million readers. Although not an ordained pastor in the traditional sense, to his disciples he became known as Pastor Russell.

The followers of this charismatic leader were simply called Bible Students. They did not consider themselves a new denomination. They regularly met in groups to study the Bible, as members of the early Christian church might have done. These congregations had leaders who, although not seminary-trained, committed themselves to intense study. My mother's father, Grant, was such a leader, in addition to his job at a musical instrument factory.[2]

∾

When my grandparents, Effie and Grant, were married, my grandfather was a dashing young man, with eyes that could peer into one's soul or just as quickly signal indifference. With his hair slicked back just so and a bow tie mounted prominently against his starched white collar, he was a man of authority. That authority came with the territory. He had been a preacher since the age of seventeen, when his father, also a preacher, died and passed the responsibility to him.

Using a heavy wooden table as a desk, Grant stacked cushions on his black chair to elevate himself to write out his sermons in comfort. Pastor Russell's books and other reference materials were stacked nearby. As he sat hunched over in his suit and tie, crafting each enlightened message with a fountain pen, a simple reminder hung on the wall above his head: God is Love.

"We went to 'meeting' on Wednesday nights, Sunday mornings, and Sunday evenings," my mother recalled. "Daddy was the elder, preaching the sermons. He was a good preacher and remained a preacher almost his entire life."

Although my grandmother's ancestors were Quaker, Effie's parents also followed the popular Pastor Russell. As Effie's and Grant's respective streams of family influence converged in marriage, they and their three little girls inhaled each word that had been exhaled by Pastor Russell.

They studied his deeply analytical reasoning, the research, the calculations, and diagrams. It required a committed and critical mentality to unravel the mysteries within. Russell's intellectual, comprehensive view of God's majestic plan for humanity fed minds as well as souls. Although my mother's family did not play cards, smoke, or drink, discovering their truth was intoxicating.

Mom felt fortunate to be born into a family where both sides for generations believed in the Bible and its prophecies. She said, "Within that environment, I was told about all the good things that were to happen on Earth after the resurrection, to which I avidly listened. Many times as a child, I heard of the worldwide Garden of Eden in which there would be birds and animals for people to enjoy."

By the time she was ten years old, though, simultaneous cracks appeared in my mother's foundation. Her mother and father divorced and the Bible Students suffered a similar fate. A new leader emerged after Russell's death, and he turned against some of the group's tenets. The association split, and a new group formed called Jehovah's Witnesses. It was an irreconcilable separation in my mom's family. Grant moved to the Jehovah's Witnesses and Effie remained a follower of Pastor Russell. Since Effie was no longer welcomed in her ex-husband's congregation, she and the girls stopped attending church altogether.

Reeling from the pain of divorce, the separation from her church, and the existential threats from the Great Depression, the family of young women found hope in Scripture which assured them their wounds would one day be healed.[3] Effie continued to provide biblical instruction enlightened by Russell's teachings. She supplemented their training with other books, sermons, and radio programs. They learned to debate the infinitesimal details, looking for clues to meaning, and how to defend their views with Scripture and logic. They fiercely competed with each other to demonstrate who possessed the greatest knowledge, insight, and ability to sway others. It was family sport, a sport in which my mother excelled.

☙

Just as Mom's spiritual journey began before her first breath, she believed it would continue beyond her last. Her childhood experiences of seeking biblical truth melted into her DNA. As a child longing for food, shelter, and stability, it's easy to understand the appeal of the promise of a perfect life here on Earth: a beautiful garden, abundant food, no disease, sadness, or pain, in a sanctuary filled with birds and animals to enjoy… and a Father who loved her.

CHAPTER 6

New Adventures

My mother's faith and her grandparents' farm were the saving grace from a fatherless and threatened childhood in the city. These enduring experiences drew her to the Stevens' farm as an adult, yet prevented her from fitting in. Although my parents' dream of living on a farm had been crushed, they were determined their vision would not slip entirely from their grip. When they left the farm, they chose to see the end of life's tumultuous spring as an opportunity for a new adventure.

Dad took a job building homes with LaFree Construction in Bremen. He worked outdoors much of the time and was able to apply his knowledge of construction, electricity, and plumbing that he'd acquired while farming. They lived in a rented house near Bremen. As a sign of confidence in an unknown future, Mom gave birth to my sister, Julie, their sixth and last child.

Eventually, they found a piece of "farmland" at the corner of Elm and Shively. It was three acres of unusable lowland, a marshy spot overtaken by tall canary grass, and disparate from the productive fields around it.

With the money from their farm auction, Mom and Dad, now in their early forties, took this rejected piece of ground and refused to let it stay in its depressed form. Out of the swamp eventually rose a beautiful new home, built entirely by the hands of Dad and my brothers, Mike and Pat. Although the interior was not fully finished, on July 4, 1963, our family of eight moved in without fanfare or fireworks because there was something more precious to celebrate than the birth of our nation. The resurrection of hope had been snatched from the jaws of despair.

Although this new home represented a new start, my family was unwilling to let go of what they loved most about their old lives. Soon after we moved in, Dad tilled up a patch of ground almost two-thirds the size of a football field to make a garden large enough to feed eight people. Mom got sixty feet of clothesline to dry all our clothes. Then Dad, Mike, and Pat fenced in some of the land for a pasture for a Guernsey dairy cow and beef steers. When the Guernsey had a calf, we also had fresh milk. Along the way we even got a herd of sheep, for reasons I never understood. And it wasn't long before chickens arrived, which scratched for food in the flowers Mom grew to bring beauty to our place.

My family had been taken off the farm, but the farm could not be taken out of my family. We were country folk and that wasn't going to change. On our little piece of land, my family created a miniature version of what we had lost.

∝

Our new home was a healing balm, but as a four-year-old, unaware of the affairs of adults, I needed no salve. This was the fertile ground in which I grew, a happy child fed by adventure and my mother's love.

But there was one challenge over which I had no control. Long after my siblings drifted to sleep, my alert mind still gushed with ideas. Annoying as it was to lay awake in bed, it also brought blessings. My mother had similar nighttime patterns, so it was not uncommon for Mom and me to be up together at 1:00 a.m. while the world dreamed. I'd often cuddle at my mother's bosom in the living room, swaying in the rocking chair as the wooden runners squeaked. A dim light from the kitchen struggled to bend its way into our sanctuary. It was a time of silence, whispers, and soft laughter. Above all, it was a time of unconditional love, which still lingers with me like the fragrance of my mother's perfume.

One night, though, was like no other. It was a magical adventure, revealed here in a story my mother wrote called "The Night the Mouse Sang."

The witching hour was nearly upon us. The deepening night had long since snuffed out lights as it crept across the neighboring fields. We alone, my youngest son and I, were the only ones up for several miles around and were about to step over the threshold of a unique adventure. Earth-shaking it was not; in fact, it was seldom believed. But the adventure wrapped us in a warm, enveloping blanket of magic where the world could not follow and where the memory of that midnight shall never dim.

We built our house on a small tract of land and moved into it as soon it was habitable, working at it during our spare time. It became my habit to work on into the night to finish certain jobs before retiring, and often the four-year-old night-owl would keep me company. We were very close and he never seemed to tire. He could go to bed with the latest and bounce up with the earliest the next morning, so he was often allowed to stay up.

On this particular night, I pushed myself to finish sweeping up sawdust and was utterly exhausted. Kerry and I had much conversation and thoroughly enjoyed each other's company. We turned out all the lights except one lamp in the living room and intending to unwind a minute or two before going to bed, I found myself too tired to make a move.

Finally, I told him, "Kerry, I'm just too tired to get up and go to bed. Why don't you rub my back a little and then I'll feel better?"

He, being an obliging little friend, did as asked. Sitting beside me as I was stretched out on the sofa, he quietly rubbed my back. No conversations, as we both were nearly half asleep.

Gradually, I became aware of a slight sound—familiar, but unfamiliar. I listened in silence for a few minutes when suddenly Kerry whispered, "Mama, do you hear what I hear?"

"Well, I hear something," I whispered back, "but what do you hear?"

He whispered again, "It's something singing and it sounds like a mouse, but mice don't sing."

This night of magic should have made me throw caution to the winds, but I held back. "Yes, whatever is doing that singing, is doing it with a mouse voice, but mice don't sing."

Again he whispered, "Let's go see if we can find what it is and maybe we can tell whether it's a mouse or not."

Like a couple of conspirators, we tiptoed across our plywood living room floor and into the dining room from where the sound seemed to be coming. Again we listened.

With eyes saucered in wonder and awe, Kerry whispered, "Mama, he sings just like our canary does." Indeed, he was right. It was an odd little voice. It was like a mouse squeak, but melodic. It went up and down the scale and varied in volume. Our nocturnal serenader would start out in the merest whisper of a song, as though his singing was for his benefit alone, and then soar up and out in the pure happiness at being alive.

"Let's turn on the lights and look for whatever is doing that," I suggested.

With the light on we pinpointed the sound as coming from behind a pile of lumber standing in the corner of the room. Kerry crept up to it and rattled a board, and sure enough, out popped a little mouse that ran behind the bureau. With little four-year-old eyes shining, he clapped his hands and exclaimed, "Look, it was a mouse. He did sing!"

Still the magic of childhood had not yet burst over me. Again I said, "Wait a little bit and see if the singing starts up behind the bureau and if it does, then we shall know for sure."

So, very silently we stood, scarcely daring to breathe, waiting. In a short time, as though nothing had interrupted the midnight concert, the little singer started in again—low and tremulous at first, but building up to a glorious miniature climax, but from behind the bureau this time!

I capitulated, "It is a mouse, it is! But mice don't sing! Can you imagine that?"

The little tyke was beside himself. "Mama, I never heard of mice singing, did you?"

"No," I said, "I never did, but that has to be coming from that mouse." Wanting to share our discovery with the rest, I added, "Let's wake up the others to hear it."

We rushed to wake my husband first. Man-like, he grunted around and when I did get him aroused enough to tell him what it was all about, he groaned and without bothering to get out of bed, he answered, "A mouse singing? You've been reading too many library books."

Then I remembered—only the week before I had read a book to the children about a little covey, or herd, or whatever they call bunches of mice, that had been singing at midnight and little m-m-m's were ascending to the sky. But I had forgotten all about it. "No," I assured him, "this is not my imagination. Come quick and listen to it and you can see for yourself. Hurry, hurry, before he stops."

To no avail he only burrowed deeper, with no vestige of youth nor sense of adventure. To give him his due, how many people would wake up out of sound sleep for such a tomfool thing as a singing mouse?

Next, we flew to the sleeping children. I managed to get son No.1 out to listen, but alas, or perhaps luckily, there was no sound for him. No tiny throat spilling out tiny notes. He hung around for a while and finally growled, "Awrghh, you just imagined you heard something." And off he went back to bed. The remaining sons and daughters we couldn't even budge and the baby wouldn't know anything anyhow, so back we went to listen by ourselves.

Truly, the magic was just for us. What other mother and little son had ever had the privilege of listening at midnight to a furry, four-footed singing creature who didn't sing?

Gone was the bone-aching fatigue. I grabbed the broom and swept the kitchen floor while listening to the little soloist.

Kerry sat and listened quietly. In the midst of the concert we heard a clattering in the woodpile in the basement beneath and knew that the cat had just chased a mouse and probably caught it and that would, in all probability, be the fate of our furry friend. This prompted Kerry to beseech, "Let's try to catch him in a jar and keep him. Maybe he'll keep on singing for us. We can make a pet out of him."

"No," I told him, "let's don't. Let's just listen to him now as I have never heard one before and we may never again. Who ever heard of mice singing?"

And so we were a captivated audience of two. Sometimes the music would stop and we'd wait and think it was all over, and then he'd start up again. Lacking a tape recorder, I tried to analyze the sound so I could tell everybody about it. As near as I could tell, it seemed to be very much like standing on a squeaking floor board and wiggling it harder and faster and slower and lighter so it varied in pitch and volume.

Proving that even too much of a good thing can become boring, Kerry began to tire, so we turned out the lights and went to bed with the mouse still singing. Never again did we hear the little fellow, though we listened for him other nights.

And as for telling the world, we soon found out that the stardust was sprinkled only on us, a mother and little son, and only on that midnight, The Night the Mouse Sang.

SUMMER

Summer Prelude

Summer brings fullness of life. In a flurry of growth of mind, body, and spirit, it bursts into full bloom. Colorful gardens here, starlit nights there, learning and writing, Mom's summer was vibrant.

As a mother, she skillfully balanced her personal influence with the freedom she granted me to explore my childhood. But through her ceaseless teaching, nurturing, and companionship, my life was rooted in my mother's animated summer.

Mom was love in motion.

CHAPTER 7

Freedom Unlocked

*Lock up your libraries if you like; but there is no gate, no lock,
no bolt that you can set upon the freedom of my mind.*

—Virginia Woolf, "A Room of One's Own"

The spirit of my youth roamed with the winds, unbound by convention and fueled by curiosity of the mind. Mom passed this cup of freedom to me because she tasted such liberty in childhood on her grandparents' farm, infused by the pages of books, and fermented by adversity. I drank from the cup deeply.

Since my mother understood the power of knowledge to unlock the mind, she read to me regularly. And when I learned to read, I consumed books like candy, becoming the class reading leader in second grade. My inquisitive mind never turned off and kept me awake long into the night, thinking of new ideas and adventures. With daylight came the opportunity to investigate what my mind had only imagined. And like Sherlock Holmes, my best friend, Bryan, served as my Watson, assisting with each new investigation.

Bryan sported a dark buzz cut and lived within walking distance from me. I was a skinny towhead. Although he was a year older, Bryan's quiet personality often gave way to my ambitions. We were nearly inseparable.

"Hey, Bryan," I said on the bus ride home from elementary school one day. "I've got a great idea on how to make an automatic hot dog cooker. Come over after we get home so we can work on it." I had recently learned something about electricity and was eager to put my knowledge to use.

Bryan showed up dutifully. In Dad's workroom, we attached two vertical boards to a block of wood like the sides of a box, a hot dog-length apart. I drove a nail completely through each vertical board so its sharp end protruded toward the other in the opposing board. Next, Bryan screwed a ceramic light bulb fixture onto the same block of wood, which completed the mechanical part of the design.

"How are you going to hook up the electricity?" Bryan asked.

"We just need to make a loop of wire so the electricity flows down one wire, through the hot dog, then back to the wall through the other wire," I said.

"Is that safe?"

"Yeah," I replied. "We're just cooking a hot dog."

"What's the light for?"

"When the light turns on, we'll know the electricity is flowing, cooking the hot dog," I said, trying my best to sound like Albert Einstein.

I found an old extension cord and cut off the receptacle end, exposing two bare wires. I connected one bare wire to one terminal on the light fixture and attached the second bare wire onto the protruding head of one of the nails. With an extra piece of wire, I connected the head of the other nail to the remaining terminal on the light fixture, creating an electrical loop.

"Can you see how the electricity will flow?" I asked. Without waiting for his answer I continued, pointing as I spoke, "When we plug in the cord, electricity will come from the wall down one of the two wires in this cord. It will pass through this nail and into the hot dog. Because the hot dog is wet inside, the electricity will flow through the hot dog and into the other nail. From there, it will go to the light, and then back down the other wire in the cord into the wall. It's simple."

"Hmm," Bryan replied.

We carried the contraption upstairs from the basement, and I got a spare bulb from the linen closet. As Bryan screwed in the bulb, I fished a slippery, cold hot dog from the refrigerator. We plopped down in the hallway next to an outlet and spiked the hot dog between the two nails. With a hopeful glance at Bryan, I plugged the cord into the wall outlet. The light flashed on. Electricity was flowing!

"See! It works," I shouted with a smile.

Soon the frankfurter began to sizzle where the nails pierced its ends. Then a lovely spicy aroma filled the hallway. Eager to see how hot the meat was, I squeezed the center of the wiener.

"Yikes!" I shouted as a lightning bolt of pain shot up my arm, and my hand was thrown back like an exploding grenade.

"Huh!" laughed Bryan. "I knew something was gonna happen… What happened?"

I rubbed my hand and checked for burns and found no damage. "Well, I guess the electricity liked me better than the hot dog. But it looks like I'm okay."

With everything still in order, we waited on bended knee as the wiener cooked. Then, as if it had been designed to do so, the light turned off after a crust burned around the nails blocking the flow of electricity, signaling the hot dog was finished. It didn't concern me that I, too, could have been finished if I'd hung onto the electrified hot dog a bit longer, or touched one of the exposed nails, which were no different than bare wires plugged into the wall. But I didn't die, and my hot dog was cooked. I called that a success.

∝

Mom seldom intervened in my ventures. That freedom of mind I was granted was matched only by the unbridled liberty to explore the physical world beyond our home.

With no spoken goals, on weekends and summer days Bryan and I meandered down gravel roads, walking sticks in hand, uncovering in the side ditches and fields treasures of rusted cans, putrid mice trapped in empty beer bottles, and nudie magazines cast aside by teenagers in the night. The horizon was dotted with farm buildings and towering gray silos that stood like rockets ready to launch from a verdant sea of corn. Billowing clouds of brown dust alerted us to approaching cars long before their arrival. Willowy grass grew alongside the fencerows where red-winged blackbirds warned us away from their nests, rabbits hid their young, and migratory Monarch butterflies laid eggs on milkweed as part of their journey north. Wherever our legs could take us we went there without permission, supervision, or parental knowledge. After we journeyed beyond the sound of my mother's shouts or the clang of the bell, a summons went unheeded.

But our favorite hangout was the deep ditch, cut through the farmland many years before to drain the once-soggy soil. Muskrats and groundhogs lived on its banks. Grunting frogs, crawdads and fish called the water their homes. We climbed down its slope through the scratchy grass to build earthen dams, catch fish, or just skip stones in the gently flowing creek. We were Davy Crockett and Daniel Boone rolled together with Lewis and Clark as we explored every bridge, every tree, and every sun-dappled ripple for a mile in each direction. We simply called this stretch of paradise "The Ditch." It was our home away from home, from the whispers of springtime to the howls of winter.

CԾ

"Kerry," Dad shouted through the screen door one August Saturday, "come out to the patio. I have a surprise for you."

Dad *never* had a surprise for me, so my eyebrows nearly touched my scalp in wide-eyed disbelief. I scrambled from my TV chair and ran upstairs with my older brother, Tom, and my younger sister, Julie, racing beside me to see what our dad had done. We burst onto the patio where Dad was standing proudly beside a poorly painted green and gold yard sale bicycle.

"Happy birthday," he said to me, as Tom's and Julie's heads turned simultaneously from the bike toward Dad, and then to me.

"Uhh, Dad…it's not my birthday," I said. "My birthday is in November, when I'll turn eight. Today is Tom's birthday."

Silence filled the air as Dad looked at Tom, who stared back blankly.

"Oh," Dad said, finally, certainly embarrassed by his mistake in the midst of his highly unusual generosity. "I guess Kerry's going to have to ride it because it's too small for you, Tom." And with that, Dad walked away. There was no apology and no promise to "make it right," which later became a source of family laughter.

I was as stunned by this sudden turn of events as Tom was disappointed. There was nothing he or I could do to fix the situation. And to be honest, my concern for Tom's welfare quickly faded as I realized I now had a bike! My exploration was no longer limited to only where my feet could walk. Now I could ride with Bryan, who already had wheels.

Bryan and I rode like the wind, flying past Holstein cows whose black and white hides looked like living Rorschach tests, past neighborhood teens sweltering on flatbed wagons as they grabbed and stacked bales of hay machined from the fields, and cruising alongside wildflowers basking in unseen glory in the roadside grass. To saddle up and ride four miles around the country block without adult permission was as commonplace as breathing fresh air.

But with this freedom came danger on four paws. Dogs. Big dogs. Dogs that lived to devour little kids who dared to ride through their domains. Although Bryan and I attempted to sneak past known "kidnivores," my skin crawled when these vipers with fur lit out across their yards at full speed with bared fangs and flying drool. As we approached such territory, we peddled as fast as our little legs could move so that when the devil arrived at our churning feet, we could lift them out of reach and pray we could safely coast past the property protected by these thugs.

Although this fear of dogs regulated our travels, it didn't stop us from riding three miles into Bremen when the notion arrived.

Bremen was, as its motto proclaimed: "A good town." But it wasn't always such a pleasant place. Its original inhabitants were Potawatomi Native Americans who were removed from the county in 1838 by General John Tipton in the infamous "Trail of Death." Escorted by armed volunteer militia, more than forty people died on their way to eastern Kansas, which marked the single-largest Indian removal in a state named after its original citizens: Indiana.[1]

Although the Potawatomi were not welcomed by the settlers to Bremen, Bryan and I experienced no such opposition as we pedaled toward town.

"Where do you want to go?" I asked Bryan, after we got past the killer canines.

"I was thinking about a piece of candy," he replied.

That got my attention. "Maybe a Bit-O-Honey?" I asked, hopefully. I had no money.

"Nope. Licorice."

Well, if Bryan was willing to share I was willing to compromise. We extended our arms like wings on a plane and steered our bikes to town with only the sway of our bodies, inhaling the syrupy smell of the burg's molasses factory long before we arrived at Bremen's first street.

The streets, which ran exactly north/south or east/west, framed orderly blocks, similar to the country roads. Bryan and I rode our bikes toward the center of town on Center Street, past Wilson's Grain Elevator where sputtering tractors towed metal wagons filled with corn, beans, or wheat to sell. Grain dust curled into the air as growers released their golden harvest into pits before it was carried to the top of concrete silos and loaded onto train cars on the adjacent Baltimore & Ohio railway.

We crossed the tracks and moved over the Yellow River, which bordered a city park. "You know," I said. "Our ditch dumps into this river somewhere, but I don't know where." Bryan was quiet, apparently pondering his licorice. "And another thing," I said, as I contemplated the world as my playground, "I don't understand why people need a special place to go play...like at this park."

Bryan had no answer as we pedaled harder up the slight incline toward the town center.

We passed near one of my favorite places: the library. Although it was a municipal amenity, it didn't lock its doors to country folks like us. Just as Mom had done with her sisters in childhood, she and I regularly plucked food from its shelves for our ravenous minds.

Flanking each side of Center Street, were simple but elegant two-story homes. Some had tidy flowerbeds that surrounded white columned porches where residents relaxed on swings or comfortable chairs on pleasant evenings. This town's tranquility and safety, reinforced with the moral fiber of its fifteen churches, are what drew many of these families to Bremen. Dr. Otis Bowen, who brought my cry into this world with a spank to my behind, and who went on to become Governor of Indiana, lived in one of these homes.

Bryan and I churned our way up Center Street and into downtown where the molasses smell of Bremen's present was overcome by the smell of Bremen's past. Our town's first settlers found the swampy marsh around the area was ideal for growing mint. Farmers set out the plants and the area soon became the "mint capital of the world" until Verticillium Wilt, a deadly fungus, took its toll in the 1950s. But Center Street still held in its palm a remnant of the faded industry. Stored inside a small warehouse were fifty-gallon drums of concentrated mint oil used to make a delicious hard candy nicknamed Bremen Mints. The aroma of the mint oil was so strong it penetrated the metal drums, seeped from the brick and mortar storage building, and filled the nearby sidewalks and streets with the smell of happiness. As Bryan and I drifted down the street, I closed my eyes and imagined I was floating on a giant mint candy.

Candy was our purpose and the source was at the intersection of Center Street and Plymouth Street. Here, Bremen's lone stop light controlled the flow of noisy cars, trucks, tractors, and the frequent Amish horse and buggy. This was "downtown." On the four corners were Bremen State Bank, Dietrich's clothing store, which opened in 1855, a hotel, and the corner store, which sold newspapers, cards and offered up a rack full of sticky pleasures.

"Let's go get our licorice," Bryan said. We parked our bikes on the sidewalk. He paid the clerk a nickel and received three strands of cherry-flavored licorice. We stepped outside to the sounds of progress, and Bryan tore off one strip and handed it to me.

"Thanks," I said. We stood there enjoying a piece of Heaven and watched the passersby.

More than a dozen small businesses were clustered in just a couple of blocks. Occasional hitching posts for the neighboring Amish horses stood in front of awning-covered storefronts. Many brick façades were topped with stately patterned cornices and fluted friezes. Hoople's Tavern, the oldest family-owned bar in Indiana, survived as a pool hall during Prohibition. It would have gone out of business, though, if its income depended on my family of teetotalers. Nearby was Koontz Hardware, Odiorne's paint store, and Berg's Appliances. But I was most familiar with the dime store, where my Mom often shopped.

Along the railroad at each end of town, where Bryan and I seldom rode, were business parks. Places like Gray Iron Foundry and TV Time Popcorn provided good-paying jobs for the adults, although some companies, like Bremen Products, sought only married men as employees in the 1960s.

Bremen was a small town with roughly 3,000 residents surrounded by farmland. But its dozens of businesses allowed Bremen citizens to live, work, and play inside the city limits.

My piece of licorice was now gone, but Bryan was still eating his first one. "How can you eat that so slowly?" I asked, somewhat annoyed.

"I'm just enjoying it," Bryan replied. "If I eat it slow, the goodness lasts longer."

I looked down the street to the nearby office of *The Bremen Enquirer*. The newspaper, founded in 1872, existed solely to serve the Bremen community. The newspaper's motto was proudly displayed in its masthead, a variation of the town's motto: "A Good Newspaper in a Good Town." In addition to the local news, its advertisements touted Huff's Funeral Home, which boasted without a trace of irony that it served "ALL religions: Catholic, Protestant, and Jewish." And with no apparent conflict of interest, the funeral home also touted its ambulance service. When gaps appeared on a page of news, the *Enquirer* filled the voids with words of encouragement such as: "Go to church Sunday." But that didn't discourage the boys of the Future Farmers of America from inserting an ad in 1967, intentionally styled after a slave bill that might have appeared in the South during the era of slavery. It invited Bremen's all-white community to its "Slave Auction" where the boys' labor would be auctioned as a fundraiser for the organization.

But such parodies of historical horror were not on my mind as a child. I looked forward to other events such as the Firemen's Festival, the midsummer carnival that kicked off with a parade down Plymouth Street with floats, tractors, and the high school marching band, and concluded with spectacular fireworks. Although I seldom got one, I also relished a cold ice cream cone from the Dairy Queen on the edge of town.

"Bryan, are you about done with those two pieces of licorice?" I asked, impatiently and with a bit of jealousy. I was done daydreaming and ready to move on.

"Almost," he said as he bit off tiny pieces from his last strip. He was in no hurry.

While Bremen had the atmosphere of a rural community, it boasted many features only found in much larger cities, such as the Bremen Community Hospital where I was born. Made possible by the pride and financial support of local businesses, organizations, and individuals, it opened in the 1940s and was Indiana's smallest hospital. As a sign of the town's country charm, *The Bremen Enquirer* published the names of all who were admitted to the hospital and often included their reason for being there, because in Bremen neighbors cared for neighbors.

As a country boy, Bremen was urban America to me, but not that intriguing. So when Bryan and I tired of the freedom of touring the metropolis, we turned our bikes around, steered past occasional droppings left by the Amish horses, and looked forward to retracing our path to the bucolic bliss we knew, where houses had no street numbers and the only light which controlled traffic was the sun.

❧

When I walked in the door after an hours-long sojourn, Mom didn't quiz me about my whereabouts. When I did share something interesting with her, she never expressed alarm at my wandering. She believed freedom was a necessary ingredient of life and provided me the gift of liberty that she had received as a child.

That freedom extended beyond where my bike would take me. It extended to my mind and spirit, and eventually gave me the inspiration and courage to head off to college, to leave Indiana as an adult, and to marry outside my ethnicity. It granted me permission to explore the Berlin Wall in East Germany, to befriend strangers on the crowded streets of India, and to sit reverently beside a pride of lions on the Serengeti.

But these acts pale in comparison to the courage she harnessed to raise a strong and independent child, not knowing where life may lead him.

CHAPTER 8

A Love Affair with Flowers

I must have flowers, always, and always.

—Claude Monet (1840-1926)

An explosion of passionate pink peonies wore the lipstick of God in my mother's gardens near the front of our red brick country home, an island of color in a green sea of towering corn. A moat of marigolds, the color of rich egg yolk, encircled sentinel rocks flanking our driveway. Blasts of forsythia, yellow as the sun, rocketed from the ground beneath my bedroom window. Jasmine, delicate and fragrant as the breath of angels, wound itself around the lamppost while red and purple fuchsia cascaded from hanging baskets beneath our patio's eaves. Ivory clematis climbed toward their trellised sky with outstretched petals like arms, welcoming all to Mom's world. It was as pretty as a Monet painting, and another area where Mom excelled.

It was on her grandparents' farm where her soul was awakened to the glory of nature. She found tranquility in the smooth petals and delicate scent of the wild rose, in the freshness of a summer shower, in the hum of bees in the vines of dusky grapes, and in the meadowlark's song in early morning. It was there she fell in love with God's creation, especially the flowers.

At the tender age of eighteen, she hinted at this love affair in her poetry, describing how flowers fit into her favorite parts of the day, the quiet times at the beginning and the end.

Dawn

The air was filled with soft twittering of sleepy birds.
Flowers pressed close and damp against the earth
Under the pearl grey fog.
Ribbons of light unfurled over the top of the hill,
Turning the mist from grey to apple pink,
And heralding the coming of the day.

Harvest Night

Air…cool and sweet as rain-washed flowers,
The moon…honey dropped on blue velvet.

A few years later, when Mom married and moved onto my dad's family farm, she discovered a utilitarian tribe who didn't share her passion for nature. There, plants were grown to feed livestock or people. Flowers were a waste of time, space, and energy. *What good are the flowers?* With that question hanging perpetually in the air and no one to share her love of nature, Mom felt alone and isolated, as she expressed in this poem.

Alone

He walks alone who walks with me
And sees not colored crystal stones,
But jagged rocks that bruise his feet.

He walks alone who walks with me
And sees not lovely perfumed blooms,
But weeds that clog his fields and lawn.

He walks alone who walks with me
And hears not birds who sing with joy,
But scheming thieves who steal his fruit.

When my grandfather eventually told my mom and dad to leave the family farm, it was a blessing in disguise. It unleashed Mom's passion for flowers. In her new home, she painted beautiful pictures with a trowel in one hand and life in the other, as she describes here in her own words:

It begins with a tug-of-war between winter and spring. The crocus pop open and tender tulip shoots peak out beneath shrinking drifts of snow. One morning, I awake to a dazzling fairyland. The trees, bushes—everything!—are embroidered with delicate tracery of hoar frost. Merest whisper of breeze loosens the frost and it falls like petals. The warming sun breaks through the mist and soon steals away the rest of the white lace.

Soon, the tulips are out in a patchwork of color, nodding and bowing to all who pass by, like ladies of long ago dressed for a ball. I work in the gardens when days are pleasant and spring laps at my feet. I spot a purple martin scouting a nest site, and listen to the sad, sad calls of the mourning dove. I am entranced as the warm sun touches my skin. The bees buzz through the early flowers, letting me know the temperature is above 43 degrees.

At night, bewitching sweet scents drift through the air. It is the white miniature iris. So sweet. By day, the mountain ash beguiles, if we don't get too close to its cloying scent.

Suddenly, winter is gone! The roses are in bloom. Goldfinches sail overhead, bobbing like ships at sea, serenading with sweet song. The hummingbirds zip like miniature helicopters, startling me as I come into the garden. A delicate butterfly lights on me and I stop to admire his buff-gold "feathers" and the many black "eyes" on the borders of his wings. I wait patiently and speak softly. Perhaps he was attracted to my lavender slacks. Perhaps he thought I was a flower!

As spring blossomed into summer at our home, fields of white daisies danced in the breeze like children. Blankets of maroon pansies, once the earlier pride of the garden, faded away as rivers of magenta and purple petunias flowed around the garage. Tangerine lilies tumbled down a small hill on the opposite side of the house.

But even more amazing was Mom's rock garden.

In our backyard, the ground sloped gently downward. The rock garden began at the top of this hill and was shaped like a royal train of a bridal gown, fanning out as it flowed down the hill. Using large rocks, Mom created concentric waves rippling out from the top of the hill, each lower than the previous.

She curated the stones in her garden as if they were works of art, hauled in from fields, from friends, or journeys away. There were smooth blue stones from Kentucky, rough red ones from out west, and pocked geodes hiding crystalline wonders inside. Each stone had a personality, unique to itself, whether pulled from a cornfield or carried two thousand miles home. Though they harbored no life, the garden was alive, as stones traded places and new ones arrived.

Between these lines of rock was an avalanche of flowers, which changed with the seasons and Mom's inspiration. Waves of yellow daffodil cups and rainbows of snap dragons swayed in spring breeze, sweetened by the fragrance of sky blue iris. White periwinkle twinkled like daytime stars amidst the rose and cream body of the columbine flowers that dangled menacing tentacles as if they belonged in the sea. Clusters of dainty coral bell rang with joy. Pillows of lavender phlox cascaded over stacked stones. Then balls of burnt orange mums burst into fall while asters fed butterflies and bees.

But Mom's gardens were more than dazzling displays of natural art. I believe they were the altar of her life, where she knelt on sacred ground. This is where she admired God's handiwork, spoke to the butterflies, and partnered with the Creator. And like those butterflies which supped at her flowers, the garden was Mom's feast for her soul, where her spirit renewed. It's where she dug her hands into warm soil and felt the security of the earth to which she was wed. It's where she witnessed death in winter and the resurrection of hope in spring. It's where her *knowledge* of God transformed into her *experience* of God.

☙

Mom did her best to indoctrinate her family with the love of flowers, but the responses were as varied as the plants she grew. Dad was eventually won over and Mom no longer walked alone. He helped her build beds and borders, and even grew straight rows of gladiolas in his own garden, as if they were corn. As an adult, I enjoy flowers, but I'm not a masterful gardener like my mother. The flowers in my gardens grow in spite of my actions, not because of them. And my nephew, Theodore, my oldest brother's son, learned an even broader lesson.

"Grandma took great joy living in the present," Theodore told me as we sat around his oak dinner table one late afternoon. "Weeding her gardens was far less important than simply enjoying them. She wasn't a slave to their upkeep, so weeds often lived in the shadow of her flowers. But I think there's a lot to be said about spending more time enjoying life than stressing out about perfection."

My older sister, Janet, had a much different experience than the other family members. Like a steady drip of nectar, Mom's love of flowers imperceptibly filled Janet's adult life until one day she looked into life's mirror and gasped. She saw my mother standing there.

"Just look," Janet instructed, pointing out the picture window into the backyard of her Indianapolis home where we sat across from each other in her living room. "What do you see?"

It was late morning and the ground outside was wet from an earlier summer shower. Golden sunshine broke over the tops of hickory and cottonwood trees, illuminating artistry below. A tall, four-sided trellis stood in the center of her gardenscape, covered in vines and blossoms of purple clematis. Islands of yellow lilies swayed in the breeze around the trellis, as did patches of white daisies and lavender salvia. Mounds of coral impatiens and white phlox encroached on the walkway as a hummingbird stole nectar, then disappeared. Near the edges of this colorful fairyland were ruby-red dahlias the size of dinner plates and pink Rose of Sharon. Birdfeeders, birdbaths, and benches were scattered among the life, as were large rock arrangements and borders. Although I couldn't smell the flowers, they were fragrance for my eyes. And I knew even more flowers grew beyond my view.

I slowly shook my head as the extravagant beauty made me smile. While still staring at the love of my sister's life, I finally replied to her question about what I saw. "I see Mom."

"Exactly! That's my point," she said, leaning forward and unwinding one leg from under the other. "I've become Mom… And it's not only what you see growing outside, but it's also the things I do."

Janet seemed eager to share her revelation, so I sat quietly and listened.

"See all those zinnias and gladiolas?" she asked, nodding toward the window.

I looked past Janet's paradise, into a garden where vegetables once grew, and saw rows of gladiolas that stood like sails in the wind, and a kaleidoscope of zinnias.

"I'm that person who turns those gorgeous flowers into bouquets for my friends at work," she said, "just because I know it will make them smile. Spring, summer, and fall there's always something I can share with them from my flower garden. And I'm that person who slows everyone down as we walk to a restaurant so I can inhale the heavenly fragrance of jasmine growing along the sidewalk."

She was on a roll and barely stopped for breath. Staring straight at me, with eyes wide open, she continued, "I'm that person who unabashedly leans in and smells all the funeral flowers while paying my respects. Who does that?" she exclaimed, throwing an open palm in the air.

"Mom," I answered, without thinking.

Janet huffed. "Yes, but that was meant as a rhetorical question."

"Oh...sorry," I chuckled. I had broken her train of thought and she stopped talking. I let silence hang in the air for a moment before asking, "So, do you remember when you first fell in love with flowers?"

"I do, actually. I remember my first love." Another smile popped onto Janet's face and she became reanimated. "As a teenager, I resisted Mom's efforts to get me into her gardens. But when I got engaged, I wanted to have an outdoor wedding and couldn't think of a better place to have it than our backyard oasis among the cornfields. So that's where I got married."

"Yeah, I remember that," I said. "I think I was going into high school."

"Then you probably remember Dad and me walking down those curving flagstone steps that came down the hill. At the bottom of the steps, my girlfriend sat on a rock next to the little waterfall Dad built and played her guitar and sang. I've always loved running water. I couldn't have asked for a more beautiful setting—a waterfall in the middle of flat Indiana cornfields! Go figure."

Janet seemed distracted with her memories, but I didn't interrupt.

"And, of course, on the other side of the flagstone stairs was Mom's *pièce de résistance,"* she said with a lilt and her version of a French accent. "That was her rock garden. My wedding colors were pink, purple, and blue pastels. Mom planted only those colors of flowers there that summer. Larry and I stood in the yard at the base of the rock garden that swept up the hillside behind us with all those beautiful flowers. I even wore daisies in my hair. Mom planted lots of daisies, too."

"So that's when you first fell in love with flowers?" I asked, studying her face for clues in the morning light.

"Yesss...but it was more than that. When I got married in front of Mom's gardens, I felt grateful. I knew then that she would do anything for me that she could." Janet slowly swiveled in her chair away from me and looked longingly out her window at the beautiful essence of our mother that grew in her gardens. The edges of Janet's eyes glistened in the soft sunlight as she inhaled deeply, as if smelling the beauty she saw, then sighed before continuing.

"Above all else," she said, "I felt loved. I felt loved by Mom. At the time, she had never told me she loved me. But that day she showed me. It was one of the happiest days of my life."

⅋

The portrait of Mom's life was painted with flowers. They were the perfume and smiles of God, and evidence of her partnership with the Creator when she toiled in her Garden of Eden. Flowers nourished Mom's soul like nectar for the bees, lifting her spirit. It was *love* she grew in her gardens, and the flowers were her embrace. Through them, she shared *all* that she loved with all *whom* she loved.

But not all that Mom touched in life bloomed with such beauty.

CHAPTER 9

Kitchen Complications

My mother had a complicated relationship with the kitchen. Its work nourished her body, but unlike her flowers, seldom her soul. As our family's "executive chef," her role was defined by her gender, but she chose to provide in nontraditional ways. Her kitchen was a place where new ideas and unusual experiences bubbled like boiling water.

The journey through Mom's kitchen began at the window above the sink, as she explained in this excerpt of an essay titled "My Sink Think."

I read recently that a housewife spends half her time in the kitchen at the sink. That sounds like me—but I think at the sink. Recent surveys indicate that people don't spend much time thinking anymore. What do other housewives do with their gray matter when their hands are busy doing the same things they have done hundreds and thousands of times? What a waste of valuable time if all they do is contemplate the disagreeableness of the task before them.

I am most fortunate that I have a sink that looks out over a small grove of trees; thirty trees occupy a space of a little over a half acre. I get to watch the seasons come and go, come and go. Is the repetition dull? Never. The oft-repeated occurrences in my little grove are soothing and stabilizing.

Mom contemplated more than the trees as she gazed out her kitchen window. She thought about growing and preparing healthy foods, and how to avoid illness and disease, which she learned from *Organic Gardening* and *Prevention* magazines. Then she turned these ideas into actions.

We grew our own organic vegetables, drank unpasteurized whole milk, and ate dense brown bread. Refined foods were particularly bad in Mom's view. Consuming white sugar was practically a sin, so we used molasses, honey, or brown sugar. Similarly, whole wheat brown flour took the place of white bleached flour used in other homes. Mom said that "her" flour contained all the elements of the wheat kernel and was therefore more nutritious than the white flour that removed the bran and germ.

Little yellow boxes, the size of Jell-O packages and labeled with simple names like "C" and "E," were stacked on our counter. From them she withdrew a handful of vitamins each day and washed them down with "mineral water," which she retrieved from a local spring in one-gallon glass bottles.

When in season, she prepared weeds from the yard—dandelions and lambs quarter, which she claimed were highly nutritious. She was disparaged within the family for this practice, prompting her to win over converts to the lowly plants by writing:

> Consider its uses. Many generations have eagerly awaited the earliest dandelion in the spring for eating. The leaves were eaten for greens, the bud and blossom for vegetables, and the blossom for wine. It's usually considered a lowly weed but get down on your knees—inspect the flower. Is it not a miniature sun protected by its saw-edged leaves? See, even the sunshine rubs off on your chin and gives you glow. Indeed, it's fittingly named after the king of beasts!

Mom invited me into her kitchen and taught me how to cook. She let me experiment and sometimes make a mess. "Stir things in a figure eight," she said to me as she gently took my hand the first time. "That way, your spoon covers the entire bottom of the pan and doesn't splash." She explained how to use recipes: "After you dip your measuring spoon into the spice box, level it off with the back of a knife so you get just the right amount." For her, the art of cooking was also the opportunity to share a science lesson. "When the bubbles start to appear on the uncooked side of the pancake, it's time to flip it." I enjoyed learning to cook and made my first pie by myself at age seven.

But not all my interactions with Mom turned out so well.

In early spring when I was ten years old, I visited an Amish sugarhouse and learned how maple syrup was made. I returned home eager to do it myself. The nights were still cold and the days had warmed, which meant perfect weather to entice the maple sap to flow up from the roots to feed the budding branches. With a brace and bit, my dad and I drilled through the rough bark and into the smooth heart of two maple trees that Mom often studied through her kitchen window. We tapped in metal spigots, and then hung plastic buckets from each one. Every evening, I put on a jacket and crunched through dry grass to retrieve the buckets of clear sap that seeped like tears. Mom poured the gallons of liquid, which contained only a faint taste of sugar, into our largest pot and boiled the sap to remove the water.

It takes forty or more gallons of sap to make one gallon of syrup. So as the liquid boiled down, Mom poured in more tears of the trees. For more than a week, she and I teamed up: carry-pour-boil, carry-pour-boil. With so much water to boil away, the sap-to-syrup needed to cook twenty-four hours a day, leaving the delicate aroma of maple perfume lingering in the house.

Finally, the moment of reckoning was near. The sap no longer seeped and the boiling golden treasure was getting thick and sticky, shimmering like jewels. At a precise point in the process, which we estimated would occur in the middle of the night, our gallon of syrup would be ready! Mom agreed to stay up and turn off the stove at the moment of peak perfection.

In the stillness of the night, she retired to her comfortable chair, as a lone bulb illuminated the book she read to pass the time.

It was a wonderful, caring gesture on Mom's part to indulge my project by staying up to monitor the syrup's final hours. But by the time the smell of smoke awoke her, it was too late. The syrup was ruined and nearly hard as a rock, turning the tears of trees to my tears of despair the next day.

Burning food was one of Mom's perpetual struggles in the kitchen. It happened so frequently that it sparked a family joke:

"How do you know when supper's ready?"

"I don't know. How?"

"When the smoke alarm goes off!"

Although she was the butt of the joke, Mom always laughed along with us. But in spite of her efforts, food continued to be burned and the blackness scraped off before eating. This frequently occurred with meat, which contributed to my strong distaste for it.

Whether it was chicken, beef, or pork fried, braised, or baked—none of the meat she prepared was appealing to me and not just because oftentimes it was burned. There was just nothing enticing about it. Cow tongue, a delicacy in my mother's eyes, was the worst. The stench of steamy death floated up from her boiling pot and collected under the exhaust hood, then spilled into the room. The sight of the cooked tongue laying curled on the serving dish reminded me of its life. *What barbarians cut tongues from their victims and eat them*, I wondered?

My disgust with meat as a child caused me to reject it outright. I was offered freewill and chose to exercise it. If Mom made pork chops, green beans, and corn for supper, I ate green beans and corn. No alternative protein was provided. Partly as a result, the words 'Kerry' and 'muscles' were never used in the same sentence. With ribs as visible as barrel staves, my grandmother would often jest, "One day you might dry up and blow away." Though she spoke in love, the sting never left the tease.

But there was one other source of protein that was as ubiquitous as it was unwanted: bugs.

Opening an upper cabinet door in our kitchen was like walking into a butterfly house of horrors as a puff of scruffy brown mini-moths flew frightfully into my face. Ugly brown beetles, the size of short-grain rice, lived in dry goods such as flour, cereal, and muffin mix, which we still consumed after picking out most of the insects. It was never clear where these beetles and moths came from. One could have come from the other, because we seemed to have an entire ecosystem in our cabinets. They even showed up in unexpected places.

A platter of steaming sweet corn was passed to me at supper one evening. I grabbed an ear as its hot, heavenly scent made me dreamy. Next, came the butter. I smeared a big piece up and down the ear, letting it melt in a golden embrace. Finally, the salt. Already enjoying the corn in my imagination, I liberally shook the shaker, as white and brown salt sprinkled out. *Wait!* "What's in the salt?" I exclaimed, as I peered closely at the dark specks. "Eww! It's bugs! There's bugs in the salt, and now they're on my corn," I wailed. Although I was the last in line to get my corn, I wondered why I was the first to see the bugs. I looked up the line at my dad who was happily munching away with two hands.

"Dad," I shouted, "you've got bugs on your corn, too!"

He glanced at his corn momentarily. "Yep. More protein," he said without missing a bite.

Whether food had bugs, or just a tiny bit remained after a meal, Mom was unable to throw it away. Her experience as a child with scarcity never left her. She always had a plan to use leftovers "tomorrow." But tomorrow seldom came. In our Sears Coldspot refrigerator, bowls were stacked on jars, on top of pans. Removing an item from the fridge was like playing a game of Jenga; we never knew when we might cause an avalanche.

Inevitably, all that organic material spoiled. Ancient yellow squash turned green from the blue mold. The freezer compartment fared no better. Without the "frost free" feature, growing glaciers consumed the entire compartment with no way to know what was entombed.

Of course, Mom tried to save as much of the formally-known-as-food items as possible when the fridge was cleaned out. The non-edible, non-poisonous items went to the big dog, and the rest was thrown into our compost pile to make future soil for the plants. "See," she'd say with pride and without a hint of irony, "nothing's going to waste."

One winter, Mom pulled out a few spoiled items from the refrigerator and mixed them with some dry dog food and water to make a dog stew. Because it was a bitter cold day and the dog slept in the unheated garage, she treated our dog by heating the stew on the stove. But as the sinking sun signaled suppertime, Mom realized she'd forgotten to go to the store. So she turned off the stew, jumped into the car, and drove to town. Shortly, Dad came home from a cold day's work and was delighted to find a warm stew waiting on the stove. He ladled himself a large bowl of the canine cuisine and ate it up. He had a stomach of steel, my dad.

Such complicated meals were not confined to our home. In the burgeoning era of white, fluffy Wonder Bread in the 1960s, we were socially out of step with Mom's dense brown bread. The awkwardness was particularly distressing for me in elementary school, surfacing every day at lunch.

"Fuzz, what's in your lunch box today? Another brick?" Roger chided as we sat down on the folding table-bench in the cavernous gym-turned-cafeteria of my elementary school where the chatter of young voices reverberated off the hard walls and floor.

"I don't know. We'll see," I said. But I already knew the answer. It was the same every day.

Roger unrolled his paper bag and withdrew a baloney sandwich wrapped in Saran wrap. I tried not to stare, but his white Wonder Bread gleamed as if it were an angel's sandwich sent down from Heaven. Roger slowly peeled off the clear plastic and stuffed the white fluffy bread into his mouth like cotton candy. "Mmm," he said, with eyes closed in ecstasy. "Thith ith deliciouth."

I turned my metal lunch box at an angle to block Roger's view before unsnapping the latch. David, who wore glasses and was nearly as skinny as me, sat on my other side and sipped milk through a paper straw, then bit into his baloney sandwich made from the same heavenly Wonder Bread.

I knew about Wonder Bread. It was on the commercials during Saturday morning cartoons. Wonder Bread "helped build strong bodies 12 ways!" It was soft, radiant, and almost lighter than air. It was also aptly named, because I could only wonder how it tasted. I knew the Bible said thou shalt not covet thy neighbor's things, but Wonder Bread was not on the list. I had a serious case of Wonder Bread envy.

"Fuzz, aren't you going to eat your lunch?" asked David between bites.

"He doesn't want us ta see his samwich," said Roger. "I mean, his brick."

I slowly opened the lid and lifted an orange to my nose, inhaling the crisp aroma, then set it down next to my lunch box. Next, I pried open my cold milk carton—the only thing I could buy at the cafeteria—and leisurely pulled off one end of the paper covering my straw. I blew through the straw to shoot the cover toward Roger.

I could no longer delay the inevitable. I hefted my peanut butter and jelly sandwich from the box and pulled the rubber band from the wax paper wrapping. As I set it down, the crackly wax paper unfolded itself, exposing my naked sandwich. It was made with dense pumpernickel bread and was nearly black. I blushed.

"What's that, Fuzz? Looks like a rock," Roger laughed after choking on his milk. He reached over my milk carton and grabbed my sandwich and hoisted it into the air as if weighing it. "David, you should feel this thing," he said, snorting again.

"Roger, put it down. That's my sandwich," I said, trying to replace my embarrassment with forcefulness.

"That ain't no samwich, Fuzz. That's a weapon. You should save it, in case you git in a fight. You whack somebody upside the head and they'd be dead!" Roger chuckled. "Why does your mom buy this stuff?" he asked, rhetorically.

In spite of Roger's teasing, he'd asked a good question. I pretended Mom bought "this stuff" because she hadn't seen the commercials and didn't know about the beautiful, fluffy white Wonder Bread that built strong bodies twelve ways. But, of course, that wasn't the reason. Even though it looked like the devil, dense and dark, she bought it because it was healthy. For her, there was no wondering which bread was more nutritious.

☙

Looking back, Mom was ahead of her time in many ways. She grew organic vegetables, ate whole wheat and other natural foods, avoided sugar and soft drinks, drank spring water, and composted food waste. It took years for that wisdom to catch up with me, and most other people. But I did learn pretty quickly that I preferred bug-free food.

Mom knew her legacy would not be served on a dinner plate. Though providing healthy food was important to her, cooking did not satisfy a lifelong yearning; she was expected to cook because she was a woman. Being herself meant living beyond the traditional feminine boundaries. Her kitchen was a place to ponder questions, to commune with nature, to teach life lessons in gender roles and nutrition, and to build memories with her children. The food she prepared there was not the end—it was the means to the end—the source of energy to fuel a family for the fullness of life.

CHAPTER 10

Labor of Love

It was nearly a perfect job for my mother, requiring no spatula or stove. So when she was offered the opportunity to write a weekly column in our small, farming community newspaper, she was thrilled. Although the pay was meager, it was beyond bountiful because the task used so many of her strengths. Mom was an engaging conversationalist, which this part-time work required. Propelled by a curious and probing mind, she possessed broad knowledge with an insatiable appetite for more. She relished sharing with others what she discovered and especially enjoyed writing about it. Her column was called "The Party Line," and bringing it to print was a labor of love.

To understand and appreciate Mom's column, it's important to understand its name, borrowed from our rural phone system.

A party line phone system was simply a single phone line shared by multiple homes, or "parties," where each home still had its own number. Although party lines were less costly than running private lines to the sparsely spaced farm homes, they also had disadvantages.

If a caller picked up the phone and began dialing while another party was on the line, each rotation of the dial brought a loud series of electrical clicks, grating on the ears of those already in conversation. More importantly, if someone needed to use the party line while someone else was on a call, it was impossible.

There was also great temptation to quietly eavesdrop on neighbors' phone calls, detectable only by subtle clicks of the lifted receiver and the breath of the snooper. Few members of the community admitted to listening in, although it was not uncommon to do so. Listening to others' conversations might seem a bit voyeuristic, but this transparency served as a stabilizing influence to keep the community connected. It was difficult to hide secrets.

The editor of our local newspaper, *The Bremen Enquirer*, wanted to capitalize on the irresistible pull of knowing about neighbors' lives. He envisioned a regular, family-friendly article that shared the kind of information a snooper might hear on a party line call. So when Mom stepped into his office in 1967 and asked if she could write something for the newspaper, "The Party Line" was born.

Mom's journalistic goal was simple: find something interesting in people's lives that she could write about. She believed everyone had a story to tell and her job was to entertain her readers with their stories.

It was fitting that Mom used the party line to create its namesake. Several times a week she sat in the center of our home at an antique oak school desk to make calls to members of the Bremen community. With our black rotary phone resting on the desktop, marked by decades of schoolhouse doodles, Mom often pointed aimlessly to a name in the phone book, and then dialed the number.

The recipients of her calls reflected the demographics of our community. She spoke with frantic farmers, dedicated teachers, happy housewives, merchants, and even teenagers. Although Mom believed mostly women read her column, nearly one in five of her subjects were men. Regardless of who answered her rings, the conversation always began the same.

"Hello," said the party at the other end.

Speaking into the hard, plastic mouthpiece, Mom asked cheerfully, "Hello. Is this Mrs. (or Mr.) So-and-So?"

"Yes, it is."

"I'm Berthella Stevens. I'm calling to talk with you about 'The Party Line' column in *The Bremen Enquirer.*"

From that point, every conversation was different, although there were common threads in the reactions.

Sometimes people refused to talk with Mom, responding with some form of, "Mrs. Stevens, I'm sorry. I don't want to have anything to do with that gossip column." Although she didn't appreciate the "gossip" moniker, she understood why people felt that way. Other times, some were just too nervous to talk to a "reporter."

On other occasions, but not often, Mom got the opposite response: "Oh, I'm surprised you called me. But you know what? I just knew that one day you might, so I've prepared something to talk about." That made Mom chuckle.

But most of the time, folks didn't feel worthy of speaking to my reporter-mother, saying, "Why would anyone care about my life? I don't do anything interesting." With callers like these, Mom's probing questions and friendly demeanor released interesting stories her subjects didn't know they possessed. They often left the conversation feeling like a more valuable member of the community. Mom left the conversations with a broad smile.

Some folks were nostalgic, recounting stories of their childhood, Bremen history, and even historical events across the U.S. Many spoke effusively of the positive attributes they saw in our community. Children, vacations, and animals of all types were frequent topics, as was gardening, cooking, and of course, the weather, a vital topic in a farming community. But conversations often veered far from the norm. UFOs, death and predestination, antique books, chess, marionettes, religion, writing, miniskirts, race riots, and rock and roll were discussed. It seemed no topic was beyond Mom's ability to keep up an intelligent conversation. Even I was occasionally mentioned in her articles, referring to me as an eight-year-old budding chef, chemist, scientist, or reporter, depending on my latest shenanigans.

As interviewees poured out their thoughts, Mom pinned the phone to her ear with her shoulder and furiously scribbled notes on a yellow pad in her lap. Sometimes only one conversation was needed to fill a column, but other times it took several. As soon as she felt she had enough material, or her deadline loomed, she plopped down in front of her Underwood typewriter and with a clatter of keys drafted articles from the stories she heard. She then drove the typed pages into town and handed them over to an editor who took his turn at revision.

Mom's perfect job lasted just over two years. The collection of her two hundred conversations captured the actions and intimate thoughts on people's minds, telling the story of peaceful life in rural Indiana in the late 1960s. It's a story generally untold and often overshadowed by the violence featured in big city newspapers at the time. But "The Party Line" is also an important part of my mother's story. In the summer of her life, she invested many hours to create this form of "public art" for the community to enjoy. In doing so, she was more fully alive, using many of the talents God had given her.

∞

The Party Line
By Berthella Stevens
August 10, 1967, an edited excerpt

When I called Mrs. Paul Briney she wasn't familiar at all with this column and said she had nothing to talk about— no hobbies, adventures, or good stories to tell. So I had to do some fast talking to "save the day." When we were through, we'd had a unique conversation and a barrelful of chuckles.

Mrs. Briney sounded like she had a Southern accent but she assured me that she was a native of Bremen but had spent a winter in the South several years ago so maybe some of that drawl had rubbed off on her.

While we were talking, my younger daughter Julie came up with a box complaining that there was a spider in it. Mrs. Briney heard her and thought it was someone else on the phone line (not then, but most every other time).

I explained to her that Julie was only a child who acted "typically female" about spiders and mice, even though I've tried to teach the children not to go into conniptions over insects and animals. In fact, the ladybug is known to one of our children as "My Friend."

That started Mrs. Briney talking about mice. She insisted she's less afraid of them than they are of her because she's a lot bigger. However, if one takes her by surprise she will holler and disappear fast. Rats, now, she can stay away from altogether.

She said her brother-in-law was shoveling corn once and a rat ran up his overall leg. I knew mice did tricks like that but never heard about a rat doing it. She said that when men wear those striped overalls, the legs are full and rats will climb right in. When her father gets a rat up his pant leg, he just squashes it right there inside of his overalls. It doesn't bother him.

She is a brave woman. Maybe because her husband likes guns and has taught her to shoot.

From what she told me, if I were a prowler I'd think twice before trying something at her house. It doesn't sound as if she is afraid of man or beast.

One time she heard a noise down by the barn at midnight so she grabbed a six barreled shotgun (six, mind you) and went down to the barn. Since she is polite to whom she is about to shoot, she asked, "Who's there?" Her father answered, "Don't shoot! Don't shoot!"

It was during harvest time and he was very late getting some of his chores done. He had a scare, I guess.

When we came to the end of our conversation, I reminded her that at the beginning she didn't think there was anything to talk about. She responded rather morosely, "My husband will probably shoot me (for talking to me I gathered)."

I had to laugh and told her to hide the bullets. She admitted she wasn't TOO scared, though. Thank goodness for that.

CHAPTER 11

More Than an Emotion

S now whipped insanely around our house, leaving deep drifts in its wake. The roads were blocked and nothing moved. In the gray light of daybreak, I peered out the window to a moonscape in the yard. That's when I heard the shriek. It was a shriek a mother hen might make just before the claws of a hawk carries away her chick—the cries of a mother losing a child. But the shriek came from my own mother, somewhere in our home.

ɔ

It all started with Evart Gordon. He was my mom's adult Sunday school teacher at Oak Grove Church and a close friend. He used to farm his own land, but as he aged, he relinquished the responsibility to younger men, though he still piddled around the farm buildings in his coveralls, plaid cotton shirt, and work boots. His hair was thin and balding on top, and he had thickened around the middle.

Before he retired, Evart also sold his own eggs. But now, only Bantam chickens lived on his farm. Known as Banties, these feisty fowl sported salt and pepper feathers with splotches of gold, red, blue, and green. They ran loose among his outbuildings and hid miniature, pastel-colored eggs wherever they pleased. Unlike the confined egg-producing hens of Evart's past, these chickens were more like wild yard art.

When I was elementary age, Mom and I visited Evart one spring evening. He lived in a simple two-story farmhouse with a modest kitchen and living room. I was perched in Evart's lap as he sat in his worn recliner while he and Mom talked. The aroma of fresh flour hung in the air, and soon his wife Florence joined us when she finished laying her homemade egg noodles out to dry on their kitchen table.

"I like our new house," Mom told Evart, "but I miss having chickens. When I was a kid, I enjoyed the hens and chicks on my grandparents' farm. The rooster was a good daddy and always stood guard. They seemed like a family, who…who loved each other… It made me feel safe for some reason."

"Well, why don't you get some, Berthella?" Florence responded.

"Oh, I don't know…where would they live? We don't have a chicken coop anymore."

"Yeah, Mom. Let's get some chickens!" I chimed in, kicking my little feet into the air.

"I'm not sure what your dad would say," Mom replied.

"Look, Berthella," said Evart. "Mick isn't going to mind. You guys had your own chickens on the farm. If he doesn't have to care for them, he's not going to mind."

"Well, then who's going to care for them?"

"I will," I squealed. Mom's gaze fell on my diminutive figure on Evart's lap. She blinked once, then turned back to Evart.

"Berthella, you know I've got Banty chickens sleeping in the barn. They can take care of themselves and live in the trees at your house, if you want some. They're practically wild. There's no work to be done."

That was all Mom needed to hear. Evart grabbed a flashlight and the three of us slipped on our jackets and followed the circular light beam across his gravel driveway to the barn. There, he unlatched the squeaky door and we crossed the threshold into the musty building. His light pierced the dark like a knife, searching the cavernous space for roosting chickens. It was an exciting adventure for me since I seldom got to explore a barn at night. I suspect it brought back pleasant memories for Mom.

Evart spied several hens sleeping on a feed trough on the far side. With the shaft of light as our guide, we walked around a hay wagon, stepped over the manure gutter where cows were once milked, and passed some old gates leaned against the wall. The dry air smelled of old wood, and every spider web, nearly invisible by day, was illuminated by the beam. Evart grabbed a couple of burlap feed bags as we approached the hens. "Here," he said to me, "hold this bag open." After he handed the flashlight to Mom, Evart grabbed the legs of two chickens sleeping side-by-side. They squawked and frantically flapped their wings, kicking up a small cloud of dust. Evart turned them upside down and they instantly quieted as he gently placed each one in the bag.

"How many do you want, Berthella?"

"Oh, ten or twelve, I suppose. And we need a rooster, too," replied Mom.

Within minutes, we had two bags full and were on our way home.

Evart's Banties spent the night in their sacks in our garage for safekeeping. The next morning, we released them into our yard and they became *our* chickens. Chickens are homebodies. If they're moved to a new owner, they don't walk back to their old house like a dog. They are also social, communal animals and stick together.

We had three acres of land and the flock found plenty to eat. They foraged in the yard and gardens, eating insects, seeds, and worms. They drank from decorative pools of water in one of Mom's gardens, plus other little containers that collected rainwater. They soon discovered the nighttime safety of towering trees, although some sat patiently on nests of eggs squirreled away in tall grass.

Within weeks, downy chicks arrived and mother hens began telling stories to their children, as I played in the yard and studied their antics. When the curious balls of fuzz were drawn to new discoveries, short, low-pitched clucks cautioned them, "stay close." When Mama's sharp toes uncovered a sumptuous worm or bug, a staccato, high-pitched, 'tuck-tuck-tuck' encouraged the chicks to "come lunch and learn!" A soft, vibrating 'errrr' sent chicks scurrying for the safety of mom's feathers if danger hovered overhead, and the vibrant crow of the rooster informed all within earshot that he was in charge. The cackle of pride over freshly laid eggs accented this musical score like grace notes. It was so peaceful watching these families go about their day.

As summer days lengthened, eggs continued to transform into new life. The dozen birds multiplied to fifty. Overseeing this flock was a handsome, regal rooster Mom named Blackie White Feather. He stood taller than the rest, with a stiff, pointed red comb on his head and two fleshy red wattles beneath his orange beak. Fearsome sharp spurs protruded above his feet, offering protection to his growing family. His mostly black feathers covered his manly chest and shone with an iridescent blue-green. But his tail stood out like the mainsail of a schooner. A sleek cluster of sparkling black and white tail feathers swept high into the air then curved proudly back to earth and bounced assuredly with each step. This beautiful creature guarded his flock, kept his harem happy, and helped baby chicks find their first meals. He was a Renaissance Rooster and the feathered love of Mom's life.

As the seasons progressed, the tree leaves turned crimson and gold, and then fell away as winter set in to declare who really had dominion of the land. Gone were the insects and worms; earth and water froze together. Deep drifts of snow made it difficult to walk, and the leafless trees provided little shelter from bitter cold. Winter was a tale of tragedy and hardship for wild animals, including the Banties. Some perished as they struggled in vain to find sustenance in the unforgiving weather.

That's when it happened.

We'd had a fierce overnight blizzard and school was canceled. I was elated at the prospects of a free day. I gazed out the window at the barren landscape, which reminded me of the moon, and then I heard Mom shriek.

Alarmed, I ran toward the cries coming from her bedroom. "What's the matter, Mom?" I shouted as the sound of distress rose in her throat a second time. She stared out the window to the ground below.

"There's Blackie White Feather," she cried. "He's frozen in the snow!"

I stood by her side, peering through the frosty glass. All I saw was his comb, sticking out of the drift, white with frostbite. A few inches away was the only other visible part of his body: his unmistakable tail, which twisted in the wind like a broken sail. I was distressed by Mom's screams. But Blackie White Feather wasn't the first dead chicken I'd seen. My indifference to this cruel turn of Mother Nature, though, contrasted sharply to Mom's reaction.

She pulled on her boots, wrapped a coat over her pajamas without buttoning it, and bolted outdoors without gloves or hat. In a minute, she was back in the house cradling Blackie White Feather.

"Quick," she said, "run some warm water in the bathroom sink. Not hot, just lukewarm."

I followed her instructions as she gently laid the rooster in the rising water. Blackie White Feather's eyes were frozen shut. He didn't move. As the warm air thawed his comb, it started to lean, then droop, then it just tipped over onto the side of his head. I stroked his back as Mom spoke.

"Come on, Blackie White Feather. You can do it. You're strong. I know you can do it." It seemed more like wishful thinking than encouragement. But then an eye opened. Then the other. Then they blinked.

"Mom, he's alive! You saved him!" I shouted, bouncing from foot to foot.

Indeed, he was alive, and the smile on Mom's face revealed a sense of relief and joy. She stayed in the bathroom with her favorite feathered friend all morning. She gave him food and something to drink until gradually his strength returned. Then she did what she had to do. She returned him to the hands of Mother Nature. And this time Mother Nature smiled, too. After his resurrection, Blackie White Feather flourished once more when winter finally gave way to spring. But his stiff red comb, a symbol of his virility, was permanently droopy and its fine points fell away. It was a small price to pay to vanquish death.

⋈

As a child, I watched and listened to the hens scratch for bugs and call softly to their chicks but didn't know a spell was being cast to capture my heart. I was unaware of the imprint of peace and joy being etched on my soul, just as it had been etched in my mother's. I had no hint of the years of pleasure they would ultimately bring. Whether or not my mother realized it, she helped write the first chapter in an unfolding story of my love for these feathered friends.

Mom loved these birds, too. But Blackie White Feather held a special place in her heart. Maybe it was his regal air. Or maybe he reminded Mom of the loving father she longed for. But I know that she saw her rooster as life, and life was worth preserving. And in rescuing him from certain death, I understood for the first time that love was more than an emotion. Mom demonstrated what love *looked* like. Love could be an action. Love could save lives.

This was just one of many lessons to come, though not all would be so heartfelt.

CB

The Party Line
By Berthella Stevens
February 16, 1967, an edited excerpt

Mrs. Burton Manges told of a recent exciting event. She and her family visited her parents near Milford one weekend. On Saturday, they butchered three hogs, and were all understandably tired. Just as they had retired, they noticed a fire in one of the hog houses. So back on went the clothing and pandemonium began.

Just like you read in the papers, Mrs. Manges called the fire department and got all mixed up in the directions. We always think of these things happening to "other people" until we find out that we are the "other people."

There was no connection between the butchering and the fire, she said, and there was only one hog house involved, but there was a sow with eight two-day-old piglets in it. Mrs. Manges was full of praises for that wise mother who saved every one of her piglets herself. The sow's nose was burned, and the little ones had cinder burns on them, but she had herded them all into the farthest corner of the pen and they were safe. Mrs. Manges thought that the mother was as smart as a human being.

One of her sisters rushed out and opened up six barbed wires with her bare hands to save the rest of the hogs, but no one, including herself, knows how she accomplished it as her father always had to use pliers to open them. She never cut her hands, either.

There were no animals lost, and that was good. Mrs. Manges said her father takes very good care of his hogs and some are tame. He saves all the runts by feeding them milk with baby cereal by bottle, and then puts them on calf starter. They end up as fine pigs. Right now, they have one called Clifford that comes to the back door about three times a day to get his bottle. She claims that he is just as cute and smart as the pig, Arnold, on the "Green Acres" television show. I could well believe her, as I had always understood that pigs are some of our more intelligent animals—also cleanest, if given the opportunity. Did I hear someone laugh?

CHAPTER 12

D is for Didactic

di·dac·tic

/dī'daktik/

intended to teach, particularly in having moral instruction

teaching in a way that is annoying or unwanted

Mom was a teacher, the world her classroom. Though no letters followed her name, no BA, no MS, no PhD, Mom graduated from the University of Curiosity with an advanced degree in All Things Ponderable. She had an unquenchable thirst to drink up the world and the unwavering heart of a teacher eager to share what she learned. And for those living in the wake of this journey, she left behind both waves of gratitude and destruction.

"Quick, come look," was often the way it started when Mom made a discovery. Maybe it was the first hummingbird of the season revealing his ruby red throat, or the distant honking which drew our eyes skyward to the "V" migrating north. Maybe it was just a lowly garden spider setting up home for the summer. Whatever it was, as a ten-year-old boy cut from the same cloth, I was eager for new discoveries.

On a sunny summer weekday morning as I sat indoors watching *Captain Kangaroo* on TV, I heard Mom's call through the open window. "Kerry, quick, come look!" I leapt from my fuzzy gray chair and bolted through the back door where I saw Mom in her work pants kneeling in the garden.

"Kerry, come sit here quietly for a moment," she instructed. She was digging out weeds and planting pink petunias behind the garage. Bees buzzed nearby. "Watch this spider," she said in a voice laced with mystery.

I knelt beside her and felt the soft bare earth beneath my knees. In front of us perched a black and yellow spider as big around as a cookie. It looked scary with its contrasting colors and sharply pointed legs that formed a large X as it vibrated its web strung between the iris leaves. "She's shaking her web like that to scare us away. She wants us to think she's bigger and more threatening than she really is," Mom said.

I resisted the urge to knock the spider to the ground and squash it and remained quietly by Mom's side. The spider eventually sensed we would do no harm and returned to her task.

"Now see what she's doing? She's building her web again. How do you suppose she's doing that?" Mom asked.

I leaned in for a closer look. "She's using her thread to weave it," I replied.

"Where do you suppose she's getting her thread?"

The spider was still a little frightening, but I put my face as close to her web as I could without making both of us jump away. She made no sound, but I could see a filament following her as she stepped gingerly from strand to strand in her delicate net, laying it down in silky concentric circles across support lines radiating from the center.

I turned to Mom who was watching me watch the spider. "She's making it, I guess."

"That's right. Spiders produce silk from their spinneret glands located at the tip of their abdomen," she said. "And she makes different kinds of silk for different purposes. What do you suppose she's making now?"

I thought for a moment as we knelt side-by-side in the warming morning sun. "Well, she's probably making sticky silk to catch something to eat." I paused. "Let's see what it does if we throw it something," I said enthusiastically. I looked around the green plants for an insect or moth but saw none. "How about an earthworm?" I suggested.

Mom turned over some musty dark soil with her trowel and uncovered a brown worm. I grabbed it quickly before it slipped away and brushed dirt off its undulating body, then flung it into the center of the web. In a flash, Mrs. Spider dashed to her unexpected dinner guest and frantically began to entomb him in silk as the web bounced with her rapid movements.

"See what she's doing?" Mom asked. Her words quickened and her voice became elevated as if she was wrapping the worm herself. "Now she's using a different kind of silk to wrap him up, like a cocoon. She's going to save him to eat later."

I was captivated by this struggle for life that was way more interesting than *Captain Kangaroo*. But the spider was having a difficult time. The slimy worm was wriggling free about as fast as she could turn her spinnerets. Soon the worm dropped to the ground and slipped away. His life had been saved. But my life had been changed by those few minutes spent in Mom's classroom. The garden spider transformed from something deserving death beneath my feet to deserving life and observation.

CB

It seemed most days brought new lessons like this. I learned how eggs formed in chickens, how bees pollinate flowers, how monarch butterflies need milkweed to survive, and how to identify a geode rock. But Mom's instruction extended well beyond the natural world and encompassed our kitchen, as well.

One late afternoon, I was sprawled on the living room floor in front of the large picture window, reading the comics as the light from the sun repeatedly appeared then disappeared behind drifting clouds.

I could hear Mom in the kitchen moving pans and plates. I smelled sliced potatoes frying.

"Kerry, could you set the table for supper, please?" she asked from the kitchen.

"Okay. As soon as I finish the comics," I shouted from the floor.

I must have been a slow reader, because she cried out again later, "Kerry, could you please come set the table? It's time for supper and your dad will be here soon."

This time I got up and dashed to the kitchen and began pushing aside old newspapers from the white laminate table as Mom turned the potatoes in her frying pan. I jerked open the silverware drawer, causing utensils to rattle in place, and grabbed two handfuls.

"Set it up like you'd see in a restaurant, Kerry. Like I've shown you before," Mom said. "The fork goes on the left and the knife goes on the right. Remember? Turn the knife so that the blade faces the plate… Also, we're having soup. Do you know where to place the soup spoon?"

"No. Where?"

"Put it on the right side of the knife."

We seldom went to restaurants, and she wasn't just being obsessive about setting the table. She was preparing me for life, so that when I left our country home I could feel confident in other settings. And this lesson continued as our family sat down to eat and I slurped my steamy cream of mushroom soup.

"You know you're not supposed to slurp from the spoon," she reminded me. "But do you know how to get the last bit of soup from the bottom of the bowl?"

I shook my head and she proceeded to demonstrate as she spoke.

"Tip your bowl away from you with your left hand so the last drops of soup collect in the corner," she said as her metal spoon clinked against the bowl. "Then gently dip it up with your spoon. Don't tip the bowl toward you because you might accidentally spill it on yourself."

Learning to set the table and how to eat in public without embarrassing myself were just two of many life skills Mom taught. But her most consistent lessons centered on language. If I asked how to spell a word, she sent me to the dictionary, the second most important book in our house after the Bible. Saying "ain't" nearly warranted soap to the mouth, while lessons in grammar were never-ending.

One day, Mom was sitting in the rocking chair reading a magazine. As the aluminum screen door slammed shut behind me and I stepped into the living room where she read, Mom asked, "Did you just come back from Bryan's?"

"Yeah. His mom gave Bryan and I some 7UP!" I said with glee and a small bit of guilt. It was a warm day and the cold drink had been refreshing. But I knew Mom frowned on drinking such unhealthy things.

Mom looked up from her magazine. "His mom gave Bryan and *me* some 7UP," she replied.

"No, Mom. You weren't there," I said, shaking my head. "I was there. She gave Bryan and I the 7UP." Although perplexed, I was glad she wasn't angry that I drank soda pop.

"No, that's not right, Kerry. It's 'Bryan and *me*', not 'Bryan and *I*.'" I stared at her blankly and she sensed my confusion. "If you want to know how to say it correctly, remove 'Bryan' from the sentence." She paused, then asked, "Which of these would be correct: 'His mom gave *I* some 7UP,' or 'His mom gave *me* some 7UP?'"

"The second one," I spouted.

"So, say the sentence again but with Bryan included."

"His mom gave Bryan and…*me* some 7UP." I said with my head held high.

But not all of Mom's lessons had such happy endings.

Each summer we loaded up the Ford Galaxy 500 for a family vacation. Mom put boxes of belongings in the foot well of the back seat and covered them with a board and thick blankets to make a large comfortable pallet for my younger sister and me. Then, to while away the hours to our destinations, she read books aloud to entertain and educate while Dad drove. During our annual sojourns, we ate boiled peanuts in Mississippi, stood atop Stone Mountain in Georgia, climbed the stairs of the Washington Monument, rubbed our hands on the glass buoys of lobster traps in Maine, shrieked at a too-close black bear in the Smoky

Mountains, and peeked through the windows of the Gateway Arch in St. Louis. But it was at the World's Fair in Texas in 1968 where Mom learned the limits of her lessons about animal husbandry.

It was a humid day. Dad, Mom, Julie, and I had just come down from the top of the Tower of the Americas that overlooked the sprawling city of San Antonio. Julie and I wore shorts, while Mom was in a sleeveless dress and Dad in long pants. I stood next to Mom at the concrete base of the tower as she dropped her only coins into the pay phone to check on my teenage brother and sister who had stayed home alone.

"Hi. It's Mom," she announced to Janet. "We're in Texas. It's pretty hot here, but we're enjoying ourselves. How are things at home?"

I stood close to Mom and could hear my older sister reply, "They're fine…except for Captain Erk."

Mom's eyebrows rose. Captain Erk was her mynah bird, which she patiently trained to talk. He started out just squawking like birds do, just an "erk." But over time, he learned to converse.

"What happened to Captain Erk?" Mom was alarmed.

"He died," said Janet, with no hesitation.

"He died? How did he die?" Mom yelled into the black mouthpiece.

"He just died, Mom. I don't know how he died."

"Did you feed him?" she asked in a tone that sounded more like an accusation. Time was running out and Mom had no more change for the phone.

"Yes, we fed him," Janet replied, exasperated.

"Well, what about water?" Now there was silence on the phone. "Janet, are you still there?"

"Yes."

"What about water, did you give him water?"

"Well, we might have forgotten to give him water, Mom. But at least he had food."

As the plastic handset flattened her hair against her ear, Mom fought back tears. "Janet, he could talk! He knew how to ask for water. Didn't you hear him pleading for water?"

Then, just as suddenly as the mynah bird had died, the phone line went dead, as well.

Mom slowly shook her head as her empty gaze fell to the ground. There was nothing she could do. She hung the handset back in the cradle and let out a heavy sigh as I saw the Texas sun reflected in the tears that threatened to spill from her eyes.

ɔʒ

Although Mom's constant instruction didn't always end well, like the experience with Captain Erk, it did pay off for me. While other students experienced "summer slide," I returned to school in the fall smarter than I was when summer began. I could see it and I could feel it. My confidence increased.

But Mom couldn't have excelled in teaching if she hadn't excelled in learning. Her insatiable curiosity and quest for knowledge consumed books like a furnace burned coal. She spent her entire life feeding the fire. Books, she believed, are man's greatest invention, with the power to record thoughts and ideas and pass them down for future generations to use and enjoy. To hold her burgeoning library, which included a complete set of encyclopedias, she built massive shelves out of stacks of bricks and boards. Magazines and newspapers also fueled her burning desire to learn. Periodicals such as *Good Housekeeping, Prairie Farmer, Organic Gardening,* and religious magazines, *The Watchtower* or *Dawn,* spread across the tables like sand on the beach. Even unread newspapers, no matter how old, lay stacked on the floor awaiting Mom's discovery of some new treasure, which she knew lay buried within its pages.

"My biggest fear in life," admitted Mom, "is missing something interesting."

Her power of observation, even of the most insignificant things, taught her large lessons, as she shared in this excerpt from her story about a tiny mosquito.

Last winter, my attention was drawn to a mosquito while I, late at night, followed my favorite bathroom activity—reading. Where had the mosquito come from in the middle of the winter? The little critter hovered almost silently in front of me, never approaching. My first instinct was to smack him, but this one stopped me.

Quite a few nights he appeared and seemed to watch me while I was reading you-know-where. He actually seemed curious and never attacked. I assumed he was male since he didn't bite me. But why did he always hover in exactly the same spot and watch me? If he was watching, that manifested intelligence. And if that was so, where was his intelligence located? I could scarcely see him, let alone see anything large enough to contain that kind of intelligence.

One night while showering, the curtain was open at one end. There came the mosquito through the opening and flew right close to me and stopped. He looked at me with unseen eyes and it seemed he was thinking and I received his thoughts, *So, you're taking a shower. It's about time.* Honest, that's what I thought he was thinking, but I couldn't imagine why he thought that way since I showered daily. He hovered there a bit longer then turned around and flew back through the gap where he had entered. It struck me forcibly how that infinitesimal creature had enough intelligence to find the gap in the shower curtain, then find me, then remember how to go out the same way he had come in.

In addition to acquiring vast amounts of knowledge from things as small as a mosquito, Mom could remember and reformulate it on the fly to inculcate in her children. But she didn't teach us just for the sake of possessing information. Her teaching had a purpose. Mom wrote:

The very best thing that parents can do for their children, besides providing food, clothing, and shelter, is to teach children how to make intelligent decisions. Every waking minute we are choosing to do something—to get up, to eat, to read, to associate with—throughout our lives. How much happier everyone would be if they learned early-on how to make intelligent decisions. The Bible states, 'Children, obey your parents, that your days may be long on this earth.'[1] Based on this, we should have a family of centenarians.

But Mom's intellectual journey had a dark side. As is true for many, her greatest strength was also her greatest weakness when it ran on autopilot. Too often she seemed unable to cease or modify her approach when needed, repelling both friends and family.

It seemed nearly every lesson had to have a biblical component, a moral to the story, which was off-putting with its frequency. Even the magical moment in the garden, when Mom and I knelt together in the morning sun watching Mrs. Spider weave her web, needed a proper ending.

"You know, Kerry, even though that earthworm escaped with his life, we shouldn't be afraid to die," she told me that day. "The Bible says that when we die, we're only 'asleep in death.' In other words, we're all going to be brought back to life again, to be resurrected. Won't that be wonderful?"

Although I was a child, I knew a rhetorical question when I heard it, so I offered no reply.

"I wonder, when we're living like the Garden of Eden, what it will be like?" she continued. "Do you think we'll watch this spider again? I wonder if it will still need to eat bugs or if God will have a different way for it to eat? I just know that God has a plan."

These constant Bible stories, often unrelated to whatever subject prompted them, might have been tolerable if they weren't amplified with another set of toxic traits.

First, there were her probing questions. "She was always looking for the backstory," said my oldest brother, Mike. "'What really took place?' 'Who said what?' 'Why was it done?'" Although she was just trying to feed her inquisitive mind, her sharp inquiry crossed a personal line for some, and seemed nosy and rude.

Second, unsolicited advice rolled off her tongue with ease. She had so much knowledge in her mind, she was eager to solve other people's problems and answer questions without being asked. She was always in teaching mode. If you happened to compete on a game show, Mom was the kind of friend you wanted to call to answer a difficult question. But if you just desired to share a pleasant relationship with a friend, Mom was often not chosen because she was sometimes perceived as a meddling know-it-all.

Lastly, because she read and studied so much, she was nearly always right, and she knew it. She saw no need to back down, to extend grace to someone who might feel slighted by the onslaught of her rightness. That created walls of resistance to the lessons she wished to impart.

I call this triad the "Stevens Curse," and Mom would pay dearly for it later in life when it came time to harvest these pernicious seeds she had sown. But this disease also infected me, and nearly every one of my siblings in varying degrees. Mom's influence was so powerful that we inherited the bad with the good. And like an addiction, it's an issue for which I must be forever mindful in order to avoid sliding into toxic relationships.

I don't blame Mom for this contagion. As I examined her life I can now connect the dots and see how she arrived there. It started with the father she never had, who left her feeling vulnerable and scared. And in her mother's absence as she worked desperately for their survival, Mom had to present an outer strength to her younger sisters, though her tender heart ached inside. And the path continued to her kindred spirit grandmother, Ella May, who developed an inferiority complex because her husband bullied her. The next dot was laid down when Mom married into the Old Country Stevens family, where she was reminded daily how she didn't measure up as a proper housewife. And finally, when her children came along, even I piled on, complaining about burned meals, smelly kitchens, and clothes lost in the tangled laundry room.

In retrospect, I now see someone who felt put down all her life and struggled to lift herself up in the absence of others' praise, to prove her own worth.

"Often through the years," Mom said, "I suffered depressing thoughts of inadequacy and disappointment to my family. Even when the family started to mature and the extra time and effort I devoted to the children started to bear fruit and the hard work lessened, the idea that I should have been better still reared its ugly head."

I'm culpable too—guilty as charged, Mom. I confess that too often I found fault for the things you didn't do, chose too often to focus on the didactic nature of your teaching, and offered no appreciation for things you did well.

Although my efforts now fall short of what you deserve, I thank you for enabling me to be successful across the strata of life, to love God and appreciate God's creation—from the spider to the mosquito, and to learn to read and write in a way which honors you. Because of your instruction, I recognize that much of what is good in my own life came from yours.

Mom, you did well.

ॐ

The Party Line
By Berthella Stevens
July 11, 1968, an edited excerpt

When Mrs. Francis Rans answered the phone with such good cheer I asked how her vacation was going. "What vacation?" she countered. That gave me the picture, as I could hear in the background that rambunctious children were the only ones getting a vacation. She was happy for the children, though, especially last night when the kids got to go to the Bremen Fair and the 4th of July fireworks for about three wonderful hours.

The Rans have three children and one on the way which they hope will be a boy as "it's more economically feasible," because she has some boys' clothes left over. Her oldest child is ten and the youngest is seven and she's afraid she's forgotten how to care for a baby and will have to learn it all over again.

That reminded me of something new about diapers. In comparing how boys and girls tend to dress alike nowa-days—they wear the same clothes, have the same haircuts, and adorn the same jewelry—now diapers even come fold-ed alike. It used to be they were folded oppositely but now one might assume that the merging of the different sexes is much more serious than we thought.

This brought Mrs. Rans to exclaim how ridiculous some of the boys look with their extremely long hair and odd-looking clothes, beards, and love beads.

Somehow, she mentioned that they had recently seen a walking stick insect in their backyard and thought they were rather rare. I asked if they kept it for a pet as I had read a story about a woman who had. She had never heard about doing such a thing.

So I told her about the story of the woman who had brought the insect into her house after she found him staring at her through the kitchen window. She put him in her small greenhouse to live.

Daily, the walking stick checked each plant for harmful insects and did it so methodically that the woman could set her clock by his habits. After he rid her plants of everything harmful, she had to feed him bits of hamburger. After eating, he wiped his face and hands and then took a nap. She became very fond of the small creature and mourned his loss when he hitched a ride outdoors on the back of her coat one day.

The story had a happy ending, though, as the next fall she sensed eyes staring at her through the kitchen window and when she turned around there was her friend looking in, apparently asking to come in again.

As I finished the tale, we heard so much crackling that Mrs. Rans thought someone was trying to get the phone line. She said that sometimes she wanted to "spit fire and brimstone" when certain ones rudely tried to get the line, and when they got it, all she heard later was crunching celery and desultory talk by kids.

That rather tickled my funny bone, and I asked her to please let me know when she was about to do the fancy spitting, as I wanted to watch. She was afraid that just letting me know would burn up the line. Too bad.

CHAPTER 13

Baby

A wise old owl lived in an oak,
The more he saw, the less he spoke,
The less he spoke, the more he heard.
Why can't we all be like that wise old bird?

—Author Unknown, Circa 1875

My buddy, Mark, and I, pulled by the gravity of exploration, ambled along the seam between the cultivated field and the wildness of the woods.

Feathery clouds filtered the afternoon sunlight as spring wrestled with summer and I gazed into the trees. Suddenly, *it* appeared in the dappled light. "Stop!" I yelled in a whispered voice. My steady stare and slight nod guided Mark toward my discovery. "Look at that owl about fifteen feet up that big oak tree!"

We stood motionless, trapped between reality and disbelief, as the owl sat motionless on a branch the size of a man's thigh. It felt like a game of chicken to see who would move first. We stood our ground, mesmerized by our first daylight sighting of an owl. We expected it to launch from its perch and fly deeper into the woods. But the longer we stood still, the longer the owl remained stationary.

This act of defiance begged to be challenged. We crept closer. Dead leaves crunched under our feet as we anticipated the silent explosion of flight. But the owl never even blinked.

Is this a prank? I wondered. After all, the owl didn't look normal.

We moved slowly left, then right. The owl's head pivoted in each direction. Then we walked all the way around the owl in a circle to see if its head really could rotate 360 degrees. It didn't.

"Why doesn't it fly?" Mark asked.

"And why does it look so weird?" I added.

The bird sat very erect, like a well-behaved school kid. Its round head, with just a whisper of tufts, melted into a larger rounded bottom. The color of dirty snow, it reminded me of last season's snowman. Gold, out-sized eyes set within a dark oval peered over a hooked beak, making it look like it wore a mask. Mark and I decided it was similar to a Great Horned Owl, but it was smaller and odd-looking. Its mottled body didn't resemble typical feathers.

"It doesn't look healthy," Mark concluded. "Since it didn't fly away, it must have something wrong with it."

An unhealthy animal was fair game and opened up new opportunities in our exploration. If it was too sick to fly, then it must be a target.

We dashed back to the edge of the field and collected an armful of dirt clods the size of tennis balls. First one, then another, whizzed through the air as we took turns trying to strike the owl. It was like a game booth at the Bremen Fair where I threw balls to knock down an object and win a prize. Except in this game, the first guy to knock the owl from the tree won a real animal instead of a stuffed imitation.

Although the contest made my blood pump faster with excitement, my heart knew this was not how animals should be treated—especially sick ones. But Mark had a strong and often negative influence on me. The clods continued to fly. They went right, left, over, and then under the owl. It clung for its life to the sturdy oak tree.

Finally: bull's-eye! With a thud, the defenseless bird was struck and fell to the ground. It flapped its wings, causing old leaves to flutter;

it floundered momentarily as it gained its footing. It sat there with leaves stuck to its hair-feathers, seemingly in shock, but alive.

We had achieved our goal to knock the owl out of the tree, but we hadn't thought about what we'd do afterward. If the owl had been killed, we would have left it, or maybe brought it back for experimentation. But it was alive. And if we left it alone on the ground, it would die.

"Hmm. What do you think we should do with it?" I wondered out loud. "Should we take it home with us?"

"I don't want it," Mark responded. "What would I do with a sick owl?"

My guilty conscious caught up with my faulty actions. I couldn't leave the owl to die there in the woods alone. "Well, then I'll take it home," I expressed with more certainty than I felt.

Mark ran back across the field to his barn as I stood guard over my prize. He returned with an empty burlap feed bag, and with a bit of ingenuity, we got the owl inside. I held it closed with a tight grip as Mark helped me hang it over my shoulder. We trudged back to his farm, and then I began the two-mile walk down dusty roads back to my house.

∽

The Great Horned Owl takes its name from its large size and its feather tufts that resemble horns, which are often mistaken for its ears.

Like most owls, the nocturnal Great Horned Owl has keen hearing and sharp night vision. Its large yellow eyes, which would be the size of oranges if the bird was human, allow it to spot passing prey. And although an owl cannot turn its head all the way around, it does have fourteen neck vertebrae, which allows it to rotate its head a remarkable 270 degrees. Owls also catch their prey by using their sense of hearing. Their large ears are covered by special feathers, which allow the owl to hear even the smallest sound, such as a mouse squeaking, up to 900 feet away.

The wings have soft fringe-edge feathers that reduce the sound of air rushing through them, making it almost impossible for prey to hear the owl as it glides in to attack. And with sharp talons on its feet that can extend up to eight inches wide, the bird is a deadly predator.

The Great Horned Owl is known as "the tiger of the sky." But it's also called a Hoot Owl for its soft and gentle "whoo hoo," which can be heard more than a mile away on a calm night.

ଓ

I hollered through the open kitchen window when I arrived home, "Mom! I've got something to show you." I felt like a cat bringing a mouse home to its owner. Always eager for a new discovery, Mom opened the aluminum storm door and stepped out on to the patio as the door banged closed behind her.

"What is it?" she inquired.

"It's an owl; a Great Horned Owl, I think. It doesn't look healthy." I leaned to the right to gently let the sack slide off my shoulder, then set it softly on the ground. As I slowly opened the top of the burlap bag, I cast my transgression in the best light possible. "It fell out of a tree and I didn't want to leave it there alone."

Mom peered inside the dark bag, then folded down its scratchy sides to get a better view. With a mixture of shock, dismay, and excitement, she exclaimed, "It's a baby!" Her face lit up as she gently slid her arm into the rough sack to stroke the poor bird's hair-feathers. The baby awkwardly moved away from her hand, but being trapped in the bag, it acquiesced as Mom lovingly stroked its back, its head, and then its belly.

"How did it fall from the tree, I wonder?" Mom said.

Is this a question or just a comment? I kneeled by the bag as Mom continued her communion with the owl. Finally, with as much nonchalance as I could muster, I replied, "I think we scared it when we threw something at it." I glanced at Mom's face for clues about what would come next. But I only saw a look of loving concern for the animal at her feet.

"It's just a baby, Kerry. That's why it looks funny. At first, like other baby birds, it has that fuzzy down; then, the feathers slowly come out. It just takes longer for owls. It's still losing its down. And see that whisper of tufts?" She gently touched the top of its head. "Those will get bigger as it becomes an adult."

I listened intently to my mother's wisdom.

I peeked into the bag and now saw a different owl. I saw a creature a bit more vulnerable than I had seen earlier. "Do you think we should take it back to the woods?" I asked.

My mom sighed, and then looked off into the distance momentarily before looking back at the baby in the bag.

"No, I don't think the momma will take it back," she replied, a bit of sadness in her voice. "It would probably die, even if we had a way to get it back up into its nest."

"Well, then we just need to take care of it ourselves," I announced.

With that pronouncement, Mom and I were a team on a mission. We devised a plan. "If we're going to raise an owl, the baby needs a name," Mom said. She'd named most of our pets, as I recall. And the names she bestowed usually reflected some physical attribute. This owl became known as "Baby."

Next, Baby needed food and shelter. Mom and I began to brainstorm. In the woods, Baby would have had limited shelter from the weather, but the high perch in the tree would have provided protection from varmints. We settled on an abandoned rabbit hutch, which was twice as tall as Baby, and nearly six feet long. It offered plenty of space to move around and grow and was mounted on legs safely off the ground, with lockable doors.

I rushed to the backyard and hurriedly cleaned out the cage, knocking the dried rabbit poop through the wire mesh floor to the ground. I then dragged it behind the old sheep building where it would have more protection from the elements. When I was done, Mom carefully reached into the burlap bag with two hands and gently cradled Baby's wings so he couldn't start flapping and hurt himself. I opened the cage door and Mom slid Baby inside. We stood there waiting to see what Baby would do in his new home. Nothing happened, which we took as a good sign.

Shelter? Check. Now all we needed was food.

"Owls eat small mammals, like mice, rats, and rabbits," Mom coached. "Plus birds, and snakes. They're carnivores. I think baby owls could probably eat a dozen mice a day."

"Well, we have plenty of mice and rats," I suggested, "but I don't think we can catch 'em every day. We're going to have to think of something else."

In lieu of mice, Mom and I decided that hamburger, and later, kidneys, would have to sustain Baby. Under her instruction, I ran into the house and grabbed some hamburger from the fridge, along with a bowl and spoon. Then I flew back to the owl cage. Mom put a spoonful of hamburger into the cage with one hand, and carefully pulled it apart with the other, dangling the bit in front of Baby's beak. "When parents bring their catch back to the nest," she said, "they rip it apart and dangle each piece in front of the chick to encourage it to eat."

Baby moved his head, first one way, then the other. Mom pulled the morsel of hamburger away and rubbed the sides of Baby's face with the back of her hand, then moved the meat back to Baby's beak.

"Come on, Baby. It's time to eat," she coaxed in a higher pitched voice—part cooing and part hooing—as she assumed the role of the mother owl.

Baby responded with a look of indifference and annoyance.

After several failed attempts, Baby finally grabbed a piece of meat and swallowed. Soon, more was gobbled down as Mom picked up piece after piece and Baby ate from her fingers. In that moment, Baby found a new mom and Mom found a new baby.

"He's going to survive!" I interjected in the midst of the bonding.

CR

Mom and I took turns feeding Baby a couple of times each day. Eventually, he no longer needed to be hand-fed and ate his meat from a bowl. His body began to fill his cage, and we took him out to exercise. His talons clutched a thick leather glove on one hand while we held his legs with the other so he couldn't fly or fall as his four-foot wings beat against the air.

Baby grew into a stunning creature. His enormous yellow eyes were amplified by an orange facial disk outlined in black. The hues of browns and grays with black bar markings on his body allowed his white throat to show prominently. He stood nearly two feet tall, with protruding tufts resembling horns.

Over the summer, Baby became an adult, and we knew it was time for him to return to the woods. I never had any expectation that he'd become our pet. He was a wild animal and deserved to live as such. One evening at dusk, my mother and I and other family members gathered around his cage to bid farewell. There was a slight chill in the air as the sun settled below the horizon and hues of red and violet faded to deep blue. I opened the doors to his cage and stepped back from the burst of flight to follow, imagining I'd wave goodbye as Baby flew off into the sunset.

It would have been a great ending had it happened that way. But Baby stood motionless in his cage watching us watching him. The game of chicken was on again. This time I tired of waiting. This time there would be no dirt clods thrown or banging on his cage to bend his will toward mine. No, we let him win and walked away with the doors of his cage flung open. His future was before him, and he was allowed to choose.

The next morning, I threw on my clothes and ran out to the cage. Baby was gone.

I was surprised to see the cage so empty when it had once been filled with life. Baby had become my friend, and I missed him. But he became almost like a son to my mother. She simultaneously nurtured Baby as she nurtured me, feeding Baby with food, gentle talk, and affection, while feeding me with knowledge, self-discipline, and a love and respect for animals. She watched us both grow, nourished by her love. While I hadn't left her home yet, Baby had, and her heart was broken.

I wonder what would have happened that day when Baby appeared on our patio if Mom had gotten angry and chosen punishment instead of mercy? What if I chose to tune my mother out and not watch and listen to what she modeled? I wonder now, *who was the wise old owl?*

After Baby left, Mom stood out on the patio after dark, alone, and called for him. "Baaa-byyy! Baaa-byyy!" she shouted into the night. "Whoo-hoo, whoo-hoo!"

But Baby didn't call back. Her pleas for companionship floated away into the ether. I heard her nightly cries from inside the house and thought it was silly. And the neighbors, who could hear it all, thought Mom had lost it. Maybe she had. But she didn't relent and faithfully stood out on the cold concrete and called, "Baaa-byyy! Baaa-byyy! Whoo-hoo, whoo-hoo!"

Then one night, after bellowing for Baby, she rushed into the house, shouting with childish glee, "He's back! Baby's back! He's answering me."

Not stopping to put on a jacket, I dashed outside to join her and listen. She tilted her head back slightly, cupped her hands around her mouth to amplify her voice, and called, "Baaa-byyy! Baaa-byyy!" The warmth of her words became visible in the chilly night air.

We waited silently.

Then we heard it, about a half mile away in a neighbor's woods, "Whoo-hoo, whoo-hoo," came the gentle reply. I turned and looked at my mother. From the faint light of the house I saw a broad smile on her face, with eyes as big as an owl's. Baby was back.

⚃

The Party Line
By Berthella Stevens
June 27, 1968, an edited excerpt

The first number I called this week turned out to be not only a home phone but a business phone, as well, and I found myself talking to Charles Kramer, Jr., himself.

Although he was working, he said that he could take just a few minutes to talk to me, but what did I want to talk about?

After explaining to him the purpose of the column, he replied that the main thing that occupies his interest these days is the turmoil in the world now. It is exceedingly depressing to him; he can't understand the extreme restlessness of mankind, nor does he know how to help.

About five or six years ago, he wasn't much concerned about what was going on in the rest of the world. He felt that any trouble was of their own making and that the opportunity existed for anyone to make it if they wanted to. But now he has gotten to the point that he just does not want to hear of what is going on in the world: the war, assassinations, and social unrest. He wants to shut all the terrible things out of his mind and feels that there must be something wrong with him to be so worried about the fate of mankind.

I disagreed with him on that point. I felt that it was not what was wrong with him but what was "right" with him to be so concerned. It is the ones who think of others—the tenderhearted, the sympathetic—who are sickened by the present mess. They are the ones who suffer. It is the callous and uncaring who say, "So what? What's it to me? Let the other fellow look out for himself. I'm not my brother's keeper," who can live through this and be unscathed.

Even industry, labor, and management can't get along, he stated, and this directly affects everyone. At the root of most of the trouble, he feels, is the love of money and what can be done with it.

He didn't believe that love of power motivates our leaders, though. He was quite firm in his belief that our leaders are good men, earnest in their desire to make things better, but they can't seem to do it. Also, he questions a lot of 'progress' in so many things—it seems to be steps backwards to him. He wishes so fervently that all the money, time, and energy devoted to killing (on any scale) would be channeled into eliminating the diseases that plague us. He is positive that it is still possible—when man becomes fully educated—that this world can be made a healthier, happier place to live where a man feels no need to kill those he disagrees with.

I asked if he knew what he was looking for and he replied he guessed it was Utopia.

Well, that is a pretty good thing to look forward to. To twist the old saw around, "Where there is hope, there is life."

CHAPTER 14

Crazy for Life

"Chinese fire drill!" older sister Janet shouted unexpectedly when our family car stopped at a traffic light in the bustling city of Indianapolis.

Four doors flew open and all of us countrified kids leaped out, as cross traffic flew by in front of us and a blue Dodge Dart pulled up behind our Galaxy 500, still idling in the street. Laughing loudly, my older sister, the teenage instigator, dashed around the front of our car from the passenger side and jumped into the backseat on the driver's side. My younger sister's flats nearly slipped off her feet as she sprinted around the rear of the car in the opposite direction then stopped momentarily in the exhaust. Less familiar with the game, she shouted between squeals of laughter, "Which door do I go in?" All of us, dressed in our Sunday best for a wedding, rushed through the chaotic routine like ants on a hill poked with a stick.

Young people loved to play this simple prank, oblivious to the racial insensitivities of its name. But this game was different. One of the players was a mature adult woman who hustled around the car in a pink floral dress, with beads and heels, grinning and giggling at the spontaneous pleasure. That woman was my mother. She loved to have fun, especially when it was least expected. She was crazy for life.

☯

Our three-acre homestead in the country was stately. A towering syca-more tree visually anchored the front yard, and two large rocks flanked the driveway like sentries. The U.S. flag flew proudly from a pole on the patio. During the day, clouds of dust drifted from the gravel road in front of our house when cars passed. But during the night, our yard often became the playground for Janet's teenage friends.

Janet was quite popular in high school, and along with the at-tention came a prank called "toilet papering." After a night of frivolity, streams of toilet tissue fluttered from the branches of the sycamore and our yard looked like a winter wonderland made of paper. It was nearly a weekly event and my dad got so tired of cleaning it up, he stuck a sign in the front yard after each episode that read: "Free TP. U-pick." But Mom took a different tack.

As the family wound down one Friday evening around 10:30 p.m. and the aroma of the nightly popcorn subsided, the action outside picked up. Mom was silently lying in wait.

"Give me another roll of TP," Susan whispered to a friend in the dark. "The last one got stuck in the tree and won't come down."

"Geez. How many are you going to use? I'm still on my second roll," replied Cindy, as she quietly lofted her roll as high as her thin arms allowed. It swished back down between the leaves.

Meanwhile, Kathy giggled to herself as she hurried back and forth along the row of shrubs in front of the house, placing her flat strips of tissue like icing on a cake.

The trio of TPers worked quietly, assuming they were alone ex-cept for the chorus of crickets. Suddenly, Mom leaped from behind a large bush and flipped on a flashlight. "Ah-ha! I gotcha!" she shouted as she waved an empty BB gun in their direction. In the dark, they couldn't see the sparkle in her eyes or the smile about to break loose. "Now what are you going to do?"

The girls shrieked and took off running down the dirt road to their car. Gravel cracked beneath their feet and rolls of toilet paper dropped in their wake. Mom just laughed, knowing she gave the girls a great story to tell their friends in school, and that they, or others like them, would probably be back the next week.

One April Fools' Day, when my younger sister, Julie, was still in elementary school, she decided to get in on the fun. Mom had just gotten into the tub when Julie dialed our telephone number on the party line system then hung up, causing our phone to ring. She then "answered" the phone and pretended to have a conversation with someone needing to speak with Mom. Knowing Mom could hear the whole thing, Julie ran to the bathroom to implore her to come to the phone, cold and dripping with water, wrapped only in a towel.

As smart as Mom was, I'm confident she understood her young child was pulling a prank, at least after the first time it occurred. But she continued to play along in subsequent years so that Julie would have her own prank memory.

"Somehow she fell for that trick every year," Julie said, mystified by the repeated success of her childhood caper. "But Mom always knew the difference between fun and disrespect. If someone pulled a prank on her she'd just come back with something fun of her own."

⚬

We lived in a 3,000-square-foot, red brick, ranch-style home, which had been well-constructed by my father and two oldest brothers. With four bedrooms and three baths, each sibling had a bedmate when all six children lived there. A colorful paint-by-number Mediterranean fishing village scene adorned the coral wall in the kitchen. A white brick see-through fireplace separated the dining area from the formal living room, clad in turquoise carpet. Earthy geraniums and other potted plants soaked up sun through windows dotted with royal-blue glass bottles on their sills. Downstairs was a family room, laundry room, "fruit cellar," and workshop.

When it was clean, our home was lovely. But often, clutter multiplied like mosquitoes in a stagnant pool, especially when Mom's focus veered from cleanliness to fun. That was never more true than the day of The Great Garbage Fight.

I was a skinny, blond, nine-year-old and my oldest brothers, Mike and Pat, were away at college when Mom yelled up from the bottom of the stairs to get my attention. "Kerry, can you come here for a second?" I left my chair in the living room and stood at the top of the stairs, looking down at my mother who had been tidying up the family room in the basement.

"Catch this apple core and put it in the garbage pail in the kitchen," she instructed as she the tossed the fruit's remains to the top of the stairs. "And if the pail is full, take it out to the compost pile."

Although I caught the core midair, it seemed as if she threw the sticky nub *at* me. Impulsively, I flung the core back down the stairs, smacking her in the chest.

Mom's body jerked and her eyebrows rose. "What are you doing?" she said in a higher pitched voice. Then she zipped the core back my way with a stronger overhand pitch. This time I missed the catch and it splatted on the wall behind me and dropped to the floor.

"Mom! Look what you did!" I wailed with a grin, pointing at the explosion of apple and juice on the wall.

That caught my younger sister's attention. She believed a game had started. Before anyone could react, Julie grabbed the two broken apple remnants near me and lobbed each piece at our mother.

"Take that!" she giggled, as her blonde pigtails swayed with her throw. The first chunk hit the wall next to the stairs and then bounced onto the handrail, leaving a slippery trail. The second piece missed my mom as well and hit the bathroom door behind her with a hollow thump.

"What are you kids doing?" Mom chortled, trying to suppress a grin. "You're making a mess!"

While Mom bent down to pick up the bits of spoiling fruit, I fetched more ammo from the smelly garbage pail in the kitchen. Flinging a brown banana peel like a Frisbee, I shouted, "Look out below!" It split apart in flight, and one segment draped over the top of a door near me while the other floated down and grazed my mom. I punched the air in victory and laughed at the rotted peel hanging on the door. Before

Mom could react, Julie appeared next to me at the top of the stairs with a handful of slimy cantaloupe seeds she'd pulled from the garbage pail.

"Now you're going to get it!" Julie snickered. Her childish throw was more like a splatter gun, ending with orange strings of white seeds sliding down the walls on both sides of the stairs. She and I burst out laughing.

My brother, Tom, came out of the upstairs bathroom, saw the fight in progress, and grabbed some three-day-old slippery cobs of sweet corn. He spun one at Mom as she returned fire with one of the banana peels I previously threw. With three kids emptying the garbage pail on her, she fought her way up the stairs under attack, grabbing as much garbage as she could and throwing it back. When she reached the top of the stairs we surrounded her with giggles and pelted her with orange peels, egg shells, and rotten tomatoes as she did her best to pick up each piece and return fire.

It was a riot of refuse and laughter when my teenage sister, Janet, arrived home. Quickly seeing but not understanding what was happening, Janet laughed, ran to the refrigerator, grabbed a cache of munitions, and flung fistfuls of cold mashed potatoes at everyone.

When it was over, we had slop in our hair and on our clothes. Garbage was stuck on the ceiling, smeared on the floor, and hung from the curtain rods. Mashed potatoes stuck to the walls. The house looked and smelled more like a landfill than a home. But a home it was—filled with joy from a unique experience shared between a mother and her children. Mom was not angry, and no one got into trouble. I'm sure we all helped clean up the chaos, but I don't remember that part. I just remember the incredible time we spent with Mom in The Great Garbage Fight.

She believed that the relationship with her kids, which included doing outlandish things, was more important than egg shells on the floor and banana peels on the door. She believed in spending time in the present with the people she loved. Mom was crazy for life.

But I must admit, her response to a crisis in my childhood caused me to wonder if she was simply just crazy.

ભ

The Party Line
By Berthella Stevens
April 6, 1967, an edited excerpt

Mrs. Barbara Hirstein said that as far as interesting things happening to her, they don't. Her entire life consists of working. But we found plenty to discuss.

She spoke of her childhood, struggling during the Depression and how different it is for our children today. It used to be when something needed doing, they did it, and did not have to depend on others. Children went barefoot all summer to save shoes for school, and when the shoes wore out, the fathers cut out a piece of leather for a new sole and tacked or glued it on. If they couldn't afford leather, they drew a picture of the child's foot on a piece of cardboard from a cracker box, and then cut it out and placed one or two of these inside the "holey" shoe. "This made the person feel almost as good as having new shoes," Mrs. Hirstein said.

I can remember so clearly during the Depression that we couldn't afford to buy bread and how my eight-year-old sister made all the bread for the whole family. While she did very well for her age, a lot of bread was lumpy and hard, or was off-flavor and spilled over the sides of the baking pan. That bread was never thrown away. We ate it all with soup poured over it. It was good, usually, and when it wasn't good, it was nourishing.

118

Times were certainly hard in those days for so many, but there was so much that was good, and there was time for so many things that there is no time for now.

Mrs. Hirstein brought this out when she reminisced of the chores they had to do, such as chopping wood, making soap, and filling the water reservoir on the stove. There being nine children in her family, each of the older ones was responsible for a young one to see that he or she was clean, dressed, and taken care of.

She told how they'd put a line and hook in the ditch, then go take care of the cows. When they came back that way, they checked to see if they had snagged an unwary fish. At night, the boys went down to the ditch to bathe and swim and the girls had a shallow spot elsewhere to play and swim.

Mrs. Hirstein believes that the families got along better then, too. Now, she feels that brothers and sisters fight more than they used to. Nature meant for the father to maintain discipline and mete out punishment and the mother to provide warmth and sympathy. More and more, she said, the modern mother must try to do both jobs at once and then the children don't respect either parent. There goes the family and there goes the nation.

I believe there is a great deal of truth in what she says.

CHAPTER 15

Crisis and Credibility

"Mom!" I yelled toward the kitchen upstairs where she was preparing supper. "Something's wrong with my leg!"

There was no response as I lay helplessly on the concrete floor of the family room in the basement of our home.

"Mom," I shouted desperately again, "I can't walk!"

> ❧

Aside from being a little achy, less than thirty minutes before those screams for help, my eight-year-old world had been perfectly normal when Mom asked me for help preparing supper.

"Kerry, can you pick some strawberries for supper before the rain comes?" I heard Mom yell from the kitchen to the family room downstairs. Strawberries grew like jewels in the treasure chest of our garden, putting a tasty dessert always within arm's reach.

"As soon as my program is over," I yelled back from my fuzzy gray chair. I loved cartoons and summertime meant more Donald Duck, Bugs Bunny, and Road Runner. A lazy day of cartoons to kick off the summer was a sweet life.

The show was over a few minutes later and I dashed upstairs, through the kitchen, to where Mom was snapping early beans for supper. I went into the garage to find a container and grabbed a white enameled wash pan with a red ring around the edge and sprinted outside to our garden.

Our summer produce department was about two-thirds the size of a football field and contained nearly everything the grocery store carried: from sweet corn to squash, melons to beans, and, of course, strawberries.

Dark clouds gathered overhead as I searched the strawberry rows to see where the last person stopped picking. When I found the spot with ample red berries, I dropped to the ground. My bare knees left imprints in the soft warm soil. Crawling along the row, I smelled the musty earth and watched ladybugs scurry out of my way as I turned over strawberry leaves to uncover the sweet hidden treasures. *One for me, two for the pan*, I recited mentally, unable to resist the heavenly morsels. *One for me, two for the pan.* As the tender berries piled up in the pan, the rain came down. It wasn't a storm, just an almost-pleasant summer soaking, the kind of warm rain that brought life.

Despite the rain, I finished picking my row then jogged up to the garage as the raindrops washed the mud from my knees. I was soaked. I shook my body like a wet dog, and then dumped out the rainwater that had collected in my pan. I slipped off my rubber flip-flops in the garage, dropped off the strawberries in the kitchen for Mom, flew to my bedroom for a quick change, then bolted downstairs two steps at a time to continue my cartoons until supper was ready.

That's when it happened.

During a commercial, I got up from my comfy chair to go to the bathroom and fell to the floor—surprised but unfazed. *I must have tripped on something*, I thought. I tried to stand but fell again. My right leg was loose and floppy like a rag doll. There was no strength, no rigidity, nothing.

"Mom!" I yelled from the concrete floor of the family room, toward the kitchen, upstairs where Mom was preparing supper. "Something's wrong with my leg!"

There was no response.

"Mom," I shouted again, desperate, "I can't walk. Something's wrong with my leg." I heard metal pans and lids rattle as she closed the pullout cabinet shelves, then her heavy footsteps come down the wooden stairs to the family room.

Even with me lying on the floor in front of her, she asked with more puzzlement than alarm, "What's the matter, Kerry?"

"I don't know. My right leg just stopped working. I got up to go to the bathroom and just fell down. I can't make…it's just wobbly."

Growing up in the country can be hazardous. In our family, if there was no gushing blood or protruding bones, it wasn't considered a serious problem. So I didn't panic as Mom helped me back to my chair and casually examined my leg, pushing and pulling.

"You might have caught a virus, or something," she said. "I knew you shouldn't have been out there in that rain."

She found me a good walking stick, and I quickly learned to hobble around the house the rest of the evening on one appendage. With Mom's assured response, the experience felt like an adventure; I was a pirate who had misplaced his wooden leg.

If this episode brought back frightful memories for Mom, she didn't reveal it to me.

The next morning, my condition hadn't improved and there was deep pain in my floppy leg. Mom took me to see Dr. Wilcox, our family doctor who was a chiropractor. He was the only doctor we saw. His office was on the ground floor of an old brownstone home in nearby South Bend, twenty miles from home. He had removed some of the walls to create a wide-open space with exam and treatment areas separated by movable curtains. The wooden floorboards squeaked with each step, and in spite of the windows, the wood-paneled walls made the room a bit dark. His treatment tables were long and slender and moved from a vertical to horizontal position with a push of a foot pedal to help patients get on and off. Since I couldn't stand very well, he lowered the table to the horizontal position, boosted me onto the vinyl-clad table, and began his examination.

Dr. Wilcox could have come directly from Central Casting. He was tall, with broad shoulders and creases of wisdom in his face. His glasses and white lab coat spoke with authority, as did his deep voice. A slight limp, a soft chuckle, and a smile on his face let those in his care know he was trustworthy.

Mom trusted Dr. Wilcox. But she didn't trust doctors of traditional medicine. She distrusted MDs and the medical profession so much that she refused to have me vaccinated for polio, diphtheria, and all other childhood illnesses, fearing they could cause the very illnesses they were designed to prevent.

Mom had valid reasons to fear vaccinations, especially for polio. In 1935, when she was fifteen years old, two separate organizations tested vaccines on thousands of children. Several died of polio and many were paralyzed, made ill, or suffered allergic reactions. Tests the following year with a different vaccine proved just as disastrous. By the 1950s, just weeks after a new vaccine had been declared effective and safe by the government, more than two hundred polio cases were traced to batches of vaccine contaminated during the manufacturing process. Most became severely paralyzed. Eleven died. The United States surgeon general ordered all inoculations temporarily halted until the problem was corrected, and not a single case of polio was attributed to this vaccine afterward.[1] But with institutional distrust seemingly innate, and evidence to reinforce her suspicions, Mom resisted vaccinating her children. I was an all-natural child.

Dr. Wilcox gave me a thorough examination, including checking my vitals, flexibility, and strength. It didn't take long for him to diagnose my condition. With raised eyebrows, he stared over the top of his glasses at my mother's face, "Berthella, this boy has *polio*."

There was no surprised gasp from Mom, or eyes widened in alarm. She seemed to take it all in stride, as if this was old hat. "You need to bring him to my office three times a week for an adjustment and therapy," he instructed. "And we'll start right now."

Dr. Wilcox helped me off the adjustment table and with assistance I hopped across the wooden floor past a vertical partition to his therapy table. There, he put a hot pad on my right leg until it was toasty, easing the ache and preparing it for physical manipulation. He began by putting one hand under my right knee and lifting, while his other hand pushed the bottom of my foot, rocking my limp leg back and forth as if I were walking. He pushed my leg high into my torso, which caused me to gasp from a shooting pain. He then pulled my leg back to the table, stretching and massaging it as he went. He repeated this motion, back and forth. Other techniques exercised my leg muscles while also measuring my range of motion.

In the midst of the turmoil, my mother remained calm. With competent adults in charge and possessing little knowledge of the seriousness of polio myself, I was optimistic. After all, I had no gushing blood or protruding bones.

⅓

When I hear the word "polio" today, it causes a visceral reaction like the words "cancer" or "heart attack." I think of the pictures of kids imprisoned in iron lungs. Although I know that polio has been eliminated in the United States, if my child contracted polio I think, like most folks, I'd rush to an MD rather than a chiropractor.

The potential consequences of her decision to consult a chiropractor for medical care were enormous. It never occurred to me to ask her why. As an adult with a very different view, I decided to examine her decision.

My search for answers began with Mom's ninety-two-year-old sister, Joy. "In the 1920s, when our little sister, Dorothy, was quite small, she fell down some steps," Joy revealed. "As her condition deteriorated, it was obvious that something wasn't right. My grandpa said 'get that child to a chiropractor.' He knew a gentleman nearby, Mr. Eaton, who was a railroad engineer, but who provided chiropractic treatment on the side. We visited Mr. Eaton—we were not allowed to call him 'doctor' because he wasn't one—and soon Dorothy recovered. Mr. Eaton told my mother, 'Effie, if you hadn't brought your daughter here to me, she would have died.'"

Because Mr. Eaton saved Dorothy's life, it made a believer out of my grandmother, Effie. So later on, when Aunt Joy had a bad fall and her back throbbed for days, off they went to see Mr. Eaton. He provided spinal manipulation three times a week until her pain disappeared. In return, Effie, a divorced single mom, did his laundry and cleaned his house since she had no money for payment. For her, "the proof was in the pudding." Chiropractic care worked.

But Effie was in the minority. Chiropractic care was controversial from its outset near the turn of the 20th century. It began with a battle with the American Medical Association, which took steps to limit the number of doctors in the U.S. because the oversupply reduced physicians' income. "Organized medicine," as this nascent industry of MDs became known, called chiropractic care an "unscientific cult" partly for its early mystical practices, but also for its new innovations in treating the musculoskeletal nervous system. [2]

I believe the opposition to chiropractic care by the medical establishment reinforced Effie's belief in chiropractors rather than diminished it. She had an "anti-establishment" world view born from her deeply-ingrained religious instruction from Pastor Russell, who opposed "organized religion." So if "organized medicine" opposed chiropractic care, then chiropractors must be doing something right.

Convinced she possessed the truth, Effie saw no need for doctors of medicine, and chiropractors became her family's sole doctors.

As her family of girls grew, so did the fear of polio in the U.S. The disease had no known cause or cure. The epidemic seemed to increase in the summer—swimming pools closed, theater goers avoided sitting next to each other, and some parents were afraid to let their children play outside for fear of catching this crippling and deadly affliction. At its peak in 1952, 60,000 children were infected, thousands paralyzed, and more than 3,000 died. [3]

Chiropractors had some success treating polio over the years, but it wasn't well-researched or documented. And of course they ran into opposition from the medical community in the U.S. But in Australia, Elizabeth Kenny had clinical success with her technique of using "exercise" instead of immobilization. She came to the U.S. in the 1940s to share her technique with medical doctors. She was a determined, outspoken woman, who was medically unaccredited, and claimed her treatment was superior to that of the male-dominated, educated medical community. She was widely panned from coast to coast.[4]

But the chiropractic community saw the merits of her techniques, which aligned with their own methods of physical adjustments. Soon, chiropractic care became the go-to treatment for many families with polio.

Although the medical community initially resisted Ms. Kenny's unorthodox treatment, she became Gallup's most admired woman in the U.S. in 1951 because of her well-publicized successes. Eventually, the Mayo Clinic endorsed her work, paving the way for her techniques to become the physical therapy widely used today.[5]

When the epidemic peaked in the early 1950s, my mother's family was hit hard.

"Suddenly, my mom couldn't get out of bed by herself," recalled Aunt Joy. "We girls were all married by then, so Mama was living by herself. But then my sister, Dorothy, came down with it in her arms, so I went to help her since she had little kids. During the night, my husband, Hank, got it real bad. I had to go to the neighbor's house to call the doctor, but Hank was dead by the time the doctor arrived."

The doctor treated Joy's mother, Effie, who fully recovered. He treated Dorothy as well, although one of her arms remained weak. Their family doctor was a chiropractor, as it was their entire lives. And for those familiar with chiropractic care, they knew chiropractors had the best treatment for polio. The doctor who brought them healing from the fearsome foe of polio was Dr. Wilcox.

ॐ

When my leg suddenly stopped working in childhood, surely Mom recognized the signs. She knew it could be deadly. She knew it could bring lifelong paralysis. She knew it was serious and needed the best treatment available, so she turned to the person she knew who could provide it: Dr. Wilcox.

After speaking to my aunt, I no longer believed that Mom's choice of chiropractic treatment for my polio was a poor choice. True, if Mom had allowed me to be vaccinated, the attack would probably have been prevented. If she had any remorse or second thoughts, I saw no signs of that in my childhood.

After a summer of treatments, sandwiched between more time for me in front of the TV and less time under the sun, Dr. Wilcox pulled off a stunning success. My polio disappeared and I had no lasting impairment. Once again, his hands brought healing to the family and created another generation of believers—I still visit a chiropractor for a condition unrelated to my long-gone polio.

Aunt Joy, who grew up with chiropractic care, still visits her chiropractor once a month as well. But after Dr. Wilcox died decades ago, she had to find a new one. Her current doctor is a special young man, filled with enthusiasm and grand plans for the business he recently took over. He's my nephew, Matt. He began treating Joy when her previous chiropractor retired. Her previous doctor was Matt's father, my older brother, Tom.

And just as my grandmother used to barter with her chiropractor in exchange for services, so does Aunt Joy. Each month she brings Matt a fresh baked pie—one made with hands of love in exchange for the hands of healing now in our family.

Thank you, Mom, for loving your family in this way.

❧

The Party Line
By Berthella Stevens
January 18, 1968, an edited excerpt

During Christmas vacation, one of our boys told me that our neighbor Eldon Manges said that I should call him as he would give me a rough time and I wouldn't be able to write it.

Well, that was akin to waving a red flag at a bull, so I looked forward to talking to him. I've known Eldon quite a long time and knew he could talk well on many interesting subjects.

So he was my first call this week, but to my disappointment, he chickened out. He was only kidding my son, he claimed, and I would have to talk to Betty, his wife. She was a little leery but did talk to me—even when the rest of her family was laughing at her and trying to scare her by saying that I probably was writing down everything she was saying.

She didn't know of anything she wanted to talk about so I volunteered I knew something that was close to them right now. I've seen them out in the bitterest cold weather, still trying to get their corn picked. Betty believes this is definitely the worst year that the farmers have ever had to contend with, because it's been so wet all fall and they couldn't get into the fields. Since she said it, I believe it.

We talked about a four-day trip that they took in August to see Eldon's brother in Pennsylvania and then on up to Niagara Falls. It was the longest trip they ever took. But, as she said, it's impossible to get away when there is so much work, especially milking cows twice a day.

She told me how sorry she felt when her children were little and they went back to school in the fall and the first thing the teacher asked was where everyone had gone during the summer. The children would come home and say, "But, Mom, we can't say where we went because we never go anyplace!"

Betty then shared with me a good example of the Golden Rule in action.

She mentioned that her father has been in the hospital for the past three months and she visits him every morning to see how he faired the night. If he is not feeling very well, she stays with him for a few hours or checks back later in the day.

When I remarked what a tremendous job that was, as busy as they are, she replied that is what she would like if she were in that position. So that is what she does. Before saying goodbye, I told her that seems to be pretty good insurance that she will be treated that way when she gets old, as she is training her children by example.

Consider what a burden could be lifted from our doctors and mental hospitals if all children cared for their aged parents and made them feel wanted to the end of their days, as Betty is doing.

It's well known that babies can waste away and die from lack of love. While too much isn't known about the science of aging, I feel sure that many a parent met a premature death from being neglected and slighted by offspring.

CHAPTER 16

Au Naturel

Mom loved to go *au naturel*. It ran in her family. Her grandmother first showed her how to use what nature provided, and Mom's mother regularly used those provisions to kill germs and bring healing with onion, lemon juice, raw honey, and sassafras tea. As a young adult, Mom witnessed the chiropractors' natural and successful treatment of polio in her family while the medical establishment watched from the sidelines. So by the time I arrived in her life, Mom had firmly planted her flag on the side of unorthodoxy. When it came to remedies for what ails the human body, Mom went *au naturel*.

☙

As a child, my mother was my doctor. It seemed perfectly normal. "House calls" were simply a shout away, and no matter what problem I had, Mom had a natural remedy.

"Mom," I eked out with a hoarse, scratchy voice as I watched cartoons from the fuzzy gray chair, "my throat hurts. It's hard to swallow."

Within minutes she arrived with a kids' version of a hot toddy. "Here, take this. Tilt your head back and spoon this warm lemon and honey into the back of your throat. Let it slide down slowly. It'll kill the germs and ease the pain."

130

Cries of different ailments brought different solutions.

"Momb," I whimpered through nasal congestion, "I hab a code. I cand breehd."

"Come here," she said, pulling a kitchen chair up to the stove where a small pan of water and vinegar simmered. Mom tore a hole in the bottom of a stiff brown paper bag then turned it upside down over the steaming concoction. "Kneel on this chair and stick your nose and mouth into this hole and breathe in deeply."

I instantly gagged and jerked away, blinking my burning eyes.

"Close your eyes and just keep breathing the vapor. The vinegar will kill the germs and get rid of your congestion."

On other occasions, when I couldn't remove a splinter with tweezers or a needle, my wail yielded a remedy more disgusting than the predicament. Using her kitchen as her pharmacy, she grated an onion into a reeking mush.

"Okay," she said, "hold out your hand." I turned my face to avoid onion-tears as she spooned the slop over the splinter in my palm, just as her mother had certainly done for her many years before. "This will slowly pull the splinter out of your hand. It's called a poultice. You just have to keep it on for a while, though" she said, as she wrapped my hand with cloth strips.

Mom even borrowed one trick directly from Jesus' natural medicine cabinet after I accidentally touched a nettle plant that grew wild on the roadside. To relieve its painful welts, she mixed her own spit with a pinch of dirt and rubbed it on the wound like a salve.

While Jesus' spit cured the blind,[1] Mom's only worked on nettles. But it worked. And surprisingly, the other treatments did, as well.

Vitamin supplements were also a staple in her doctor bag. She knew vitamin A is good for your eyes and heart; vitamin B helps keep up your energy and is good for your blood; vitamin D makes strong bones and teeth. There was seemingly no end to her knowledge and miraculous claims. She was well informed from the books and magazines she read and the seminars she attended, and she even sold supplements to friends and neighbors.

But vitamin C was the superhero. It prevented and cured the common cold, lowered blood pressure, and fixed cataracts in the eyes of the aged. When mixed with blackstrap molasses, it healed skin conditions. And if I was ever stranded at sea, I knew that vitamin C could prevent scurvy. There seemed no end to its benefits. If Mom had been a real doctor, I believe her favorite saying would have been: "Take two C vitamins and call me in the morning."

Sometimes vitamins and natural elixirs weren't enough. Gadgets were needed. Resting head-down on a "slant board" realigned my spine and allowed gravity to pull my organs back into their proper position. Jumping on a mini-trampoline called a "rebounder" healed my body by stimulating my lymphatic system. At least, that's what I was told. And when an especially bad cold or flu hit, it was time to be stuffed into the steam cabinet to rid my body of "poisons and toxins."

A fully enclosed metal box about the size and shape of an oversized washing machine, Mom's steam cabinet was like a personal Greek bath in our basement. It was probably old enough to have been used by Aristotle himself. Hand-painted a faded cream color to hide the chips, cracks, and dents on its exterior, its top sloped down and opened in the center like two storm cellar doors. There was also an opening in the doors for an occupant's head to protrude. But the interior is where the action happened.

Aching from sickness and wearing nothing but a towel, I opened the heated cabinet, releasing the musty odor of an ancient gym, then gripped the sides with clammy hands and climbed into the box. I felt the trepidation of an audience member at a magic show who'd been called to the stage. But I resisted that fear and imagined I was an Apollo astronaut climbing into my space capsule. I heard the front door snap closed behind me as I turned around and sat on the adjustable bench. I leaned my head left and then right, as Mom carefully dropped the two top lids into place with hollow metallic clanks. I was locked in with only my head sticking through the opening.

A cast iron tank with water and a heating element produced the steam from under my seat. Mom tucked a towel around my skinny neck to prevent vapor from escaping. If there were any temperature or timer controls, I didn't see them. My job was to sit there and sweat. As the temperature rose inside the box, perspiration oozed from my pores and drained into a small container beneath the metal floor of the contraption. Only time, and my imagination, would reveal if I'd be sawed in half at the magic show or fly to the moon.

While I baked, Mom insisted I rehydrate.

"Are you thirsty?" she asked. She held a straw to my mouth so I could sip a glass of water. "You need to keep drinking so the poisons will be flushed out of your body."

After I was fully cooked, I felt rejuvenated and believed that somehow the "toxins" had drained away through my sweat glands.

❦

The benefits of Mom's gadgets, like the steam cabinet, paled in comparison to the power of her own hands. She was a trained masseuse who wiped away body aches and gloomy dispositions in her "massage room," where cool, gray concrete formed one wall and bare wooden two-by-fours formed another in our unfinished basement.

My mother's hands were strong as a man's—muscular, with short thick fingers that could dig deep into inner tension. Lying shirtless and face down on a massage table in the center of this space, she stood at my head and laid her warmed hands at the top of my shoulders, one on each side of my spine. Then she pressed down and slowly glided them like rollers into the small of my back, separating around my waist. My breath eased out with each press of the flesh, releasing a tiny bit of pain or cloudiness of spirit. When she found a tight muscle, she'd push down, and in a single motion squeeze and pull back, kneading the muscle until it was soft as fresh dough and my body melted into the table. As I rested peacefully, she'd finish up with a rapid percussion using only the sides of her hands, up and down my body's length like she was playing a symphony with human drumsticks. When it was over, I lay motionless with my eyes closed, lost in the moment.

I wasn't the only one to benefit from Mom's skilled hands. For twenty dollars, she treated men and women to an hour of Heaven in her massage room. To bring levity to a conversation with a prospective new client, Mom didn't shy away from using terminology which conjured up visions of the world's oldest profession.

"It's good to meet you, Berthella. So tell me, what do you do?" a newcomer asked politely.

"Well, I do a lot of things," she'd begin, without a flinch or smirk. "Sometimes I run a massage parlor in my basement."

The newcomer would gasp, wide-eyed. Silence followed.

"Well, not the kind you're thinking of, of course. I'd never do that," Mom said to relieve the tension she'd just created. "I give real, therapeutic massages."

The stranger would sigh with skeptical relief. "I see. S-s-so… you…give massages?"

"Yes. I'm a masseuse," she'd grin. "I give therapeutic massages. Have you ever had one?"

Most folks Mom met had never been to a massage parlor, the legal or illegal ones. But the courageous or curious took Mom's bait and engaged in this most-unlikely conversation.

"So why should I get a massage, Berthella? What does it do for me?"

"Well, it's the ultimate gift of pleasure and well-being that you can give your body," she'd tell them, standing with shoulders back and her chin high. "Not only does a therapeutic massage give you a sense of well-being, it improves circulation and the suppleness of your joints and tendons."

The newcomer's eyebrows would arch. "All that, just from a massage? How's that possible?"

"It's done by focusing on the much-neglected lymph system, which we've been hearing about in the news lately. That neglect contributes to our illnesses."

She was as good a salesperson as she was a masseuse. For those who transcended this barrier of intimacy, all-natural bliss awaited them.

∞

Despite the natural remedies at her disposal and her skill at therapeutic massage, it wasn't enough to resolve a debilitating issue—one that struck me like lightning.

Elementary school had just let out for the summer and the promises of freedom rang in my ears. But one afternoon the freedom I imagined was smashed by intense, throbbing pain in the center of my brain. When it struck, lights and sounds were unbearable and food was unappetizing. I lay on the couch in the fetal position, covering my head with the cool fabric of a pillow until it passed. Mom massaged my neck and took me to our chiropractor, but most days, the darkness of misery blotted out the sunshine of summer.

"Berthella," Dr. Wilcox began after another unsuccessful adjustment, "I have an idea." He walked around the treatment table, stopped by my feet, and untied and removed my shoe. Then he pinched the bottom and top of my big toe between his thumb and index finger. I screamed and nearly launched from the table like a rocket. It felt like the doctor had pierced my toe with a red-hot nail.

"That's it," he said. He tilted his head and shoulders back and peered at my mom. "Something's wrong with this boy's pituitary gland."

As my mom looked on, Dr. Wilcox put his hands behind his back and spoke to me. "Your pituitary gland is about the size of a pea and is located near the center of your head. It's often called the master gland because it controls several other glands in your body, like your thyroid and testicles."

I didn't know anything about my thyroid, but I knew about my testicles. I sure didn't want him squeezing them like he did my big toe, which still simmered with pain.

Mom narrowed her eyes. "Dr. Wilcox. What did you just do? How do you know something is wrong with his pituitary gland?"

"Reflexology. The feet contain nerve endings that go to every part of your body. Those nerve endings are roughly arranged in your feet as the body is arranged. Come over here and let me show you."

Mom and Dr. Wilcox stared at the bottoms of my feet as he pointed and lectured.

"The nerves from the top of his body—his head, eyes, ears, neck—end here around his toes at the top of his foot. The nerves from the middle of his body—liver, kidneys, gall bladder—those nerves end here in the middle of his foot. His tail bone and lower back are all the way down toward his heel. So if you know where each nerve ends, you can rub that spot on his foot, which can trigger a healing response at the other end." Dr. Wilcox studied Mom's eyes to see if she understood.

Mom tilted her head to the side. "So if there's a problem in the body, then it shows up as a pain in the foot?"

"Correct. So when I barely squeezed the region of the pituitary gland in your boy's foot, that pain indicated a problem with his pituitary, which is where he's experiencing the pain in his head."

"So I just need to rub his feet and that will stop his head from hurting?" Mom concluded.

"That's right. And I know where you can take a class so you can learn what you're doing. There's dozens of these zones on the feet, covering the entire body."

Suddenly, a new world opened to Mom, with endless possibilities. She had been shown a natural treatment for multiple ailments that was free and didn't involve medicine or an MD.

We rushed home. As I lay on the couch with my feet across Mom's lap, she began the treatment. She cupped the heel of my right foot in her left hand and gently touched the center of my big toe with her thumb and index finger like Dr. Wilcox. I screamed and jerked my foot back, nearly hitting her in the face. The pain was unbearable. After a moment, we tried again with the same result.

I shook my head. "Mom, I don't think I can do it. It just feels like a knife. You must be digging in with your thumbnail."

"I'm barely touching it, Kerry. But let's stop for now. Hopefully it will get better the longer I can rub it."

We had no other options. At least none I was aware of. Over and over I succumbed to the daily torture. At the same time, Mom took the class Dr. Wilcox recommended; she learned about all the zones and the proper technique for giving a therapeutic foot massage. When the recurring headaches inevitably crashed into my brain, we rushed to the couch. She took my feet in her hands and began treatment.

Inch by inch the headaches lost ground. They became less painful, didn't last as long, and my big toe became less sore. Mom massaged with intention, striving to clean that sore spot right off my toe and wipe away the headaches with it. By August, she had permanently rubbed out the darkness, and the sunshine returned to my life.

Buoyed by her success, she offered this new service to her clients and hung a laminated poster on the wall of her massage room to explain the location of the many zones in the foot. From headaches, to chest pains, to kidney stones—Mom had a cure. And wherever she went, including Bremen's pharmacy, she never missed an opportunity to evangelize this miraculous technique to treat almost any ailment.

"What can I help you with today, Berthella?" asked our pharmacist, fit and attractive in his glasses and white lab coat.

"Oh, nothing, Mr. Molebash. I just came in for some Epsom salt. How are you?"

"I'm fine. Thanks. But I am having a bit of pain in my abdomen. Hopefully it will pass soon," he said with a wink.

"Well, it could be something besides gas, you know."

"Yeah. Like what?"

"Oh, I don't know. But I could find out for you."

She launched into her sales pitch on reflexology, describing the many places in his midsection that could be the source of his pain. Soon, Mr. Molebash was sitting on the edge of his sales counter with one shoe off as Mom worked on his feet and other customers gawked in disbelief. I stood respectfully nearby, too embarrassed to find out if his pain passed.

∞

As an adult, I have mixed views on Mom's all-natural approach. Like her, I take a fistful of daily supplements and can see benefits of each one. I'm seldom sick. When my daughter was young and had congestion in her chest, I pulled a kitchen chair up to the stove and had her breathe steaming vinegar. While I don't see the medicinal benefits of a steam cabinet, I must admit I've never researched it. And although my scientific mind can't understand the physiology of foot massage reflexology, I remain open to the mystery because it worked in my own life.

Mom's life may have been simpler if she'd just taken me to the doctor and had me pop some pills when I sniffled or my head hurt. How much easier might it have been if she hadn't gotten involved in massage and reflexology and used her own hands to wipe away my pain? I'm sure there were many other things she could have done with her time. But her investment allowed me to grow into a happy, healthy man.

Mom's actions were love in motion and yielded more than physical benefits. They also nourished my soul. Through her gentle touch—skin on skin—she renewed a primal bond of physical connection shared only by a mother and child. Too often, we break that natural connection when we decide we've grown too old to be cradled, or too mature to kneel at the feet of someone we love. Mom and I never broke that bond. Through the seasons of life, she continued to rub my feet, back, and neck, and I returned the gestures when I could. Her hands brought wholeness of heart and health as her touch warmed my spirit.

There's nothing more natural than a mother's touch.

CB

The Party Line
By Berthella Stevens
June 8, 1967, an edited excerpt

I had a delightful conversation with Mrs. Jennie White this week. I found her just full of interesting things to know and in a reminiscent mood.

She announced that she was baking pies and had just fixed some dandelion greens for her son-in-law. I expressed surprise that she still had dandelion greens tender enough to eat. To my further surprise, she said that she picks lots of them when they are plentiful and young, blanches them just like any other greens and then freezes them. That way she has them on hand all during the winter. They are delicious and cost her nothing.

It really was amazing to find someone wise enough to utilize modern methods on such an old-fashioned food, which just happens to be one of the best all-around plants. As far as I know, the only parts that don't have some use are the flower stalks and the seed head.

The young leaves make one of the most nutritious and tasty greens, the unopened buds make a delicious and tender boiled vegetable, and the juice from the roots has been considered for centuries as a "cure-all." It's still used in various medicinal and nutritional preparations today. Then, of course, the blossoms are good in various ways, the most notable being dandelion wine.

So what do most of us do with the plant? We poison it, spray it, plow it up, dig it out and otherwise show our contempt for a great bonus given to us by Nature. Then proceed to go to the store and BUY something that can't hold a candle to the "lowly" dandelion.

Mrs. White said she guessed that it was the Indian blood in her that prompted her to gather and enjoy such things.

This started her remembering things dear to her heart—starting with her grandmother.

As a child, she could remember the summer kitchen where her grandmother dried all her herbs and plants she used for tea, medicine, and salves, such as rue and pennyroyal. As a child, all the children would chew on pennyroyal and slippery elm as they went about their day. If you notice, the slippery elm is still included in modern-day throat lozenges.

Then she mentioned curly dock, and how she loves that. Since they grow just about anywhere, you can have them on the table, cooked and ready to eat in less than 10 minutes as it takes only about two or three minutes to cook. Can you get anything much fresher—except maybe catching a newly laid egg?

We also talked about how curly dock will often be found growing near nettles and how the crushed dock leaves can be rubbed onto nettle stings to relieve the pain.

I have never used that method yet. Any time that I was careless enough to get stung by nettles I would spit in the dirt and rub the mud on the sting. It always worked for me.

We agreed that for all the hard work our happiest memories stemmed from such times and places. We wondered if our grandchildren would have such nice memories of us.

CHAPTER 17

Gifts of the Sky

*The heavens declare the glory of God, and the sky above
proclaims His handiwork.*

—Psalm 19:1

The gifts from the sky came with no ribbons or bows and were often a surprise. A disappearing sun, stars falling at night, or rivers of undulating color filled Mom's life with joy and intrigue. As the handiwork of God, they were too special to keep to herself, so she readily re-gifted them to me. This chapter is the story of a collection of unusual gifts, blessings that can never be repaid.

ღ

"Guess what I saw?" Mom asked as she sprang from the garage into the house with a sack of groceries. It was a common question.

"The Loch Ness monster," I replied. I glanced up from the apple I was devouring at the kitchen table and smiled.

"No, better than that. Besides, that's in Scotland. Guess again."

"A ghost."

"No, silly. I saw the gold at the end of the rainbow!" she exclaimed.

"Did you see leprechauns, too?" Tom asked with a smirk as he sauntered into the kitchen.

"Funny. I didn't say I saw a pot of gold. I just saw the gold."

I gave her a quizzical look.

"I was just driving home with this light rain and the sun was shining, and across the fields, I was watching a rainbow following me. Suddenly there it was! As I was passing a large grove of evergreen trees in the distance, there was the end of the rainbow! At the very end were golden sparkles like the ones which dance from the Fourth of July sparklers. They were quite delicate."

I contemplated her words and remained silent.

She bolstered her case by adding, "There's not really a pot. I think that over the generations that just got added to the story."

Recalling Mom's delight in seeing the gold, or whatever it was she saw, still makes me smile. She never tired of these gifts of the sky, and though sometimes I laughed at her escapades, I'm thankful she chose to include me, as she did one brisk Saturday in early March.

Mom gathered our family on the patio for a momentous event that day. The trees in the yard still stood naked as the sun's rays warmed our cheeks and the "cheer, cheer, cheer" of a cardinal pierced the air. I waited in the sunlight as my friend, Bryan, walked over from his house, joining us for the excitement.

"Fuzz, why aren't you wearing a jacket?" Bryan asked as he stepped onto the patio.

I looked at my uncovered arms and down at my sandaled feet, noticing for the first time the poor choice I'd made. "I don't know. I guess I just ran out here so I didn't miss the eclipse."

Even Dad stopped his chores to watch the sun grow dim at midday, along with my siblings. Of course, they were all dressed warmly.

"Okay," Mom called. "You can't look directly at the sun or it will burn your eyes. So everyone needs to use these." She handed each of us several sepia-colored strips of negatives of our family photos that she had removed from a desk drawer. I quickly stacked three strips together, held them to my eyes like sunglasses, and glanced at the sun.

"No, not yet, Kerry," she admonished. "There's still one more step. Go in the house and get a big pot of water." I did as I was told, and Bryan held the storm door open as I carried it out. "Now dump it out on the patio," she instructed.

"Just dump it out anywhere?"

"Yes, just pour it on the concrete."

The water glistened in the sun as it spread across the cold, hard surface, creating a coarse mirror for the sun to reflect in the water, and absorb some of the harmful sun rays.

"Okay," Mom said. "We're ready."

As we donned our film-glasses and peered into the water-mirror at our feet, the invisible moon slowly chewed off an ever-growing chunk of the resplendent ball of fire as it passed in front of the face of the sun. The light of day faded away as we watched and left me with an enduring memory.

∞

Eclipses and rainbows only sporadically grace the sky, but the sun itself brought frequent joy as it bid goodnight to the firmament with kisses of color. Delicate splashes of pinks and blues appeared around the edges, with deep and passionate bursts of oranges and reds near the disappearing heart of the sun. A large, west-facing picture window in our living room provided Mom a front-row seat to this daily love affair, causing her to name our home Sunset Manor.

When the sun's last kisses faded away, the sleeping stars came out to play: bright lone stars that shouted, "look at me," families of stars with infinite twinkles, and stars that became animals and men in the imagination of the night. In the deep darkness of the unlit country, these dots of white light became my friends, introduced to me by my mother.

"Do you see the Big Dipper, Kerry?" Mom asked as we stood side-by-side in the front yard and stared into the jewel-studded blackness. Crickets serenaded us in the warm summer night.

"No. Show me."

She extended her arm and pointed north, midway in the sky. "See those seven stars right up there? They're brighter than those around them. On the left are four stars that form the curved handle of the Dipper. Do you see them?"

"Yeah…I think so," I replied, as my eyes adjusted to the darkness and I searched the heavens.

"Okay. The last one on the right end of the handle is also in the cup of the Dipper, along with the remaining three. The four of them together almost make a rectangle. That's the cup. See it now?"

"I do, I do. I do see the Dipper now, Mom," I said, bouncing lightly on the tiptoes of my bare feet.

Mom continued her sky tour. "Now, draw an imaginary line connecting the two stars on the far-right side of the Dipper straight up into the sky. Follow that line until you get to another bright star. See it right there?" She pointed higher and to the right of the Dipper. "That's called the North Star. If you can find that star, you'll always know which direction is north. And if you know where north is, then you also know all the other directions. People used that star to guide them all the way across the ocean by ship," she counseled. After we basked in a silent embrace of the stars, Mom turned to me and added, "If you want evidence of God, Kerry, just look at the sky. This is God's handiwork for the world to see."

I eventually learned to identify other stars like Sirius, often one of the brightest lights in the night sky, and another favorite constellation, Orion, spotted by first finding the straight-line triplet of stars that form his belt. Mom called these The Three Sisters, who stayed close together, seemingly talking through the night. I think these celestial bosom buddies reminded Mom of herself and her two sisters. She longed for relationships and The Three Sisters provided her comfort each night when she and her own sisters could not be together.

But stars don't always behave well when they're playing at night. Sometimes they stumble and fall from the sky. Those are special nights. The beauty of "falling stars" inspired a poem Mom wrote in high school.

Late Reflections

I was not dreaming!
I saw her, that Lovely Lady of the Night,
Reach up and loosen those twinkling stars
Caught in the balsam tree,
And drop them into my garden pool.

Nights of falling stars are predictable as Earth passes through remnants of ancient asteroids in its circular journey around the sun. Mom knew when those events occurred just like she knew when the first day of summer arrived. She eagerly awaited those tiny bits of gray rock being pulled into our atmosphere, bursting into flames as they fell to the ground.

The best summer show of falling stars occurred in August when we spread our blankets across the damp grass and plopped our bodies down to stare into the eyes of Heaven, listening to the haunting calls of an owl. In November and December, armed with coats and hats, even Old Man Winter couldn't keep us from the ritual. But whether we relaxed in the humid air of summer or the chilly crystal-clear nights, we gathered for the drama, unwrapping one more gift of the sky.

As we lay side-by-side, conversation came in short bursts like the falling stars.

"Look. There!" Tom might shout as his arm stabbed eastward toward the flash.

"There's another one!" I'd shout at a second streak of white.

"See that? Wow!" Julie would declare.

Misbehaving stars that fell from grace weren't the only moving lights in the night sky. Flying saucers, now called UFOs (Unidentified Flying Objects), regularly flew by our house—at least according to Mom. She wasn't immune to the excitement of the 1950s and '60s when sightings popped up like weeds. The anti-establishment sentiment in which she was raised also fueled her suspicion that the government was covering up the facts. Conversations at our house became more bizarre in 1964 after she read *The Hollow Earth*, which purported our planet had a hollow and habitable interior with a small sun in place of a molten core, from which "super humans" flew their flying saucers to visit the "known" Earth.

I also saw strange lights in the dark sky, but when I saw UFOs, I was WUI (Watching Under the Influence) of my dear mother. Today we know it's plausible that life could exist beyond Earth, based on the sheer number of Earth-like planets in the universe. Perhaps Mom did see new lifeforms investigating us in their flying machines.

Although shooting stars and flying saucers captured my imagination as a child, another moving light called to me with the seductive song of a siren: the Northern Lights. Each unpredictable appearance was enchanting. It caressed the sky with rivers of light the colors of romance: reds and violets atop stems of green. The luminescence could leave as quickly as it arrived. Mom never missed a chance to glance at this late-night art in motion.

Mom would wake me with a nudge and a whisper. "It's the Northern Lights. They're beautiful. Come quickly."

I'd stumble out of bed, shove my feet into slippers, wrap a blanket around me like a cocoon, and silently follow Mom through the dark house.

The delicate scent of Mom's night-blooming flowers tickled my nose and woke my curious mind as we stepped away from the canopy of trees and into the open yard.

I remember the first time. Above my head, majestic curtains of violet and lime saturated the velvet sky. I held my breath in disbelief of the enormity of the rippling lights. While I never took my eyes off the grandeur unfolding above us, my curious mind awakened and questions began to flow.

"What causes the Northern Lights?"

"Energy from the sun is hitting the magnetic poles of the Earth."

"Well, how does it make the colors?"

I heard my mother sigh softly as she reveled in the extravagance overhead. "I don't know, Kerry."

"Why are some colors different from others?" I persisted.

"I'm not sure," she said, without taking her eyes off the sky. "Let's just sit here quietly and soak up the beauty."

As we sat alone under the mysterious lights, I felt like a favored son, the biblical Joseph receiving my coat of many colors, a precious gift. I wanted to immerse my hands into the mystery, to feel the softness, to see if red felt different from green.

I heard a symphony playing in the lights. The piano began, bass notes at first, drawing a ribbon of green from the sea of stars. Slowly, the ribbon grew as the high notes of the piano's right hand joined the left with pale yellows and lime. Then the cello emerged, the deep slow cello, turning the ribbon to a river of deep green, as the bow of a violin danced with its strings and the river began to undulate, first this way then the other, back and forth like draperies blowing in the wind. The pace quickened, and the trumpets brought colors of red as the river ran wild and flowed over its banks in a crescendo of colors. The silence of this symphony was deafening.

⋐

As an adult, the sky still holds a special place in my heart because of this collection of gifts bestowed by my mother. I can still identify major stars and planets in the night sky. And I keep track of the phases of the moon and stop to admire solar or lunar eclipses or the passing of a comet. Sitting quietly beneath a sea of stars still leaves me in awe. Although I have not seen the Northern Lights since childhood, a yearning continues to tug at my soul.

Over the years, I've passed along these gifts to close friends and taught my daughter how to find the North Star as we lay on blankets in the backyard to watch shooting stars. But one extraordinary moment occurred when I had a chance to share my own gift from the sky with Mom.

During the Space Shuttle program, returning astronauts sometimes landed the shuttle in Florida, though rarely at night. On one particular flight, not only did they land after dark, but they were predicted to pass above my home in Central Texas on their approach to Florida. On this particular summer evening, Mom and Dad were visiting from Indiana.

At the appointed time I said, "Let's go outside now." I held Mom's arm and she stepped carefully from the house lights into the darkness. I guided her through a grove of live oak trees in the backyard, then into a clearing. The rhythmic hum of cicadas filled the humid air, and the sky was awash with our familiar friends.

"Look toward the west, just above those cedar trees," I told Mom as I pointed to the patch of dark sky from which the shuttle was to emerge. Then, as scheduled, it appeared, a bold point of golden light.

"Do you see it, Mom? Do you see it?" I asked eagerly.

"Oh, yes. I do. It's quite bright," she said, as she stared skyward.

As we watched, the point began to lengthen like pulled butterscotch taffy into a bright solid line of sparkling gold on an ebony sky.

"Oh, Kerry. That's beautiful! It's the color of the end of my rainbow!" she squealed.

It was as if a spider was silently releasing a long golden thread on which it would hang its web to capture the stars. But there was no spider. It was the distant supersonic flying machine whose wings ionized the air they passed through, creating the golden glow.

"I don't think I've ever seen something so amazing," Mom said as her gaze lingered on the growing trail of light. "The color...the immensity...the silence..." her voice trailed off. "It's almost as if God is underlining the glory of His handiwork by dragging His finger across the sky...just for me."

In the starlight, I could see a broad smile on Mom's face, transfixed on the heavens, as she stood motionless, bound by awe and wonder. She had been blessed with a gift from the sky. And I was blessed to show her that gift.

∽

The Party Line
By Berthella Stevens
February 8, 1968, an edited excerpt

Thanks to a lot of people not being home when I called, I got to talk to a Mrs. Delbert Doty, a very interesting mother of four boys.

Mrs. Doty had often thought about what she'd talk about if I did happen to call but had not decided on anything. So she was caught off guard. However, it didn't take long for us to get in the thick of it.

Mrs. Doty is a bookworm, as am I, and I believe that all bookworms feel a kinship. A thought came to me in thinking over our conversation—do enriched and cultivated minds go with easy talking?

Books are a problem at her house. She loves them and has them all over but has run out of room to keep them. Already she has started to put them in boxes in the attic, which is no way to care for them, she believes.

I told her how I partially solved the same problem.

Since bookcases will probably be the last thing done to our house, I scrounged around for bricks and boards of the same length. Using an old bookcase headboard as a foundation, I built shelves clear to the ceiling of our family room. With the ivory bricks that match the fireplace, natural-color boards, a few curios and a pretty vine, I created a rather attractive corner—and it didn't cost me a penny.

She then told me a story about one night when they were driving. One of her younger boys asked what the moon was. That surprised her. It seems that the first child gets taught everything and then the assumption is that the rest all know it automatically. 'Tisn't always so.

I told her of a time like that for me. Our youngest son, Kerry, had taken a fancy to a group of three stars, and one night when we were coming home late he saw his 'friends' again. Instead of putting him to bed, we got the encyclopedia out on the kitchen table and spent at least a half hour running in and out of the house and identifying his 'friends' as Orion's belt, and all the rest we could find. He has never forgotten that and he still has a fondness for those stars.

We usually watch for the announcements in the paper concerning the meteor showers, also, and run a contest to see who finds the most shooting stars. One night we took the lawn chairs, wool blankets and hats and set up business in the driveway. My husband came home late and found the whole bunch out there, star gazing. I guess he thought we were a little bit loony when we could have been in bed, warm and comfortable. There have been some memorable nights watching the Aurora Borealis, too. I wake up all that I can if there is an outstanding night sight.

Children need their parents to point out such things and explain them more than just reading about them.

CHAPTER 18

Feathers of Love

If there is a hell for chickens, I've been there. It's the opposite of Heaven I witnessed in the skies. Absent of fire, the stench of brimstone and ammonia inflamed my lungs and burned my eyes as I crossed the threshold into this darkness. Unable to see, I felt filth cling to my clothes like a frightened child clenched to his mother. Slime sucked my feet to the floor and made walking as difficult as breathing. The suffocating silence was interrupted only by the haunting sound of an open door banging in the wind. As my eyes adjusted to the dim sunlight that pulsed through the open doorway, the torment which once dwelled there was revealed.

To my left and right were metal cages connected in rows the length of a football field. The cage doors were ajar and the bodies were gone, but clumps of manure and feathers spoke to the horror of this place. This had been an egg farm, which had gone out of business a week earlier, and the building was abandoned. I saw a semitruck hauling away the chickens.

Bryan and I were about twelve years old when natural curiosity drove us to investigate the aftermath of this failed venture only a couple of miles from our homes. We had no agenda or goals beyond simple exploration as we entered Hades.

"There must have been tens of thousands of chickens in here," I sputtered between coughs. "This is horrible."

"I wonder why they left?" Bryan said, through his hand held over his mouth and nose.

Up to three hens would have lived in the cages the size of hat boxes, stacked three tall, back-to-back and side-to-side, with openings between the wires for them to poke their heads through for food and water. Droppings from chickens in the top cage hung like stalactites into the middle cage below. The poor chickens enslaved in the bottom row received a shower of excrement. Most of the manure squished between the wire mesh and piled up on the concrete floor that supported the battery of jail cells.

Triggered by the rising sun, a well-producing hen can lay one egg nearly every day. But the absence of windows told us the hens in this house were tricked to produce eggs more frequently by cycling the artificial lights off and on more often than once every twenty-four hours.

That's how they lived—survived actually. For months, the prisoners could stand or sit, and maybe turn around. But there were no roosters, no chicks, no sun, no bugs, no outstretched wings, no scratching the fertile earth. The place was trashed, the electricity was shut off, and the doors left open. Only yellow tape was missing from what felt like a crime scene. The catacomb was empty—or so we thought.

"This feels like a spook house," Bryan said as he pinched his nose to the piercing smells. "All we're missing is a corpse or a ghost."

"You shouldn't have said that. Look here." Through the faint light I spotted a chicken lying motionless in a cage and then one lying on the floor. "Look at the bent wings on that one…and that other one's leg looks broken." I felt nauseous from the scene and the stench. Suddenly, a ghost with white feathers slipped silently through the darkness on our left.

"What was that?" Bryan asked.

We crouched low to peer under the cages, careful not to kneel in the slurry, and saw a chicken stumble aimlessly over piles of poop.

"He looks terrible," said Bryan. "Look how dirty his feathers are. And he's missing all the feathers on his head."

"That's what happens when hens are trapped together with nothing to do. They just peck on each other and pull out their feathers," I said.

The place felt like a death chamber as we walked its length and encountered more escapees left to die. The way these chickens were treated was inhumane. I shook my head in disbelief as I breathed through my shirt sleeve and wiped my watering eyes. I was reared to respect life.

Sunlight blinded my vision when finally we exited Hades through the banging door. Even there we found a few more hens huddled in tall grass, dazed and confused by freedom. Although these chickens were bewildered, suddenly I was not. In a moment of clarity I remembered when Mom had snatched Blackie White Feather, the leader of the Banties that once roamed our yard, from the jaws of a frozen death.

"Bryan," I exclaimed. "We've got to rescue these chickens!"

By the time we rode our bikes two miles back home and returned with sacks to carry them in, I hatched another idea: *This is a good business opportunity.* The people who had owned this dilapidated chicken house clearly didn't care for their birds, so it was no wonder they went out of business. "I can do better than these guys," I told Bryan with certitude, as we liberated about a dozen unhealthy birds.

"What are you going to do with them?" Dad asked that evening when he returned from work.

My skinny chest puffed up. "I'm going to start an egg business and make a lot of money."

"I see," he replied with a shallow nod. "What are you going to keep them in?"

"I figured they could just stay in the busted-up sheep building."

"Well, that doesn't offer much protection. They really need a chicken house," Dad said.

Dad liked my idea of going into the egg business. Maybe he thought I was following in his footsteps. He soon found a traditional unused chicken house on a neighboring farm, pulled it down the road with his truck and set it up in our field. Unlike the coffin in which they'd previously lived, this house had four south-facing windows, which cast out the stench and darkness of death. Multi-tiered wooden perches on one wall provided places to sleep at night, and a set of dusty nesters created a safe haven where the hens could jump up to do their daily duty. The biggest change: the refugees had freedom to waddle in and out of their new home through a special chicken-sized door.

As I set up shop, I estimated my income. A dozen eggs could be sold for roughly a dollar. The hens were older and didn't lay very well, so I figured I might get two or three dozen eggs a week, if they didn't hide them in the grass. If I was going to make real money selling eggs to my neighbors, though, I clearly needed more chickens.

Mom found an order form for baby chicks in the back of *Prairie Farmer* magazine. Unsexed chicks were half the cost of sexed chicks, so I ordered fifty unsexed Rhode Island Reds using the little bit of money I'd saved. It wasn't long before the mailman drove into our driveway and carried a cardboard box labeled "Live Chicks." The chick chatter ricocheted inside the box like a busload of school kids.

As the chicks grew under a warm light in our basement, I decided I could save money by grinding my own chicken feed at the Bremen grain elevator instead of buying the premade kind. Using farming magazines around the house, Mom helped me research which grains, legumes, and supplements were the most nutritious for the secret recipe. I recorded it on an index card and tucked it away in a tattered recipe box. I kept records on each of the individual chickens already on my "farm," noting size, health, and whether or not they were laying eggs. I was fairly certain the guys who went out of business had not prepared as thoroughly, and that my diligence would pay off.

When the chicks feathered out, I moved them to the chicken coop, which was surrounded by an enclosure my dad and I built. The little ones danced their days away, jumping with the joy of childhood in the tender grass. The discovery of a new insect brought a cluster of friends to investigate. Nubbins of little combs sprouted from the heads of the young boys, as they stretched their necks to the sky in anticipation of a mighty proclamation of their manhood.

I drew joy from the happiness in the chicken yard. It fed my soul to care for living creatures and watch them develop. Like the Banties before them, these chickens spoke to my being. But unlike the Banties, these chickens had no parents to care for them. I was their provider.

And the more I learned about them, the more I loved being with them.

As they grew, so did my feed bill. Even while the chickens slept, feed disappeared, stolen by rats that fed their families on my tab. That prompted me to create a new record: notches on the side of the coop for each rat I killed. My spirits remained high, though, because soon the hens would lay big brown eggs.

Gradually, the young roosters began to find their voices. At first their crowing sounded like teenagers with bad colds—more phlegm than masculinity. But eventually their voices deepened and each morning a choir of riotous roosters greeted me. Their firecracker-red combs and sweeping black tail feathers signaled their machismo and accented the satin rust of their body feathers. They were half of my flock. Combined, I estimated the total flock could produce nearly two dozen eggs every… single…day. The thought of earning nearly sixty dollars a month made me crow with pride.

I read in the *Farmer's Almanac* that my hens could begin laying eggs at eighteen weeks old. So on the first day of the eighteenth week, I walked in the coop, head held high, expecting to be rewarded. But there were no eggs. *Nada.* On day two I marched into the coop looking for the first gleaming brown egg. *Nada.* No eggs. On day three, now certain of the pending achievement, I discovered…*nada.* No eggs. Disappointed, I remembered the book said it could take up to twenty weeks. So each day, chickens scattered as I charged into the coop, only to find empty nests. At twenty-one weeks, I was disheartened. *Surely, I couldn't have an entire flock of late bloomers,* I thought. At twenty-two weeks, as the feed bill mounted, so did my angst. Then week twenty-three came and went with nothing to show. By week twenty-four, I had less optimism than eggs and could no longer deny the catastrophe.

"Kerry, why aren't your chickens laying any eggs?" Dad inquired.

I looked up at Dad and thought, *Well, that's the one hundred dollar question!* "I don't know, Dad. I don't know what to say. They're just not laying any eggs," I sighed, obviously upset.

"Well, let me see if I can help," he said, calmly.

Dad returned from work the next day and announced he had a solution.

"I stopped and talked with Howard Stratford, where I got the coop, and told him about your predicament. He just laughed when he heard the story, and said the answer is pretty simple."

Dad had my attention. I liked simple answers. Simple sounded inexpensive. Maybe free. "Well, what did he say?" I asked impatiently.

"You have to kill the roosters," Dad said.

My eyes widened. "What? How come?"

"Well, one rooster can breed up to twelve hens each day. You got the same number of hens and roosters. So they're breeding the hens all day long, keeping the hens from laying eggs."

I was shocked, but relieved to have a solution to my mounting debt. But killing the choir that serenaded me, the guys I raised by hand? *That makes me no different than the egg man down the road who walked away and let his chickens die,* I thought.

For a day, I wrestled alone with the moral dilemma of killing my friends to make a buck. *In the country,* I reminded myself, *farm animals lived and died so that humans may thrive.* Reluctantly, I let the sound of cash drown out the crow of the roosters, and that Saturday, nearly all my roosters lost their heads. I grabbed each rooster, one at time, and wrapped a twine around its neck, and tried to think of it as an object rather than a living creature with feelings, feelings like my own. My dad held its body as I pulled the twine taut with its neck laid across a log. I turned my face away as Dad's hatchet landed the deadly blow. When Dad released each headless body, it first spun like an acrobat as blood spewed from its open neck like water from a hose. Then it tumbled and ran, first left, then abruptly right, then a flip, then a sharp left again. When it was all over, the carnage on the battlefield sickened me. I felt as dead on the inside as the headless birds around me.

Dad and I worked mostly in silence as we dunked each carcass into boiling water that Mom brought from the kitchen, and we plucked off their feathers. After each bird was gutted and its feet removed, Mom took them to the freezer.

After church the next day, with the cloud of death still hanging over my head, I ran out to the chicken house. I flung open the door and peered into the nester as hens scurried away and dust flew. There lay four, clean brown eggs. One was still warm. They sparkled like pure gold to me. *Four eggs!* On the second day, ten more eggs graced the place. And soon all the hens were doing what I rationalized God intended them to do—make money for me.

My chickens were free-range and organically raised. They scratched for bugs in the earth, saw the sun rise, and laid eggs with deep orange yolks. Until I could walk or ride my bike to sell the eggs to the neighbors, I stored the bounty in our old refrigerator in the garage, which Mom helped me clean out. The neighbors raved about the thick brown shells and the firm yolks. Business was good. I had repeat customers. Finally, money flowed in both directions on my egg farm.

But another painful lesson lurked just around the corner. When I purchased the chicks I didn't spend the extra money to have their wings clipped, which would have curtailed their ability to fly. So some of the hens literally flew the coop and laid their eggs in the tall grass near their enclosure. Although I frequently searched the grass, it was like hunting Easter eggs and I didn't always find them. When I did, I wasn't sure how old they were. And because I kept a couple of roosters in the flock, the eggs were fertilized. Occasionally, baby chicks started to form in blood-red sacks before I uncovered a hidden clutch. After I learned that customers didn't appreciate having their breakfast eggs served bloody-side up, I tried to candle all my eggs for better control over the quality.

I also discovered what supply and demand meant: I needed more neighbors. Twenty-five healthy hens can lay up to fourteen dozen eggs a week. Every week. In the sparsely inhabited countryside, I didn't have enough customers to consume all my eggs, especially after demand dropped when some folks received eggs with beating hearts they weren't expecting. So my eggs accumulated in the smelly old refrigerator where they acquired a taste like dirty socks.

My production costs with my custom-made feed were also way out of line with my income. I needed to earn two or three times the supermarket price for eggs just to break even, and that wasn't possible.

My costs were out of control, my quality was poor, and my chickens laid more eggs than I could sell. It seemed my fate was the same as the egg man down the road. I couldn't stay in business. Now I understood why the owner jammed his hens into tiny rooster-less cages, blocked out the sun, and pretended that night followed day more quickly in the egg factory. It didn't make things right, but it brought new insight.

Even with my current dilemma, I knew I would never treat my birds like the neighboring egg man. With a heavy heart I released my hope of a thriving business to the winds and my feathered friends joined their *compadres* in the freezer.

My egg business wasn't a total bust, though. It came with an extraordinary benefit. It was the only experience I can recall where my father was physically and emotionally engaged in my life. When he ran our family farm before my birth, farming was his primary means of relating to his kids. Any of us who were old enough were involved in some way. My oldest brothers have fond memories of my father and hold him in high regard, largely due to their childhood experiences. They worked together daily and he helped them with their ag-based projects, like raising pigs. There was an unbroken bond between them. But when Dad lost the farm, I believe he also lost the tools for connecting with his younger children. Absent were conversations about school, friends, books, or games. He was physically present and provided well; but without the emotional connection, my relationship with him lacked depth. Then, when my interest in chickens entered the picture, he was present and accounted for, tools in hand, ready to help me build that business. He and I talked, worked, and even sat silently together enjoying the simple gift of presence. It was a blessing.

Dad enabled, while Mom inspired. I was happy to have two parents actively involved for the first time in a common cause with me, each sharing something bigger than mere business acumen. They shared themselves and provided another enduring reason for me to cherish chickens.

❧

In adulthood, chickens reemerged in my life. I built a small chicken house in our backyard modeled after the one in my failed business and filled it with chickens of all types. Some had fuzzy black heads and others had feathers on their feet, and some were just the ordinary Rhode Island Reds of my childhood.

But these birds were not for business. They were raised as a reminder of the light of Heaven I received from birds rescued from the darkness of Hell. They were raised for the memories and rekindled joy of the Banties, which preceded them in my childhood, and for the patient hens that sat on eggs for twenty-one days to bring forth new life. For peace that settled in my soul when mothers called softly to their chicks. For the amazement when the young ones discovered their first bug, their first flower, their first bee. For the safety hidden in soft warm feathers. For the optimism of the rooster who greeted the rising sun, and the security he brought with watchful eyes on the sky. For the awe of simply being present with these living creatures.

These chickens reminded me of my own mother and father, covering me with feathers of love.

❧

The Party Line
By Berthella Stevens
April 20, 1967, an edited excerpt

If I picked one theme that has cropped up more than any others in this column, it would be "How much we like Bremen." I found another one this week.

Mrs. Wayne Gaby said that they are comparative newcomers to these parts. They used to farm in Logansport and came up here after finding the farm through an ad in the *Prairie Farmer* magazine. They didn't know a soul up here and friends and family could not figure out why they wanted to go where they knew no one, but they are not sorry. I'll bet she told me five times during our conversation how well the family likes the area.

Mrs. Gaby thinks that their farm is 250 acres and probably won't know for sure until she gets on the tractor this spring. I told her it will probably seem like 500 if she has to find out that way! She said driving the farm machinery from the old farm 70 miles away, was quite a job. Whew!

She also mentioned that she sells eggs and how the farmers' prices are so low for everything they sell, but you couldn't tell that by the high prices in the stores.

Mrs. Gaby was sewing a dress for her mother when I called and said that she really likes to sew but doesn't want to do anything else when she IS sewing. I asked if she sews as much for her two boys as she does her girl, and her answer was typical of the average sewer—"It's not as easy to sew for boys, so, no, I don't." My own boys feel rather left out when I sew dresses, so I bought some material to make surfer shirts for them. They felt a little more important, then, but, alas, they are still sad lads as the material is still in the sack, and there are four spring dresses in the works.

That reminded Mrs. Gaby of something. When she was in the hospital (or maybe just came home), after the birth of one of her children, her husband was "chief cook and bottle washer." He went to town one night ostensibly to buy shoes, but the next day a dishwasher arrived at the home. Then, another time, when she had another child, he bought her a sewing machine. That tickled me and I told her I thought she had a pretty good system going there. She laughed and said that all good things must come to an end some time, but, seriously, she doesn't believe men actually realize how hard women's work is until they have to try it. Then when they do, they try to figure out an easier way to do it.

When we said goodbye, she told me that she felt like she had made another acquaintance as she felt like she knew me already from reading "The Party Line." I liked that.

CHAPTER 19

A Greater Love

As the Father has loved me, so I have loved you.

—John 15:9

We hurtled down the hard concrete, Mrs. Smith behind the wheel, striving for a balance between pain and expediency. Fence posts whizzed past my window. The jolt of each uneven seam in the road brought moans and groans, punctuated by outcries when a tire hit a hole. My arms rested on a pillow that appeared when I was eased into my teacher's car amidst the ensuing crisis. But the pillow might as well have been made of bricks as jolt after jolt electrified my arms.

☙

Recess had always been a joyous time, and that day had been no exception. When the bell rang, I threw on my jacket, slapped on my gloves, and raced for my favorite playground equipment called the witch's hat. My fourth-grade buddy, Roger, joined me as we grabbed the large horizontal ring above our heads suspended by chains from a center-pole, which formed the 'hat'. The metal ring quickly chilled my hands as we pushed off with our feet then picked them up to twirl around the pole, floating inches above the frozen ground. The sky was overcast and piles of snow decorated the playground like discarded wrapping paper after Christmas. As we spun endlessly in a circle, sounds of glee floated on our breath in the frigid air.

A couple of other boys joined our circle of fun, which balanced the swaying ring and sped us onward. Then Bob showed up. Bob was in sixth grade—two grades older—and had also been held back a year, but he was everyone's best friend on the playground. With his size and strength, he reminded me of the Jolly Green Giant, and instantly transformed any schoolyard ride from mere fun to exhilaration.

I was thrilled when Bob joined the group. No longer did we need to kick the ground with our child-sized feet. He turned that ring like a windmill in a storm as the centrifugal force pulled my body, legs outstretched, to a nearly horizontal position. Only a death-grip on the ring kept me from launching across the playground, as screams of elation flew skyward.

Then Bob tried something new. Rather than spinning the human blender horizontally around the pole, he tilted the twirling ring so our knees practically banged against the ground on the low side, and we seemingly touched the clouds with our feet on the other. 'Round and 'round he pushed with seemingly endless energy. As the force pulled my body away, I gripped tighter, not wanting this ride to end. But as my grip began to fail, my screams of encouragement changed to screams of panic. "Stop! Stop!" I shouted amidst the cacophony of voices. "Stoooop! I can't hang on anymore!" And with that, my human rocket left the launchpad at the top of the arc, feet-first, seeking orbit. But within seconds, I crashed to the frozen earth.

Stunned, disoriented, and embarrassed, I leapt to my feet and stood motionless as my world closed in. I no longer heard the shrieks of children playing. I focused only on my hands.

Roger rushed to my side, concerned by the spectacle. "Are you okay?"

"No, I'm not," I eked out. "I can't move my hands."

Roger quickly examined the situation and assured me with his fourth-grade diagnosis. "This happened to me before. Just move around a little a bit and they'll be okay."

I wanted Roger's words to be true. But I wasn't that strong. His diagnosis didn't stop the pain and the tears from welling up. Anguish spilled from my eyes, leaving frozen drops of terror on the ground. Mrs. Smith, the teacher on duty, rushed to my side. Her car became my ambulance as we bolted to the only doctor's office in the community, while someone else called my mother. The doctor provided the real diagnosis: two broken arms. He said I'd need casts and six weeks of healing.

When Mom brought me home from the doctor's office, Julie was already back from school. Her blond pigtails bounced as she ran to the kitchen to greet us. "What happened to you?" she asked, staring at my casts. "I was scared when you didn't get on the bus to come home."

Julie wasn't the only frightened one. I couldn't use my hands and didn't know what I was going to do. My mother stepped in and took control. The first time Mom squeezed my runny nose with her hankie and told me to blow, I became a frustrated toddler once more. I felt like a baby bird as she fed me one spoonful of food at a time at mealtime. And Julie, who was only trying to be helpful when she took her turn, would add, "Here comes the airplane," as her forkful of food zoomed through the air toward my waiting mouth. "Open wide so it can land."

Everyday activities, like eating, drinking, dressing, and using the bathroom required ingenuity, patience, and humility for all involved. Activities, which normally took one minute now took five. My world slowed down.

My mother already had a full life, which included writing "The Party Line." But that labor of love consumed more time than she had available. She asked the newspaper if she could take a short break and focus on her wounded son. They agreed.

When I eventually gained enough dexterity to manage most of my activities, and it was time for Mom to return to her column, things had changed at the paper. They no longer needed "The Party Line," she was told. Months passed before she received an explanation from the editor who said the weekly feature, "…did not achieve its purpose." She heard through the "real" party line, though, that a powerful woman in the community had complained that the newspaper didn't have room to publish an article about the woman's recent vacation, but they had room for "that gossip column."

Maybe that was true. Or maybe my mother's columns were too long or touched on topics beyond the local issues that didn't achieve the editor's vision. Regardless, my broken arms marked the end of my mother's sojourn in the newspaper business.

It must have been embarrassing and painful for her joy to be crushed so publicly. She'd poured so much of her life into the column, only to have it rejected. But unlike her young child, who cried in anguish with each bump along the road, I never heard one word of despair leave my mother's lips with the passing of "The Party Line." On the surface, she picked herself up, shook it off, and looked forward to the next thing that God might place before her. It seemed as if Roger's diagnosis of my broken arms was really meant for her: Get up, keep moving, and it will be okay.

Though my arms healed fully, I don't believe the wound to my mother's heart ever did. "The Party Line" had been the perfect opportunity for her to express so much of who she was: a conversationalist, teacher, and writer. It nourished her soul and brought her joy. It was a great love in her life. But she sacrificed that love for a greater one, for which I'm eternally thankful.

FALL

Fall Prelude

Fall is filled with the harvest from the promises of spring and the fullness of summer.

It brought freedom to Mom. She enjoyed the changing colors of this season, which allowed her to express the writings in her heart and listen to the music in her soul. But the fruits she gathered in her storehouse were both bitter and sweet.

I spread my wings during this time of maturity, discovering myself and the threatening blights that grew unnoticed in the fields of my youth. No longer seeing through the lens of childhood, my adult eyes saw my mother anew.

Autumn brought wholeness to my love for my mother.

CHAPTER 20

Riding Through the Rainbow

by Berthella Stevens

What is as glorious as a long drive in the country during the heart of the color season, particularly when the sun shines? The great banks of woods and forests, the windbreaks, the lawn trees, all ablaze with heart-stopping color!

Autumn is so beautiful in this part of the world that it could easily be an incentive to live just one more year—just one more autumn.

Who could possibly dream up the sublime picture of a magnificent golden-hued maple with half its leaves on the ground so that the whole lawn is the same color and texture as the tree, pierced by a shaft of golden sunlight? Such a place is where one could easily fall to his knees in worship.

One of the most attractive places is along highways that cut through, or in close proximity to the woods, where one catches all colors and shades of the rainbow in passing. There!—the yellows of the poplar and maples, the golds and bronzes and browns, the blazing scarlets and oranges interspersed with the still-unturned greens and the velvety richness of the pines. Here!—a rose-crimson, a purple-wine, a claret, corals and ambers and, yes, an occasional pink. And when one has seen them all, the very next woods elicit the same pleasure and awe. This whole kaleidoscope of colors painted against a blue, blue sky has no equal, no comparison to anything else.

I wonder: Why has our Creator made such a panorama? What useful purpose does it serve in Nature's scheme? Is there any benefit to the land, the creatures that inhabit the land, or to us? The only answer that I can come up with is that God planned and executes this display for our pleasure only. He gave us the eyes to see it, the brain to register the minute differences in shades, and the emotion to enjoy it.

So do—do enjoy your ride through the rainbow.[1]

CHAPTER 21

Sounds of Silence

Silence is the melody of nature. It's the music of the rising sun and unfurling petals warmed by its rays. Silent notes float with butterflies and white clouds in azure skies. What tune is heard when summer strawberries blush and fall leaves change to the colors of passion? Or when snowflakes tumble to the ground and greet their friends on starlit nights? That is the sound of silence.

Silence was my soundtrack of country life. It provided space to dwell in the quietness of nature and listen to myself think. But when I left my country home for college in the city, my silence was battered and broken. Days and nights without ceasing, engines revved, "Go, go, go," while horns blared, "Get out of my way!" Ambulances screamed, "I have an emergency!" while fire trucks shouted, "Something's burning!" And it seemed everyone but me ignored the lonesome ka-chunk, ka-chunk of metal wheels on rails that echoed from passing trains. It was difficult to sleep; I was drowning in the noise of the city.

In the midst of this urban cacophony I met a young woman named Karen. She was smart, fun, had long brown hair, and came from a suburb of Detroit. She was also a freshman, and we immediately started dating. Later that autumn, I invited her to come home with me to enjoy some peace and quiet.

I was proud of where I grew up, only a two-hour drive away from the university, and eager to introduce Karen to country living.

After our ride home through the rainbow of fall colors, we greeted my folks, and then walked around the front yard to smell the last flowers in Mom's garden. A car passed by, kicking up a gritty cloud of dust. I waved and the driver waved back.

"Who was that?" asked Karen.

I shrugged my shoulders. "I don't know. I didn't recognize him."

"Then why did you wave at him?" It was a simple, logical question, but it stopped me in my tracks. *Why did I wave at him?* That question had never crossed my mind.

"I don't know," I confessed. "It's just what you do. Isn't that what you do at home?"

"No. We don't wave at people. Especially if we don't know who they are." After an uncomfortable pause she continued, "So…you just wave at everybody?"

"Yep. Pretty much. I thought that's what everybody did. Besides," I added, "we usually know nearly everyone who drives down our gravel road, so it isn't much extra effort to be friendly to the few strangers who pass by."

Karen's query marked the first time I seriously pondered who I was. As that conversation lingered in my psyche throughout the day, it slowly opened my mind and my ears to prepare for the bigger challenge she was about to bring.

The crisp air, low humidity and delicate breeze kept the insects at bay that evening. It was a perfect fall night, and the stress of school slipped away with the setting sun. At bedtime, Karen slept in my childhood room while I used the downstairs bedroom, which each of the boys inherited as we grew up. Our house had no air conditioner, so I opened Karen's windows before I retired to allow a blanket of serenity cradle her to sleep.

The next morning, after a peaceful sleep, I greeted Karen as she stumbled from her room, a bit blurry-eyed.

"How'd you sleep?" I asked.

"Terrible. I barely slept," she said, with a husky voice.

"What? What happened?"

"There was so much noise all night long. Didn't you hear it?"

"No. I didn't hear anything. It was quiet."

"Quiet? Didn't you hear dogs barking, over and over? And the cows…bellowing? Why aren't they sleeping? And those bugs!" she said, spitting as if she'd swallowed one. "I guess they were crickets. They never shut up until sunrise. They kept making racket the entire night. And then the frogs chimed in. You must have some big frogs out there. They…"

Karen shook her head, sighed, and didn't finish her sentence. Maybe her brain was too fuzzy from the lack of sleep. Or maybe she thought it impolite to complain so much. But the words had already left her lips, and there was no taking them back. She described the sounds of nightlife in the country in a way I'd never heard.

We didn't resolve our different perspectives then, but Karen's comment that morning caused me to listen to my world with new ears. *Was the music that played in the background of my life really that noisy?*

After breakfast, we dawdled outside and I pondered the sounds of the day. *What did I really hear?* Like the cars in my college's city, I heard engines. But one of those engines was from Eldon's International tractor hauling grain to sell in town. And the other was from John, disking up his empty wheat field across the road with his green John Deere. It wasn't noise; it was our neighbors' working, taming nature to support their families.

As Karen and I swayed on the porch swing I listened anew and heard the buzz of bees' wings as they bobbed between fading flowers, delivering pollen and retrieving the last drops of nectar to carry back to their hive. And the giant leaves of the Sycamore tree, mostly dry and brown, rustled together as the breeze pushed them first one way then another.

When light finally turned to darkness, I lay in bed with the windows open and listened with fresh ears. I heard dogs barking. First, a hound a half-mile to the north spoke up with a deep bark, and then his neighbor a bit west responded. Soon, a companion three fields east had something to say.

In the distance, a dairy cow let loose a long, soulful cry. I recognized her grief-stricken bellow. Her calf had been taken away to be weaned so Eldon could claim the mother's milk. And I heard an even fainter, high-pitched cry of the calf that missed the wet, warm nuzzle of its mother. I knew it would soon enjoy its bottled formula, and its separation anxiety would subside.

I heard a symphony of crickets rubbing legs together to attract mates. As the temperature dropped, I knew the rhythm of their song would slow and finally fade away as they participated in the circle of life. Frogs competed for attention as they, too, sought companionship in the marshy low spots.

These were the sounds of work, grief, companionship, and love. They were stories of life Mother Nature read aloud to me as she rocked me to sleep. They were the sounds of the country. The sounds that I once heard as silence.

I was not the only one pondering the sounds of my environment. I discovered my mother also contemplated the sounds she heard, comparing the vibrations of man to the music of nature in the following poem:

The Looms of Life

Man's looms hum with industry;
Noisy, chugging, dirty,
By the minute, by the century.
Who has not heard them?
Who has not helped them
          Making things:
Things to eat,
Things to wear,
Things to live in,
Things to play with,
Vibrating, squeaking, roaring, deafening.

But who has ever heard the
    Orb of the sun as he steps over the
    Circle of the East and weaves from

Threads of life
Our vestments of

     The days?

Or who has heard the voice that whispers
  Down the ear of earth,
  Silently,
  So silently:
  "Awake, awake,
  And don your verdant

     Attire?"

What finely attuned ear
  Has ever heard the looms working in the
  Trees of orchards as they labor
  In season?
    From air and sun
    And sap and ground,
    First the bud and then
    The leaf;

      Then dappling fruit.

Who could say
  I gave the order,
  I helped it grow,
  I made it sweet?

Or who has heard the flapping of
  Night's wings as they bore him
  Over a slumbering land
    Mending here,
    Healing there,
    Tying up the knots;

      Freshening?

Through her poem, my mother expressed the silence she also heard in nature. It reflects my experiences of how sounds of silence brought healing to my own soul as "Night's wings bore me over a slumbering land." But my friend, Karen, found comfort in the looms of city life.

Are the sonic expressions of the country better than the city? I wondered. *Without the looms of industry and the sounds they produce, what would we wear? And without the labor of orchard bees or the calf crying for its mother, what would we eat or drink?*

In my first semester in college, I decided there was more to life than I'd imagined. I only had to open my eyes and ears to understand it. I decided that city and country life *both* bring something valuable to our lives. Silence may be perceived differently, but the sounds of the city were the harmony to the melody I heard in the country. City folks and country folks may not always understand each other, but humans have more in common than we might think. We love and care for our families, enjoy the dignity of work, and eat and drink so our bodies are strong. These are the blessings of the sounds of silence.

CHAPTER 22

Spreading Wings

When I graduated from college, I bought a used car, packed my bags, and left Indiana on a wing and a prayer with a heart filled with hope. I left without an ounce of hesitation. There was no looking back; I saw only in one direction: forward. I left so quickly I never saw Bremen in my rearview mirror.

I had an internship in Tucson, Arizona the summer before graduation, which led to my permanent job there. I had friends waiting for me. I knew where to find a cold beer. There was fulfilling work. The mountains formed the backdrop for the life I had only imagined.

I don't remember much of my goodbyes, and I don't know how my mother felt about my departure. The promise of tomorrow blinded me to the blessings of today. But, surely, she saw her reflection in my face and held back tears of sorrow mixed with joy.

Yes, four of her offspring had previously left home. But aren't all children special? Does each departure leave the same break in a mother's heart? Does the last son feel different from the first?

I wonder, as she clumsily hugged me goodbye, if she remembered the magical night we shared when the mouse sang? Did she quietly reminisce about rocking together in a house of silence beneath the midnight moon? Did she reflect on stumbling through the dark in Evart's barn, gunny sack and flashlight in hand, looking for Blackie White Feather? Did she recall Baby and the joy her miscreant son brought her by bringing home that owl? Did the memory of the long-ago pitch of the apple core make her wince? Did she turn her head and shed an unseen tear as I backed out of the driveway? Did she share in my joy—in the promise of the future? Was she proud that she raised a strong and confident son who had wings to fly? Was there remorse that I failed to listen to the Lord, or did she maintain hope that God was not yet done with me?

I have no doubt I broke my mother's heart, aching with unspoken love. She was a woman with an endless vocabulary, but she was unable to give voice to any words of endearment. I left Bremen with no deep hugs, no tears, no *I love yous.*

Still, as she stood, waving goodbye until my car passed over the horizon, it warms my heart to imagine she offered this silent prayer:

Oh Lord, release me from the overwhelming grief right now, and replace it with hope and excitement for his new life.

Help me put one foot in front of the other and release my tears AFTER I hide in my bedroom and cry on my pillow instead of making a scene in front of others.

Release me from being broken-hearted if I don't hear from him as often as I'd like.

Release me from worrying about things beyond my control and remind me that despite the inevitable challenges he'll face, that You're directing his path.

As he leaves my grip, remind me I've raised a young man who's ready to spread his wings.

Oh…and one more thing, Lord: Hold me tightly in Your peace and comfort tomorrow as I release him to You today…even though he's always been Yours.

Lord, in your mercy, hear my prayer. [1]

CHAPTER 23

The Belt of Truth

Therefore put on the full armor of God, so that when the day of evil comes, you may be able to stand your ground with the belt of truth buckled around your waist and with the breastplate of righteousness in place.

—Ephesians 6:13-14 (paraphrased)

"If you died today, Berthella," asked Evart Gordon, the teacher in her adult Sunday school class at Oak Grove Church, "do you know where you'd spend tomorrow?"

"Of course I do," replied Mom with her chin held high and a slight frown. If there was one thing Mom was confident about it was her knowledge of the Bible and God's plan for humanity.

"Well, where would that be?" Evart pressed.

"If I died today," replied Mom, "tomorrow I'd be at Huff Funeral Home in Bremen."

After a stunned silence, chuckles of humor and disbelief sloshed around the classroom like waves in a pool. They subsided quickly, though, when Mom pointedly challenged Evart, "Do you know where *you'd* go?"

The question I imagine Evart posed is a classic query for some Christians and central to Mom's essence. Traditionally, in the Monopoly game of eternity you either land on "Free Parking," or you "Go Directly to Jail." But Mom grew up with the teachings of the late Pastor Russell and did not share this conventional vision of the Christian afterlife. Russell referred to traditional views as muddy waters to be washed away. With the "belt of truth" buckled tightly around her waist, Mom was prepared to enlighten anyone whose beliefs fell short. Although her religion also instructed her to go into the world to make new followers of Christ, her unyielding use of her Truth created more animosity than disciples.

CR

Mom's father was a preacher, but when her parents divorced, her mother took over as the sole source of biblical upbringing. When Mom married and moved to the country with Dad, she lost much of that biblical nurturing. Although my dad's family was Catholic, he disassociated himself from Catholicism because of painful childhood experiences. Soon, Mom became spiritually isolated with no religious connections. So when Evart Gordon became aware of Mom's presence in the community and invited her to nearby Oak Grove Church, she was eager.

Oak Grove was a small, non-denominational church built to serve the farmers in the area. It sat on a small hill at the corner of Shively and Beech adjacent to the white clapboard parsonage. The sanctuary, filled with the earthy scent of old hymnals, had no more than a dozen rows of worn wooden pews on each side of a center aisle with a balcony in the rear. A dark oak pulpit stood center stage, flanked by a small organ and a piano. A scratchy hemp rope hung through a hole in the vestibule's ceiling. At precisely 9:00 a.m. the preacher pulled on the braided rope and the iron bell in the steeple announced the start of the worship service. For nearly sixty years, Mom and Dad worshipped and attended Sunday school at Oak Grove Church, along with us children when we were young.

Like most churches, Oak Grove required aspiring members to recite a specific "profession of faith." But Pastor Russell, who informed Mom's spiritual upbringing, warned against such artificial orthodoxy as being inconsistent with the Bible. So Mom refused to espouse something she believed to be untrue. For almost six decades Mom was not an official member of the church she attended and retained the designation of "visitor."

In spite of her status, Mom remained active in her church. She greeted congregants at the door with a smile while handing out paper bulletins, leaned into the pulpit as she lifted her voice in duets with my older sister Janet during worship service, and stayed engaged in her adult Sunday school, which met in a section of the pews after worship. Sunday school provided most of her peers a place to learn. But for Mom, it furnished a venue to educate others on her Truth. Unfortunately, her views were often at odds with those of her classmates.

"Berthella," Evart continued, as he tapped his fingers on the back of the hard pew to regain control of the conversation regarding the afterlife. "I'm not talking about where your *body* would be tomorrow if you died today. I'm asking about your *soul*. Where will your soul go?"

Without hesitation, my mother responded, "My body and soul are one. So the answer is the same. In the book of Numbers, God gave instructions to Moses on how to divide the spoils of a battle they'd won. God referred to the captured animals—the cattle, donkeys, and sheep—as souls. Now why would a hungry soldier, a shepherd or farmer want a soul they couldn't eat or sell? And even in the New Testament, in Jesus' parable of the rich man who had a great harvest, the rich man says to himself, 'Soul, you've grown enough for many years; eat, drink, and be merry.' So it seems to me that self, soul, and body are one and the same."

Someone coughed and Mom looked around the room. Half the members intently studied their bulletins as if something new suddenly appeared since they received it earlier that morning. The eyes of the others drifted in any direction but hers. Dad sat silently next to her.

"So, Berthella, you don't think your soul will go to Heaven when you die?" asked Evart.

"Do you?" Mom retorted.

"Yes, of course I do."

Mom glanced at a classmate, "What about you, Fran? Do you think your soul goes to Heaven when you die?"

"I guess so, Berthella. Isn't that what we all believe?" Fran glanced around the class with a flushed face, eager to get out of the spotlight.

Mom shifted into high gear and picked on someone else. "What about you, Willard?"

"Berthella, isn't that why we're here?" Willard asked as he gently rocked his head.

"Well, I guess that's not why I'm here. I'm here to learn, to dig into the Bible to find the Truth," Mom replied. "So, Willard, do you believe in the resurrection—that we'll one day be resurrected from the dead?"

"Why do you keep asking me these questions, Berthella? They're almost silly. Of course I believe in the resurrection. I'm a Christian, aren't I?"

"Yes, I guess so. So if you believe that you go to Heaven when you die, and you also believe in the resurrection, then how are you going to get resurrected in the future if your soul has already gone to Heaven after you die?"

Willard shook his head with more intensity.

"See, the Bible doesn't say we go straight to Heaven when we die," Mom continued. "It tells us that we'll be resurrected to an earth as it is in Heaven, a fully restored Earth as it was in the Garden of Eden. That's what I'm looking forward to," said Mom as she smoothed the front of her blouse and sat down.

Edna sat quietly, like the others, but the scowl on her bespectacled face revealed her thoughts. "Berthella," she blurted, "if you don't believe we go to Heaven when we die, I think that says more about you than it does about us."

For many churchgoers, church is a place to cultivate a garden of friends who bring them beauty and sustenance and help them hoe out the weeds of life. Evart remained such a friend to Mom despite her pointed remarks. But I believe most of her classmates felt battered by her belt of Truth rather than enlightened by it. Although Mom tried to adjust her communication style, the heat of her words had a way of scorching the dialog, withering the flowers of friendship. Mom entertained leaving her church completely, but the painful loss of her childhood church family still lingered in her memory. So she remained steadfast, saying, "I love the Oak Grove people even if we don't always see eye to eye."

❧

Mom's insistence on sharing her beliefs didn't stop with her Sunday school class, or the community-based Bible studies she also attended. Her fountain of Truth flowed into nearly every conversation at home, regardless of the topic, which tested family relationships.

"How was school today, Kerry?" Mom asked after I got off the bus and marched into the kitchen.

"Fine." I dropped my middle school books on the table and prepared to make a sandwich to feed my skinny frame.

"What did you learn?"

"We learned about idiots," I said with a wry smile. "I mean, idioms. Do you know what those are?"

"I do. It's a phrase that means something different than what words normally mean if they're used by themselves. What idioms did you learn?"

"A penny for your thoughts, and actions speak louder than words."

"Those are good ones," Mom said, nodding. "There's also a type of phrase similar to idioms that expresses a general truth or some practical advice. Do you know what that type of phrase is called?

"I have no idea, Mom. Idioms was all we learned about."

"*Were* all we learned about," she corrected.

"Were."

"Have you ever heard, 'early to bed and early to rise, makes a man healthy, wealthy, and wise?'"

"Of course." I said, turning my body slightly away from her.

"That's a proverb. You know there's a book in the Bible called Proverbs where you can turn to find wise sayings to help make life easier. The Proverbs in the Bible are inspired by our Maker so you can depend on them for true guidance." she concluded.

At times like this my reaction varied between silence and resistance, depending on my mood. This time I expressed indifference. "Okay, Mom."

ᘓ

One time in high school I sold boxes of candy to raise money for a choir trip. If we didn't meet the goal we couldn't go on the trip, and I wanted to "get out of Dodge." In the evenings I drove around the neighborhood and on Saturday spent time at local businesses. I sold a lot of candy.

"You're pretty enthusiastic, Fuzz," remarked Julie. "I'm impressed. You must really want to go on this trip."

"Yep, I do. And I'm gonna go, too!"

"You know where the word 'enthusiasm' comes from?" Mom interjected as she stepped into kitchen where Julie and I were talking. Mom had a habit of starting conversations with a question.

I turned my head so only my sister could see my eyes roll. "No, Mom. Where does the word 'enthusiasm' come from?"

"It comes from the Greek word *entheos,* which means 'God in you' or 'full of God.'" She paused so I could say something that would prompt the rest of her story. I remained silent, but she continued. "The Bible tells us that God is love. So enthusiasm is akin to being full of love for something or someone. It's truly one of God's greatest gifts."

If I had engaged her, I'm certain she could have given me an entire exposé on the biblical understanding of enthusiasm. Instead, I ignored her, full of annoyance instead of love.

ᘓ

Adulthood offered no escape from the perpetual drip-drip-drip of indoctrination.

As a young adult, Mom offered me a laminated copy of a document called, "Chart for the Ages." It graphically illustrated God's master plan for humanity, described by Pastor Russell. It was filled with clusters of time-based arches and showed Jesus' "second coming" had already occurred in 1874. Levels of humanity, starting with Adam and Eve, pointed the way to eternal life on Earth, restored to the condition of the Garden of Eden. Humans who "rested in death" would be resurrected at that time, according to the chart, and be given a second chance to accept Jesus Christ as their sovereign ruler, if they hadn't done so before they died.[1]

"Chart for the Ages" was Mom's treasure map, her personal declaration of independence from the false orthodoxy of the Church, and from the confines of mortality itself. It defined her world view, formed and severed relationships, and shaped the spiritual lives of three generations in her family. She made herself a large color copy and laminated it for durability. It was the most precious piece of plastic she owned. Although it could have been mistaken for a placemat, for my mother, it was the bedrock of her life. She made identical copies for each of her six adult children. When the day came, she handed me mine.

"Here, Kerry," she said, extending her hand with my copy.

I was home for a visit. "What is it?" I asked, glancing at the plastic seemingly covered in hieroglyphics.

"It's the 'Chart for the Ages.'"

"Okaaay." I accepted the cold stiff plastic with a sigh I hoped was inaudible. "What am I supposed to do with it?"

"This is yours to keep. I want you to know about God's plan for our lives."

"Oh, good, I was wondering when he was going to tell me that." *Oops.* The sarcasm was too strong.

Ignoring my rudeness, she said, "If the Creator can swing the stars on such a precise and unerring timetable that humans can predict the position of any heavenly body, isn't it reasonable to suppose that He has as tight a schedule for the affairs of man? And wouldn't He furnish us with such a plan if we desired it?" She had masked her statements as questions but knew I wouldn't respond.

"When the Word of God is studied in depth, this is exactly what we find." She looked into my eyes to see if I was listening before continuing. "To me, it seems that we are right here on God's timetable," she said as she pointed toward the middle of the timeline, "where man's rule is coming to an end. We are in the tearing down process, waiting for the final blowing away in the wind of anarchy before Christ raises up his other 'living stones' to prepare for the promised new World Government."

I understood no more of what she said than if she had spoken Russian. But I accepted her chart and quickly closed the conversation.

"She was always teaching the Bible," Julie remembered at a later visit. "I got tired of it. It seemed all conversations somehow got turned to the Bible."

My adult cousin, Debby, on Mom's side of the family, was further removed from the situation and extended more grace to my mother. "Yes, Berthella could go on forever talking about the Bible," she said. "But that's what she grew up with. That was a big part of her upbringing. She and her sisters all got it from their mother, from our Grandma Effie. Effie's life was turned upside down when she divorced and had to raise those three girls alone during the Depression. Studying the Bible became Effie's 'go to' place for sanctuary… It was an anchor because she had nothing else."

∽

Regardless of its source, Mom's insistence on sharing her Truth cast a shadow of varying shades over us children. Most of us rejected all religiosity. Although we had been raised in the Church, every one of us left when we were able, and only one eventually returned, although several claim the mantle of Christianity. Some of my siblings still struggle to find the words to express their frustration with Mom's actions and the effect it had on their lives.

Mom's insistent actions created space between us, but I regret tuning her out and not honoring her with a more open heart when it came to such an important part of her character. At the time, it was a matter of preserving family ties and avoiding conflict. But in spite of straining under the weight of her Truth, looking back, I admire the thoroughness on which she formed her opinions, the courage she demonstrated in speaking out, and the strength it required to endure the consequences. The clarity of her vision was astonishing.

Did Mom harbor a heavy ache of disappointment and failure for not instilling her faith fully in her children? If such profound sadness dwelled in her heart, she didn't share it with me. Nor did she dwell on the loss of deep friendships at Oak Grove, though that, too, must have been painful. She never let any person keep her down because she knew God wouldn't let her down. The grace of God was the shiny buckle that hung at the center of her belt of Truth. She believed we'd be given a second chance at the time of the resurrection. This freed Mom from living in a place of fear or anxiety. Instead, she lived into the hope of the future. Her joy came from knowing this world is only temporary and that one day she would be with God in a garden brimming with love.

CHAPTER 24

Mirror of Prejudice

"Eeny, meeny, miny, moe," I said as my pointed finger moved past the first four classmates during recess on a sunny spring day. "Catch a nigger by the toe. If he hollers let him go. Eeny, meeny, miny, MOE!" After going around the circle, pointing to a different kid with each word in this lyric, the last "moe" determined my choice for the kickball squad. On the surface, it was a benign playtime activity with no consequence beyond the selection of a team. But below the surface, a dangerous cancer of prejudice grew silently into my adulthood, pushing away important relationships just as my mother's religion had done to her.

⁂

She had dark hair and deep brown eyes, with a tan the color of rich honey. Standing five-foot-two, her gregarious personality and infectious laugh filled the room. I was only in my mid-twenties when I fell in love with this woman named Gloria in a whirlwind romance. I wasn't born in Texas, but this Central Texas lady made me glad I arrived. Nothing in our nascent relationship, though, prepared me for what lay ahead.

Growing up in large families, we shared stories about our common experiences over dinner one evening. "Do you want to see a picture of my brothers?" Gloria asked.

"Sure, that'd be great." I was eager for more information about her and anticipated our bond would take root.

When we returned to her apartment, she emerged from the next room, picture in hand. The smooth snapshot passed gently from her hand to mine belying the grenade about to explode.

The photograph was at once shocking, confusing, and repulsive. There were five brown-skinned men, almost black with hair to match, standing shoulder-to-shoulder with arms around each other. My soul was sick and verbal vomit spewed from my mouth.

"These are Mexicans!" I hissed like a snake.

It was a visceral reaction out of my control. I was panicked and disoriented. *If Gloria's brothers are Mexicans, then she must be, too.* I had fallen in love with a Mexican. *How did I not know that? How could I fall in love with a Mexican? Why is this happening to me?* The questions piled up. My gut ached and my heart labored faster than my brain.

"Gloria, these are Mexicans," I repeated, as if she somehow missed my earlier insult.

We don't often get a chance to see our prejudices so clearly as I did that day. They often just peek out around the water cooler, in jokes with friends, or in the lack of eye contact at the supermarket. Seldom is the curtain of our soul pulled back so brusquely, exposing all our darkness to the light of day. But there I stood that day, culturally and racially naked. Later, as I examined my life in the mirror, I peered at that nakedness for the first time, and like the biblical Adam, I felt shame. *Where did this sin come from?* I wasn't raised this way. *Or was I?*

After insulting Gloria, I spent the next several weeks searching for answers and failed to uncover a single word or deed of my parents that I could label as racist or even "off-color." But as I dug deeper more subtle signs emerged.

I recalled telling and listening to "Polack jokes" as a child and often turned to my joke book when the moment was right. I often hung out in our family room with Bryan and Tom and let my jokes rip.

"Why do flies have wings?" I'd ask.

"I don't know, why?" answered Tom.

"So they can beat the Polacks to the smelly garbage cans," I triumphantly recited amidst the ensuing laughs.

"What does the garbage company do when a Polack quits paying his bill?" I continued. Without waiting for a response I answered my own question, "They stop delivering garbage!"

These were hilarious jokes in my non-Polish circle. Although there was a Polish community in the regional city of Mishawaka, I never wondered what a boy my age might think about my derogatory ethnic barb.

As my reflection progressed, I remembered a silver metal nut-cracker that sat in our nut dish in our dining room at home. It was made of two strong handles, each nearly as big around as a finger, with intricately knurled patterns. The handles were joined together by an equally sturdy joint, producing a crushing jaw that devoured any nutshell with a satisfying crunch. But one type of nut was tough-as-nails. The size of a big toe, its three sides were rough and deep brown. Cracking this nut required strong and skillful hands. These nuts often escaped carnage, lying forlornly at the bottom of the nut bowl after all the good nuts had been eaten. No one seemed to like them. We called them "Nigger Toes." It was the only name I knew for Brazil nuts. To me, it was simply a descriptive name, like "sunflower." It was never voiced that this epithet might be a racial slur.

Probing my newly-discovered prejudices, I tried to remember my interactions with black people growing up. *What were they like?* In my first eighteen years of life, I remembered only one interaction with a person of color. In Bremen High School an African-American girl transferred in for a few months. I didn't know where she came from, and when she left I didn't know where she went. She was just a girl passing through the halls and through my life. Her appearance and disappearance were a mystery because I never spoke with her, nor did anyone else I knew. Almost like she was just a black stain on our white paper, which we were glad to have wiped away.

I was aware of black people from the news, though, as racial riots lit up the nation. "Those people" rioted in the streets, burned cars and buildings, and were dirty and poor. Gary, Indiana, a gritty suburb of Chicago, seventy miles west of Bremen, was widely defined by the blackness of its people and the grunge of its steel mills. Those folks didn't even merit the level of respect afforded to the so-called Polacks.

I had subconsciously constructed an orderly hierarchy of races. Whites were on the top and blacks below them. Although I never met a brown person, I had a vague awareness. They slinked around in the background of our community, almost invisible, as migrant farm workers. I recall seeing some in the distance, stooped over, picking strawberries in a commercial field. It was like sighting a strange animal in the woods. These peculiar brown people were at the bottom of my hierarchy.

Even Oak Grove Church, which I attended as a child, unknowingly reinforced my social hierarchy. With the gusto that only a group of rambunctious Sunday school kids could muster, we stood in front of our little wooden pews in the basement of the church and sang:

Jesus loves the little children,
All the children of the world.
Red and yellow, black and white,
They are precious in His sight.
Jesus loves the little children of the world.

This foundational song was intended to impart a message that we are all God's children. But because it left out a large segment of God's creation, it had unintended consequences. Red and yellow kids seemed rather abstract to me at the time, while black and white children were real. *But why were brown children excluded?* Evidently, they really weren't children of the world, or Jesus didn't love them.

As I continued my journey into the looking glass, I saw layers of bias laid down like sediment during my life, cemented into a foundation of prejudice. The day "these are Mexicans" spewed from my mouth was my moment of truth. I had fallen in love with someone I had learned to despise. But Gloria's grace-filled response determined what I did with that truth.

"What did you expect?" she replied, calmly to my cancerous comment. "You didn't know I was Hispanic?" She was just as dumbfounded by my reaction as I.

"No," I admitted. "Then why do you have an American name?"

Although she was hurt by my comments, Gloria patiently explained that she was indeed an American, was married before and retained her Anglo husband's last name. And because I was blinded by love, the color of her skin offered me no clues.

For the next month, I wrestled with conflicting emotions and dug deep to unearth the roots of my prejudice, which threatened the promising relationship with Gloria. As I came to terms with my illness, I resolved to be transformed and offered her a poorly chosen peace offering: a taco. She didn't think it was funny, but to her credit she stayed by my side as I began the process of redemption. As proof that love heals wounds, a year and a half after we met, Gloria and I were married, launching me into a life of cultural exploration and revelation.

My first revelation occurred with Gloria's large extended family, where a cousin celebrated a special event at a VFW-type hall on the outskirts of the small town of Caldwell, Texas. The cavernous room was dimly lit and filled with raucous laughter, lively music from a band of brothers, and words spoken or sung in Spanish. Rice, beans, and bowls of menudo were spread out on tables as men embraced each other, and families of children and adults danced across the concrete floor as if no one was watching. Everyone in the room that day had brown skin with dark eyes and hair, with one exception. I was the only blond, blue-eyed guy whose white skin flashed like a single firefly in the night. I felt alone and isolated in a sea of joviality.

"Hey, looks like you need a beer," said Gloria's brother, José, as he sauntered my way with a crooked smile on his friendly dark face. I was sitting at a long wooden table, quietly observing. Everyone else near me was involved in conversation. The meal was over and the party was ramping up.

"Nah, I'm fine. This water's good for now." I said, embarrassed to share that I no longer drank alcohol.

"Well…okay," he replied.

Just then another man approached José and they embraced, careful not to spill their beers.

"Kerry, this is my cousin, Buddy," said José, as Buddy and I shook hands and said hello. "Buddy, this is Gloria's husband."

"Hey, man. Good to meet you. Congratulations on marrying my little cousin," he said with a grin.

"Thanks, Buddy." I didn't know what to say next. The social discomfort I felt prevented me from being me. So I said nothing.

"Can I get you a beer?" Buddy finally asked.

"Nah, I'm fine. But thanks for asking." Understandably, Buddy and José soon moved on, leaving me alone again.

No one did anything to make me feel uncomfortable that day, but my mind had done so on its own. I didn't understand the language, the open expression of familial love, or the strange foods. I felt like a puzzle piece that ended up in the wrong box. *I* had become that "strange animal" which "slinked around the fields" of my childhood. I was now the minority. As I sat there in my self-isolation it occurred to me for the first time that this was likely a daily experience for people of color living in a world of whiteness. It broke my heart but opened my eyes.

I eventually learned to navigate this new Hispanic realm where men hugged other men, where *cascarones* were smashed on my head at Easter, and where the rituals of the unfamiliar world of Catholicism were deeply embedded in my chosen family. Experiences such as these ultimately gave me the courage and skills to work in India and form close friendships with Hindus, to partner in my local community with Muslims, and to travel unaided and unafraid in East Africa. It's amazing to me how so much change can occur from spending time in another person's world.

Looking back at my childhood, I decided parents play a passive or an active role in cultural and racial education. An active parent takes concrete steps to positively or negatively influence a child's perceptions. A passive parent does nothing. In the presence of nothing, the surrounding community and experiences fill in the voids. When I was a child, my mother chose to do nothing, and many years after my epiphany, I confronted her, as we rocked gently on the porch swing on our front patio.

"Why did we not discuss racial issues in our family?" I queried. "Why was there no talk when Martin Luther King was killed? Why didn't you explain why black people were protesting? Or what made some so angry that they responded violently at times?"

Her answer was profoundly and jarringly simple. She looked straight ahead as she contemplated her response and then replied, "It didn't affect us."

I believe my mother's passivity in the midst of this social and political turmoil was partly influenced by her deeply held belief in the teachings of the late Pastor Russell who instructed his followers not to engage in political or social issues, saying, "This is the Lord's battle." But I also believe these issues were so far removed from life in the country, Mom really felt no connection. After all, there was no one to smash *cascarones* on her head at Easter. But she was mistaken about the lack of cultural awareness not affecting me.

As Rev. Martin Luther King, Jr. once said, "All men are caught in an inescapable network of mutuality, tied in a single garment of destiny. Whatever affects one directly, affects all indirectly."[1] Although King's statement can be difficult for some to embrace, I believe it's true. My destiny, how I understood and interacted with humanity as an adult, was profoundly affected by those who did not look or speak like me, beginning with the woman I chose to marry. Through the grace of God and the love of my wife, over the years the white threads of my childhood have been woven together with filaments of browns and blacks, to create a richly textured garment of life. For this, I will always be grateful.

CHAPTER 25

Three Loves

One love is young and tender,
  Like the first drop of dew on a wild plum petal,
  Which springs from the wildness of a soft grassy meadow.
  Like the twittering of birds as a coral dawn breaks,
  Who speak of the promises the new day will make.
It's then I taste your lips caress sweetly on mine.

One love is wild and fierce,
  Like mighty cold wind, over rocks it does roar,
    sending waves crashing against the bare shores.
  Like rumbling storm clouds, steel-blue and black,
      Rent by lightning,
      Until, tired and spent,
      they call themselves back.
It's then I feel your arms warmly wrapped around me.

One love is haunting and elusive,
  Like the lingering strains of an old violin,
  Spiraling like smoke from a fire within.
  Like the flickering light of the will-o'-the-wisp,
  Which shows us the way then fades into mist.
It's then I hear your voice calling in the darkness.

—"Three Loves Have I", adapted from a poem by
Berthella Whitmyer, circa 1940, age twenty

I struggled with prejudice before I was married. But Mom did not.
Before her first romance, my mother was in love with the *idea* of
being in love. She anticipated in "Three Loves Have I," a multifaceted
relationship, tender and soft, yet bursting with ferocity, and as elusive
as the vanishing light from a will-o'-the-wisp. It was surprisingly pre-
scient poetry, revealing my parents' story of three loves.

One Love is Young and Tender

"I still remember him strolling through the lovely high meadow
above the little lake. His shirt was off. He was all brown, mannerly,
and innocent-looking," recalled Mom of their first meeting at a group
picnic.

The attraction was mutual. "She was slender, with hazel eyes and
brown curly hair," remembered Dad. "She looked smart."

By nightfall, my future dad had a date with my future mom
for the following weekend. It wasn't long before they were married
and decided to honeymoon at the place they met, this time all alone,
walking hand-in-hand along the shore, and lying peacefully in a
hammock beneath a canopy of green trees, languishing in new love.

They seldom shared such solitude again for the next thirty-four
years. For when they married, my mom joined my dad, who was still
living with his parents on his parents' farm. Then the cries of my oldest
sibling, Mike, pierced the air a year later and Dad's parents decided to
move to a small house at the end of the lane. Babies continued to arrive
like clockwork, producing six healthy children.

Their life on the farm was a shared dream. Dad was a fun-loving
guy who drove loud tractors and rode a Harley Davidson motorcy-
cle, but he could also relax in a bubble bath after work, to Mom's
delight. Sometimes Mom found Dad where he sat and approached
from behind to wrap her arms around his strong shoulders. Likewise,

he often enveloped her slim waist with his arms where they stood. They often held hands and enjoyed free time together, picnicking with Mom's family, riding on a cool river in a motorboat with friends, or building snow animals with Mom's giggly sisters in the slowness of winter.

Dad managed the entire farm, kept the farmhouse in repair, and took care of difficult outdoor tasks. Mom provided food and clothing, kept the household running, and worked in the garden. These traditional roles suited them, and they were happy. They were also intellectually matched, both smart and curious, and each graduated early from high school.

They shared a relaxed approach to parenting their towheaded children, who helped out in the house, the garden, the barn, and the fields. Everyone joined in. Dad showed my older brothers, Mike and Pat, how to till the soil and milk the cows, while my older sister, Janet, learned to cook, sew, tend the garden, and gather the white eggs from protesting hens.

As the family grew, Dad ice-skated with the boys, pushed them on swings, dipped in the lake during a summer lull, and took my older sister for bike rides until she was big enough to pedal herself. Mom and Dad took photographs of each other hanging out with their children, while Dad shot eight-millimeter movies of milestone events in the children's lives, including the births of the fourth and fifth children, Tom and I, as we cried our way into the world.

In many ways, Mom's and Dad's relationship was idyllic as they lived the bucolic life they always imagined. But weeds sprouted in the soft grassy meadow of their young relationship.

The most devastating issue was Mom's homemaking habits. Far from magazine-style, her upbringing and her unwavering focus on her children left insufficient time to keep the house orderly. Although this undoubtedly caused some concern for Dad, they were in agreement on how the children should be raised. Her Old Country in-laws, however, saw this as an unforgivable shirking of a woman's responsibility. It was this sin that caused my grandfather to snatch my parents' dream from their grasp in the springtime of my mother's life and force our entire family from the farm when I was one year old.

I can't imagine the immense pressure Mom and Dad must have felt as they wrestled with the loss of their dreams, their severed relationship with my grandfather, and the stark requirement to feed and house a growing family. But in the heat of the moment, my parents' relationship did not combust. There was no visible evidence that my father blamed my mother for this drastic change in their lives. Indeed, it's likely their relationship was temporarily strengthened since both had been deeply hurt and neither felt they deserved to be treated so harshly.

Hope lingered in their marriage while we lived temporarily in a rented farmhouse. Within months, they conceived their sixth and last child, Julie. When they repeatedly came up empty-handed in their quest for a new farm, they still stuck together as Dad contemplated a drastic change in direction for the family.

I picture a lazy Sunday afternoon after our family had returned from church and lunch was over when my dad broached the subject. Baby Julie was napping while the rest of us kids were playing outside. Mom had changed into a faded house dress and sat on our coarse green couch. Dad was still in his good trousers and white shirt, but no tie, as he sat beside her in a matching chair. Both were quietly reading the newspaper when Dad put down his paper and turned toward Mom.

"Berthella, I've been thinking. How would you like to forget about farming?"

"What? What would we do? What would *you* do?" Mom peered steadily into Dad's eyes for clues.

"Well, I'd just keep working at LaFree's, building homes. I wouldn't go back to farming."

Mom nodded as he spoke. "Where would we live, Mick? Could you live anywhere else but on a farm?"

Dad shifted in his chair. "I've decided I could. But I wonder about you. Could *you* live somewhere other than a farm?"

Mom sighed and looked out the window across acres of corn. She remembered the years of enjoyment they'd left behind.

"We could use the money from our equipment sale," Dad continued, "to build a house in the country. We wouldn't be on a farm, but we could still live in the country." Now Dad studied Mom's face as she contemplated a new beginning.

"Okay," she finally said, as she gently bit her lip and smiled. "Let's…do it."

The decision to stop farming and build a new home was not made by the "man of the house." It was jointly made by equal partners. But the initial goodwill between them slipped away as their fresh start took shape. Whether Dad outwardly blamed Mom for the loss of the farm, I believe the issue smoldered beneath the surface and burst into flames after they settled into the spacious residence they built nearby.

One Love is Wild and Fierce

It began innocently enough from Mom's desire to waste nothing after growing up with so little during the Depression. She kept leftovers a bit too long in the fridge, slipped a collection of rubber bands over the doorknobs, and stashed scraps of paper in the corners. With the possibility of Armageddon "just around the corner," cans of food collected in the pantry until they rusted or bulged from spoiling, just as they did at her mother, Effie's, house. Habits like these started on the farm.

Eventually, Mom found it difficult to throw away anything with pretty pictures or interesting information she might need one day. *Good Housekeeping, National Geographic, Reader's Digest,* and *Life* magazines piled up on tables while drawers overflowed with newspaper clippings. The piles of school work of six kids grew along with us, and any objects owned by family members of the past were too precious to toss. Glass jars, books, clocks, old photos, and worn clothing moved only in one direction—into our house. Items from other people's garage sales rained down on our home like manna for the wandering Israelites, blessing us with aged furniture, faded artwork, lamps without plugs, and worn gardening tools. When Mom got too busy to keep up with the news, towers of newspapers grew in the living room, then moved to the dining room when the stacks threatened to tumble. Piles of her own writings on the backs of old papers were jammed into desk drawers, along with religious booklets, pamphlets, and leaflets, until the drawers no longer closed. Colorful glass figurines collected on windowsills or hung from the curtain rods, reflecting the afternoon sun, while forgotten clothing languished in the laundry room waiting to be mended, ironed, or donated. And when things broke, Mom knew one day they'd be fixed; so chairs, small tables, picture frames, and record players piled up in the basement awaiting that day which never came.

Finally Dad had enough. He was not a hoarder and couldn't convince Mom to change her ways. He'd lost the farm because of Mom's poor housekeeping and now his new home was being consumed all on its own. Dad believed that hard work never hurt anyone and was frustrated that Mom didn't work hard enough to overcome the chaos. So he took charge, enlisting our trash barrel as his ally. Although his battles with Mom started differently each time, they always ended the same: with tongues of fire and venom.

It was an overcast Saturday afternoon when Mom pulled into the driveway with a trunk full of groceries. I rocked in a tire swing, enjoying the smell of smoke from a fire Dad tended in our metal trash barrel near the garage. As Mom drove up our short driveway, crackling yellow flames shot six feet into the air from the mouth of the rusty container. This fire looked different to her.

She stopped the car without driving it into the garage and practically leapt from her seat. Without closing the car door, she marched toward the blaze as her dress fluttered behind her and large black ashes floated to the ground. Dad tossed a big stack of papers into the fire and then stepped back as flames engulfed them with a whoosh.

"Mick, what on earth are you doing?" Mom asked, curtly.

"I'm burning papers," he said, without looking up. Dressed in his flannel shirt and work boots, he meant business.

"What? You're not burning my newspapers, are you?" Her body stiffened and her shoulders pulled back.

"I'm just getting rid of the stacks of trash piling up the living room," he said flatly. He stared into the flames as if they were a crystal ball.

"No you're not," Mom asserted, glaring at Dad. "You're burning up my newspapers. I haven't read those yet!" Her volume increased with each word. "You can't just burn up my stuff!"

"Berthella," he said in a tone that sounded more like swearing, "these papers are three months old. The news is old." He looked straight at her now, and Mom could see the fire's reflection in his eyes.

"I don't care," she yelled. "I haven't read them yet. Besides, there's all kinds of good stuff in there…recipes, 'Dear Abby'…MICK, YOU CAN'T BURN MY STUFF!" Then Mom kicked the barrel and scuffed her good shoes on the hot rusty metal and nearly singed her coiffed hair. She pivoted on the ball of one foot and retreated through the cooling ash.

Other times, it began differently.

One Saturday when the day was still young, Mom was dressed in faded green slacks and was washing laundry in the damp basement when she noticed an empty space on the floor where piles of something once resided.

"Kerry," she called from the musty laundry room into the family room where I was wrapped in a fuzzy blanket watching Bugs Bunny cartoons. "Where's your dad?"

"He's outside. He came through here a while ago with somethin' in his arms."

Mom slammed the washing machine button off, and I heard the machine jerk to a stop. She stomped up our wooden steps as if she wore bricks on her feet. I jumped up to follow. The aluminum storm door had already slammed shut before I got to the top of the stairs. I burst through the door and onto the chilly concrete patio in pursuit.

"MICK!" she screamed as she rounded the corner of the garage and saw the barrel belching orange flames while it consumed an object with long wooden rods protruding from its mouth. Dad stared into the barrel with his arms crossed and didn't respond. "That's my Mom's old drying rack! That's an antique!" she said, shaking a fist in the air.

"Berthella," Dad snarled, "two of the rods are busted off and this piece of junk has been sitting in my way for *two years*."

"But that's MY stuff!" Mom shouted back. "And it's an ANTIQUE! IT BELONGED TO MY MOTHER! And who knows how old it was before that?" she railed. "MICK, YOU CAN'T BURN MY STUFF!" With that, Mom stepped into the white smoke, stabbed her hand into the flames and grabbed the unburned end of one of the wooden rods and jerked the flaming apparatus out of the barrel. Burning wood chips sprang through the air, trailing tails of smoke like missiles. But the flames were so hot Mom was forced to drop the cluster of burning rods onto the ground. Half the rack had already turned to ash. The other half lay in the dewy grass like twisted wreckage of a plane crash. Mom had been defeated again. Her chin trembled as she stumbled back a step before returning to the house, leaving footprints in the wet grass and animosity in her heart. Dad picked up the smoking carcass and tossed it back into the blaze.

This became a common occurrence as Dad repeatedly reached his tipping point from too much "junk" in the garage, the basement, or the living room. No matter how it started, it ended with a fiery argument with Mom ranting and Dad defending his actions as a necessity due to her negligence. After each episode, Mom's anger smoldered for days, then transformed to resentment. Dad's fires not only incinerated Mom's stuff, they charred her respect for the man she married.

During this age of infernos, I believe Dad also lost respect for Mom for other reasons. When their love had been young and soft, they shared a common intellect; both were curious, intelligent people on equal footing. But as troubled waves "crashed against the bare shores" of their relationship, anticipated in Mom's poetry, her intellect diminished in Dad's eyes and her credibility crumbled.

When Mom read the book *Silent Spring,* she became convinced that invisible chemicals were indiscriminately killing off wildlife and that the chemical companies knew and didn't care. Dad shook his head in disbelief. Then a bullet brought down President Kennedy and Mom, who was already skeptical of the Federal Government, believed that Vice

President Johnson conspired with the government to assassinate him. She read *The Hollow Earth* and believed that "flying saucers" flew from the center of a hollow earth through tunnels at the poles. Dad couldn't persuade her it was nonsense. Mom was living on the fringes, it seemed to him. She didn't trust the church, the government, or business.

Next, Mom complained of chest pains and needed to stay in bed longer than usual or lie down and rest when Dad thought she should clean the house. Nothing obvious to Dad explained the chest pains so he surmised they were, "all in her head." There was little sympathy from a man used to getting up before dawn to milk cows seven days a week, regardless of how he felt.

I believe Dad connected all these dots into a pattern of implausibility and colored it in with skepticism. Their communication was strained.

But nothing could have prevented the tempest that swept into their relationship with "clouds of steel-blue and black, and rent by lightning," as described in Mom's poetry. The storm was menopause. It struck Mom about the same time we moved into our new house, shortly after Julie was born. Mom was in her early forties. In retrospect, stages of menopause explained a lot of the behavior I witnessed for years. But at the time, we younger kids only knew it as a violent squall blowing through our lives. As this gale strengthened, it didn't take much to trigger a torrent of fury in an otherwise peaceful day.

I was sprawled on the turquoise carpeting in our living room after church one Sunday, reading the "funny papers." Rays of afternoon sunshine angled through the picture window and warmed the floor next to me. Still wearing his necktie, Dad sat in a wingchair nearby with his head buried in the newspaper while Mom finished preparing our midday meal. I heard the clatter of plates and clinking silverware and could smell a roast cooking in the oven. While waiting on the roast, Mom came into the living room and shuffled through a stack of newspapers next to her chair.

"Mick, where's last Sunday's paper?"

"I threw it out, Berthella," he said, without looking up.

"Did you ask me first, if I'd read it?" Mom lifted her head and stared in Dad's direction.

"It's a week old," he said through his paper screen.

"I don't care how old it is. Did you ask me first?" Her voice was sharp enough to cut through the paper in Dad's hands.

Dad lowered his newspaper and returned Mom's gaze with a frown. "I need to ask your permission to throw away an old newspaper?"

"Yes, if I haven't read it," she responded, smartly. "Is that too much to ask? What if I just threw away the paper before you read it?" Mom's words weren't a question. They were a challenge.

She got up from her chair and in three quick steps she was standing in front of Dad and grabbed the sections of the still-folded Sunday paper waiting on his lap. She charged into the kitchen, opened the pantry door, and crumbled the entire wad into the smelly trash can.

"There! How does that feel?" she exclaimed as Dad entered the kitchen behind her.

I jumped up from my place in the sun and ran toward the gathering fury.

Dad brushed past Mom and started to fish out the mangled mess from the trash. "Berthella, you're being silly."

"Well, see what you're doing? See how it feels? You cannot NOT read the paper. WELL, THAT'S WHAT YOU KEEP DOING TO ME, AND I'M SICK OF IT!"

I could hear Mom breathing as her words boomed like thunder.

"Berthella, you're acting crazy," he said as he started toward the living room to finish reading the wad of chaos in his hands. His words struck her like lightning.

"Crazy! Crazy? I'm the one who's crazy?" she ranted as her arms swept through the air. "Who's constantly burning up other people's things? You're the one who's crazy. You're making me crazy! I'll show you crazy." Her face reddened as the tension tightened. "I'm so mad at you I could throw something!" she screamed, stopping Dad mid-step.

"Well, maybe that would calm you down," said Dad, unhelpfully. Just then, he spied the plates sitting on the counter that Mom had set out for lunch. He picked a plate up from the small stack and held it out for her. "Here you go. Throw this."

I could almost hear the switch flip inside of Mom.

"I'LL SHOW YOU CRAZY!" she bellowed as she grabbed the plate from Dad's hand and flung her arm backward to prepare for an overhand pitch. The plate catapulted through the air like a UFO out of control; it smacked the hard linoleum floor and shattered into a half dozen smaller pieces of broken ceramic that skidded across the kitchen floor.

I was standing near the plate's flight path with my stocking feet, frozen to the kitchen floor, struggling to understand what happened. But when a piece of broken glass struck my skinny leg, I fled from the kitchen into the hallway and knelt behind a wall as I peered through the doorway.

"You see that, Mick?" Mom shrieked. "THAT'S CRAZY! YOU'RE MAKING ME CRAZY. You treat me like the trash in that can. I'm so mad at you right now I could smash every one of those plates!"

Dad picked up the small stack and handed her another plate. This time she cocked her arm backward with a side pitch and flung the plate like a Frisbee. It sailed through the air, glanced off the back of a kitchen chair with a thud, then exploded when it struck the wall, with little pieces cascading to the ground like fireworks.

"That's what I feel like doing to you!" she hollered.

Dad handed Mom a third plate. Without saying a word, she raised the plate over her head and smashed it straight into the floor in front of her. As if a hand grenade exploded, ceramic shrapnel ricocheted off cabinets and the refrigerator, striking Dad's black Sunday shoes and Mom's blue flats. One piece zipped by my face like a bullet. I closed my eyes.

Between eruptions of angry words, Dad steadily handed Mom our dinner plates and she continued to obliterate them as she fought to obliterate the emotion that consumed her. When the stack was demolished, Dad walked to the cupboard and took out the remaining plates. With unusual calm, and almost a smirk of amusement, Dad stood by Mom and handed her plate after plate until the floor looked like the bombed carcass of a city at war.

The rage in the room sucked the breath from my body as I crouched for safety behind the wall. Tears threatened to spill from my eyes but were too frightened to flow. My hands trembled as destruction rained down.

All the plates were finally killed in action, but the battle was not yet done. Dad improvised and unwrapped a loaf of bread sitting on the counter. He handed Mom a soft slice. She didn't hesitate to fling it across the room as she had done with the plates. It hit the wall silently and bounced to the floor intact. Dad handed Mom a second slice, and this, too, she launched with the same anticlimactic result. Now two slices of limp bread floated alone on a sea of broken china.

The shift from violent explosions to almost-comical floppy bread deflated the tension in the room like a popped balloon. As suddenly as it started, it was over. Without a spoken word, Mom turned and charged passed Dad, crunching glass beneath her feet. She bolted down the hall to her bedroom and slammed her door shut, passing by me as I cowered on the floor behind the wall. Dad began to sweep up the carnage. In the wake of her rapid steps, a small breeze swirled by my face, too weak to blow away the image burned into my memory.

⅓

Mom and Dad spent more time apart than together as the conflict increased. Dad used his free time to go bowling, added on the duties as our county tax assessor, and poured himself into creating a beautiful landscape outside our home to counteract the turmoil on the inside. Mom remained focused on us kids still living at home and started selling vitamins, aloe vera juice, and bras. She also learned foot and body massage and became an expert masseuse. Their lives diverged with fewer and fewer intersections.

Then weight began to stick to Mom like Velcro. For more than twenty years and through six children, she maintained a svelte figure, but now her hourglass shape became an oval—forty pounds heavier. Dad remained in good physical shape and regularly criticized her eating habits.

Although they slept in the same double bed during their entire marriage, Mom usually stayed up late reading in the living room and Dad retired to the bedroom alone. When they were together, I didn't see them embrace, hold hands, or hear any terms of endearment such as "dear" or "hon." They addressed each other with simply "Mick" or "Berthella." The three words "I love you" were never used in the same sentence.

This pattern persisted for many years as Julie and I grew up and left home. For her, it was particularly troubling when she was about to start her independent life.

Julie was eighteen, blonde, and energetic. On a warm summer night, a month before she was to leave for college, she'd gone to bed with her windows open so the crickets could sing her to sleep and the heat of the day might drift away. Around 2:00 a.m. Julie awoke when she felt her sheet move and someone nudge her.

"Julie," Mom said in a voice louder than a whisper in the dark room. "I have chest pains that won't go away. And I'm having difficulty breathing."

"What?" Julie said, groggily as she rolled over and saw Mom standing in her white nightgown by her bed.

"My heart," Mom said. "I'm having some episode with my heart. I'm having difficulty breathing."

"Are you having a heart attack?" Julie gushed as her own heart shifted from basal to crisis state in seconds. "What should I do? What did Dad say?"

"I don't know. I didn't try to wake him up," Mom said as she rubbed one arm.

Julie raced to their bedroom and shook Dad. "Dad, wake up. Mom's having heart pains. It may be a heart attack."

Dad didn't rouse.

"Dad," she tried again, this time harder. "Wake up." Dad never awoke. Nearly panicked, Julie snapped on the hall light and dashed to the phone to call the hospital.

"Can you bring your Mom into the hospital?" the attendant asked after listening to Julie's plea for help.

"Yes, of course," said Julie as she stood in her bare feet on the cold linoleum floor, thankful that someone was responding.

"Okay. We'll see you at the door when you arrive. Drive carefully," the stranger added.

As Julie gathered up Mom and headed for the door, Dad emerged from his bedroom in his bed clothes. "What's going on?"

"Mom's got some heart problems. I'm taking her to the hospital." Then she closed the door behind them, got into the car, and drove Mom through the black of night to the Bremen Hospital. The hospital admitted Mom and ran some tests. Julie called home about sunrise when she knew Dad would be getting ready for work and filled him in on what happened.

"Do I need to come in?" Dad asked.

Julie was flabbergasted. What did he mean, *'do I need to come in?'*

Still wearing the mismatched clothes she'd thrown on during the panic at home, Julie's shoulders slumped as she stumbled back to Mom's room and told her of Dad's response.

"Mom, I'm not going to college anymore."

"Why is that?" Mom asked, resting on her side in the hospital bed.

"Because one day you'll be dead," she said, brushing away a tear, "and Dad will go to work, come home, and wonder why you're still in bed."

"Julie, I don't think so," Mom said between shallow breaths.

"Yes, he will, Mom. And you'll be dead and he won't even know. So I'm staying home." Now the tears flowed freely.

Maybe it was the difference between youth and wisdom, but Mom prevailed after getting a prescription for nitroglycerin to treat angina, and Julie went to college, as planned. But the concerns on both their hearts remained as Mom opened up to Julie over the subsequent long-distance phone calls.

"I don't know what's going to happen to your Dad's and my relationship," Mom declared.

"I know, Mom. I worry, too."

"We've never been alone our entire married life. Whether it was his folks or you kids in the house, we've never been alone. It's been more than thirty years that way."

Julie sighed, not sure what to say next.

"I don't know what it's going to be like," Mom continued with a trembling voice. "I'm scared."

One Love is Haunting and Elusive

As the pages of the calendar changed, Mom's fears slowly dissolved. She discovered a mellower version of herself, and Dad retired and spent more time understanding life. A faint light began to shimmer through the darkness that once tied them together in knots. As the tension unwound like "smoke spiraling slowly away from a fire" in my mother's poetry, new energy took its place.

They traveled to sunny Hawaii to visit my older sister and each relished the aroma of leis placed around their necks. They scootered across Bermuda with Mom's arms wrapped around Dad's waist as he drove, and in New Zealand they were swept away by the sheer beauty of the isle. Traveling alone or with family members to many other places, they soaked up new experiences and became reacquainted.

Grandkids arrived and loved to visit, especially after Mom and Dad dug a small pond on their property, something they both always dreamed of. Mom and Dad enjoyed the reflection of the sunset in the rippling water and were excited if a wood duck took up residence there. But most of all, they enjoyed listening to nature speak in this quiet place. I believe the pond was also a pleasant daily reminder of the little lake where they first met and honeymooned.

Nature followed them to the house, as well, where my parents sat side-by-side on the porch swing, eating meals or watching birds. Ruby-throated hummingbirds vibrated in mid-air over the feeder, while a pair of swallows sat silently on a window ledge watching Mom and Dad. Orange orioles swooped in and stole strands of string Dad laid out for them to build strong nests across the road. Color bloomed in their lives once again, like the flowers they both enjoyed.

Mom retained her independence and still stayed out late, attending lectures or Bible studies, and Dad was still in bed asleep when she came home alone. But now they had their days together, and a new confidence existed between them that things would turn out right, anger would not rule.

Throughout the journey of their marriage, they appeared together at Oak Grove Church where they greeted congregants at the door, listened to the sermon, and Dad watched Mom share her Truth with their adult Sunday school class. Dad still avoided biblical talk and the preacher even wondered if Dad was a believer. But in a sign of a lifelong devotion to his wife, who valued talk of the Bible above nearly all else, he accompanied her to church each and every Sunday, even if he only sat quietly and listened.

Dad grew thicker around the middle and found Mom's heavier frame still attractive. Intimacy returned. He rubbed Mom's neck or feet when they ached, and one day I spied him placing his hand on her thigh under the table as they reminisced over old photographs of themselves. Mom remarked that they had more romance at age seventy than any time earlier in their lives, and Dad still wanted more.

This haunting and elusive era of their marriage lingered for decades like the sweet strains of a violin, longer than any other period in their married lives.

⚬⚬⚬

I grew up in the wild and fierce era of my parents' relationship where union was replaced by detachment, and communication was swept away by disagreement. During this stage, my father was not an active part of my life. He was the type of a father I might ask how to fix a broken bike but not a broken life. He didn't push me on a swing, teach me to catch a ball, or play with me in the warm lake. Dad even stopped making home movies of the youngest children, Julie and me. I have no doubts that my father loved me, but I think two obstacles kept us from bonding.

One, his primary mechanism for relating to his kids had been the farm, which offered ample opportunities to engage and enjoy life together. At heart, he was a farmer and his older kids joined him in this endeavor. So my siblings who experienced Mom's and Dad's era of young and tender love saw a side of Dad that we youngest ones did not.

And when my parents' lives diverged, I believe that created an additional chasm he could not bridge. I suspect he struggled separating the lives of us youngest children, who were very close to our mother, from the issues he had with her. So he pulled away from Julie and me, just as he pulled away from Mom, leaving Julie with a sense of paternal abandonment.

Overall, I believe I gained far more than I lost and retain no animosity toward Mom or Dad because of these experiences. The lengthy haunting and elusive era of their marriage is the one I choose to remember.

This sweeter era between my parents is the only one most of the grandkids knew. I sat with one of them, my oldest brother's son, Theodore, on a warm afternoon in late spring and we talked about his experiences with my mom.

"The two of them were always together," recalled Theodore, whose eyes smiled as he spoke. "Like two peas in a pod. I don't think I ever saw one without the other. Ever. I doubt they enjoyed wedded bliss every day…surely there must have been arguments and bad times in their marriage. But they arrived at a destination that is so difficult to find nowadays…to stay together for so long. I learned from Grandma that love overcomes everything else. She taught me the importance of family and loving relationships, and that I, too, can lead a wonderful life being devoted to just one person."

Though Mom had experienced three loves in her life, one young and tender, another wild and fierce, followed by a third haunting and elusive relationship, Theodore discovered the ribbon of wisdom which bound the phases together across a single marriage spanning sixty-five years—love endures.

However, I would discover in my own marriage how greed replaces love.

CHAPTER 26

Greed to Grace

I shuffled my bare feet in the cool dirt with the patience of a four-year-old. Sunshine entered through the open door but the empty garage felt dark and cramped. My older brother, Tom, waited next to me for Mr. Matz to arrive to pay us for picking up rocks in his field behind the garage. Suddenly, Mr. Matz appeared in the doorway, backlit by the sun. It was difficult to see his face. He reached into the pocket of his coveralls and pulled out some change. His arm moved slowly as he placed a nickel and a worn penny into my outstretched palm. Six cents! I was thrilled. The money was well earned. A sense of satisfaction settled over me like a well-worn pair of jeans.

This is my earliest memory.

☙

First memories can be dangerous. Years ago, I heard a psychologist say that your first memory reveals the prism through which you view your entire life. When I heard her bold statement I thought back to my memory of standing on the dirt floor in the garage and getting paid. What did this recollection reveal about me? *Nothing*, I concluded.

Although I dismissed the idea, the thought never fully dissolved.

More recently, I sat at my oak kitchen table with my younger sister, Julie, as the morning sun filled the room and brightened our summer day. She wore a sleeveless top and her light brown hair touched her bare shoulders. As we chatted, I happened to share my first remembrance and the psychologist's observations. Before the energy of my words subsided, Julie interjected, "Oh, that's you for sure."

"Why do you say that?" I queried, my faced flushed with surprise.

"As you were growing up, you were always looking for a way to make or save money," she said with certainty. "You raised chickens and started an egg business—to make money." She extended a finger on one hand and began to count my endeavors. "Then you raised earthworms to sell to fishermen as bait—to make money. Remember when you plastered the light switches and cabinet doors in our house with signs? The signs implored us to turn off the lights because every dollar we saved in electricity could be used for some other purpose, like buying clothes."

Julie was on a roll and barely stopped to breathe.

"In fourth grade you sold more magazines than any other kid in school as a fundraiser, although that money didn't find its way into your pocket. And you got your first real job at age twelve as a farmhand and never stopped working until you had enough money to retire at age fifty-four!" She paused, and then added, "So I think that psychologist was right. You've always been about money."

Could this be true? I wondered.

I couldn't let go of Julie's perception of me. Then I recalled a story my sister didn't know.

Soon after we were married, when I was still in my twenties, my wife, Gloria, and I traveled to Mexico. We strolled hand-in-hand from one shop to another, admiring red and orange paper flowers, straw hats, and blouses and skirts in a palette of colors. Spanish intertwined with English as merchants negotiated prices with tourists.

As we ventured to the next shop, passing from the sun and into the shade, we noticed a boy tucked into a doorway, almost hidden.

"Oh, look at that little boy with a guitar," Gloria said, softly as she nodded in his direction.

The ten-year-old boy wore a dirty t-shirt and jeans covered with holes. His straight black hair looked as if it hadn't seen a comb. As we approached, he launched into song, strumming his weathered guitar and singing with joy. A smile lighted his face as we stopped to listen. Although we didn't understand Spanish, his spirit spoke to my wife. She reached into her pocket and pulled out some change and dropped it into his open guitar case at his feet as we turned to leave.

Suddenly, my body tensed and I glared at my wife. Her simple act of charity pulled a pin on my psychological grenade.

"How could you do that?" I berated her.

"Do what? I just gave the poor kid some change!"

"You're just encouraging him to beg some more! He's just a beggar," I barked.

My harsh remarks quickly led to an unresolved argument.

That day, my inner drive to work, earn, and save came to a crescendo and reverberated inside my hollow heart. I had earned six cents picking up rocks as a kid but this boy didn't deserve a dime for singing us a song. There are many ways to find fault with my actions that day. But no matter how it's examined, it's clear that Mr. Scrooge and I could have sat together on the board of Stingy, Greedy, and Moody, Inc.

Maybe Julie was right, I thought. *Maybe my worldview has been all about making and saving money for my own use and not for others.* But why? Did it come from my childhood?

Although we didn't live in poverty when I was a kid, money was scarce. That's why, when we needed a different car, Dad sent Pat and Mom to New Jersey to buy a used pink taxi for $300. That's why I remember the smile in my elementary school picture when I wore my first "bought" shirt from Kmart, instead of used clothing from Goodwill. More than once I remember the rhythmic swish of plastic bread sacks protecting my shoes when we couldn't afford boots for my growing feet, and cardboard inserts inside my shoes to protect my socks from the holes worn clear through the soles.

I didn't dwell on those issues as a child for I understood the unspoken social contract of the community: if you worked hard, you could be successful and get what you want. So that's what I did. After I started working on a neighbor's farm at age twelve, I paid for all my personal expenses thereafter. But those values made the world all about me. Absent was any concern for others. Presumably, if everyone worked hard everything would be okay.

There was virtually no discussion in our home about giving to others. Each Sunday as we sat in the hard, wooden pews at church, Dad dropped some folded bills into the offering plate, but I had no idea how much or what motivated the donation. From Sunday school lessons and the preacher's sermons, I was aware of the biblical instruction to give ten percent, but our family's giving could not have approached that amount.

As my "life teacher," maybe Mom said nothing because we were the "less fortunate ones" and we had no money to spare. Or maybe she remembered living in poverty as a child and being humiliated when she received "handouts," so she felt her lack of donations to others actually demonstrated kindness. But when Mom got her first job after high school, one of the first things she did was give her younger sister, Joy, a weekly allowance of twenty-five cents. That clearly was an act of generosity, but it demonstrated a different value of "taking care of her own."

Throughout Mom's life, though, she drank from the spiritual fountain of Pastor Russell who instructed his followers not to engage in social issues. He taught that dealing with such things was God's work and that people should stay out of God's way, and instead should be "proclaiming the heavenly kingdom at hand as the only remedy." I suspect this perspective significantly shaped her thinking, which in turn, influenced mine.

⌘

As an adult, I wasn't devoid of understanding. Although I rejected the "ten percent rule," which seemed arbitrary, I recognized the pastor and the church's electric bill needed to be paid. So I dutifully donated a little money to my own church based on the New Testament idea that God loves a cheerful giver.[1] And over time, I even gave a little bit to United Way through my employer. But my giving was still about me, and my need to be cheerful.

In general, I had little empathy for those living on the margins of society. It seemed obvious to me, for example, that the bedraggled homeless folks I saw begging on the noisy street corners wouldn't be homeless if they just got a job. Therefore, they and the Mexican beggar boy didn't deserve any of my earnings.

But all that changed when my soul was ripped open in a poor village in South India.

I visited India several times for business and spent most of my time in large cities. Intrigued by this culture, I was thirsty for knowledge of the rural spaces where most Indians lived. So one weekend, Indian colleagues arranged for me to travel with an NGO (Non-Government Organization, aka nonprofit) to a remote village. As we drove further from the city, the smooth highway devolved into a mostly paved roadway. Then the roadway became gravel. Soon the sound of gravel crunching beneath our tires gave way as we drove slowly down parallel dirt paths. Hours after we started our journey, even the pathway disappeared when we arrived at the impoverished village.

I could see men working hard in distant fields and heard dogs bark as I followed our leader down a rutted dirt path to the meeting place. There, the village women gathered, dressed in brightly colored clothing wrapped around their bodies and heads, sitting cross-legged on the covered porch of an adobe-style home, awaiting my planned arrival. I nodded and smiled as we briefly exchanged greetings, though we spoke different languages. I was invited to sit silently at the edge of the porch while the NGO representative shared with the women brief education, unrelated to my visit, about money management and stopping sexually transmitted diseases.

When their meeting was finished, our interpreter turned to me, "Do you wish to address the assembly?"

Caught by surprise, my seated posture stiffened. The women's eyes looked expectantly in my direction, as I stammered without fore-thought, "Is there something they want to ask me?"

The interpreter turned back to the women and repeated my question in their native tongue. As he spoke to them, I imagined the intrigue my visit must have brought to this impoverished place. I was fairly certain I was the first white person and first American they had ever seen. *Would they ask me about something grand in the U.S.? About the amazing jets that fly overhead? What wisdom would I impart?*

Soon he had their question. He turned and looked me in the eye. Speaking on behalf of the women gathered there he asked, "Can you get us water?"

I gasped as if I were sucker-punched. With one question, these strangers simultaneously revealed my ignorance and arrogance.

Sensing my distress, the interpreter continued, "See that metal pipe sticking from the ground on your left?" My eyes followed the direction where he pointed. I gazed down at a small, two-foot-tall leaning gray pipe protruding out of the dusty ground. A simple faucet, like the kind on the outside of my house, was attached at the top. "That was the village water source. It's no longer working, and they have no means to repair or replace it, and nothing else nearby."

The lack of accessible clean water, the very basis of life, had a profound effect on this community. Understandably, that's what was on their minds. It wasn't about me.

This experience shifted the bedrock on which I'd built my world-view and my place in it. In that moment, I was moved to empty my pockets of my Indian currency and hand it to the NGO. That was the only thing I knew how to do. But over time, it led me to a year-long study of the root causes of poverty and how I could help without hurt-ing those I sought to assist. I learned the world is far more complicated than "hard work equals success," and that the playing field isn't always level. I also began to see my checkbook as a moral document as my donations became less about me, and more about the needs of others in relation to what I've been given.[2]

Since this experience, my financial contributions have risen significantly. My wife and I donate to international crises, national causes, and local projects. But more importantly, I've used my time to raise awareness and a million dollars to help a large impoverished community in Kenya find its own pathway to self-sufficiency, which included providing access to much-needed clean water.

I am someone who has changed. My only motivation in sharing my transformation is the hope that it might inspire others, just as another man inspired me.

John Newton was an Englishman who lived in the 1700s and spent years as captain of ships transporting slaves from Africa to America in the dank and putrid bowels of his vessels. After violent waves smashed a hole in the side of his ship, he cried out for God's mercy to save him. He pointed to that harrowing incident as his "conversion moment," which opened his eyes to the disgusting life he lived, leading him to eventually reject the vile work in which he'd been engaged.[3]

John told his story in a famous Christian hymn called "Amazing Grace:"

Amazing grace how sweet the sound
that saved a wretch like me.
I once was lost but now I'm found.
Was blind but now I see.

Like John, I, too, was once blind. But I see better now. I no longer see "just a beggar" playing music in a shop doorway. I now see a struggling Mexican child using his abilities to survive, not unlike the boy I once was picking up stones, who deserves no less than I.

I "see" differently because I've experienced grace in many forms. I've received mercy from my wife who didn't excuse my blindness but allowed me the space to stumble about on my own. I received favor from total strangers in India who pulled the cover from my eyes so the light of day might enter. And like John Newton, I have felt the unmerited love of God guide my way.

As the recipient of so much grace, it is only natural to want to return a portion as a sign of my gratitude. That, too, is an expression of grace. I'm now on a journey that started at greed but is moving toward grace.

CHAPTER 27

Love Letters

M om loved to marry words together like some girls marry Barbie to Ken. With just the right words in the proper order and cadence, they unleashed her imagination and gave voice to an unseen part of herself. She created a portrait of the joy in her soul with only a pencil and paper. And when she was lonely and sad, words also brought her the comfort of hugs. Mom was in love with words, and they with her. Written words were the love letters she gave to herself.

Mom inherited a love for writing. Her paternal grandfather was a preacher, poet, and lyricist. Her own father, Grant, also a preacher, crafted inspiring sermons once or more a week. Her mother, Effie, was a prolific writer and used her words like tools to speak truth to power, chastise family, or share information. This was the fertile ground onto which the joyous seeds of writing were scattered in my mother's garden.

Mom's voracious appetite for reading nourished her love of writing. The library, one of the few free and enriching experiences available to her during the Depression, was Mom's second home in the city. It was a bottomless treasure chest filled with hardcover jewels. They inspired Mom to evolve into a poet, novelist, historian, and theologian. Her interests and aspirations seemed to have no limits.

Poetry was Mom's first form of creative writing. It began in middle school where she wrote a poem from the perspective of a blind person about the dazzling beauty the person "saw." The teacher rejected her work and sent Mom to the office, saying Mom couldn't know what it was like to be blind. Then she challenged Mom, "How could a blind person 'see' anything?" It befuddled Mom how her teacher couldn't see what she saw. I think this experience was Mom's first clue that she was somehow different from other people. Poems continued to pour out during high school, but as she became an adult, her interests broadened into writing fiction and non-fiction—whatever touched her heart. She also took classes at a community learning center to improve her skills and joined a writers' group.

No matter what she chose to write about, each creation began the old-fashioned way with paper and pencil. During the Depression and World War II when many items were in short supply, Mom wrote on any blank space on any portion of any paper. But as the world changed and inexpensive paper became readily available, Mom's habit remained. The backs of my childhood quiz papers (which carried the scent of mimeograph blue), business letters sent to the house, and the envelopes in which they came were gathered up and became the canvas for a work of art. Hunched over the dining room table with the amber sun at her back, Mom wrote silently, up one side and down the other, until her thoughts consumed the empty spaces. Only the hushed rub of an eraser was heard, or the shuffling of papers when one became jammed with words and she'd grab another. When words stopped flowing, the table-top was covered like the desk of an absent-minded professor.

Then came the tasks of revision and transforming the cursive into the typewritten word. Mom sat like a ramrod in her straight-back chair, and with her strong hands she unleashed the fury of her Underwood. When her writing was clear, the thin metal arms of the typewriter smacked the page like bullets from a machine gun, rat-tat-tat, piercing the air with precision of thought. Sometimes, Mom's fingers flew faster than the little arms could advance and retreat after their singular duty was complete. Two or three might crash on their way up or down, halting the attack until she could untangle them. But in more pensive moments, Mom hammered on the round metal keys like a blacksmith slowly beating molten metal into an artful form, as each little letter smacked the ribbon and left behind a black image of itself. Leaning closer to the page and tilting back her head to peer through her bifocals, her head bobbed down, then up, as each word was wed to another.

Mom wrote creative non-fiction in her story "Puppy Love" about the amorous relationship of our brindle pet dog, Dudley. She wrote memoir as she recounted her life as a child of the Depression, and of her admiration for her grandmother, Ella May. She constructed theological pieces to articulate her unique understanding of the Bible. In total, she composed dozens of written works of art in addition to being a journalist with "The Party Line."

Still, it was her poetry that provided a window to her soul. She wrote poetry of all kinds, often centered on the seasons of the natural world, loving relationships, or God. Some poetry also revealed the angst that sometimes dwelled in her, such as this:

Spring Prayer

John, dear,
It's spring again.

Your empty chair
Still stands beside the open window
With the linen curtains blowing.
Under the old, gnarled cherry tree
I can see the tulips we planted,
Swaying and nodding
In the evening breeze.

The turtle doves are nesting
In our tree once more,
And mourn all day
As if they knew.
Still hopeful,

Laddie lies beside your chair
Awaiting your caress.

Oh, John, dear,
It's spring again.

She wrote children's stories, as well, such as "Jonnie McCracken," and "How the Two Billy's Got Their Blue." The latter story is about Billy Bird who made friends with a sad and colorless berry named Billy Berry. Billy Berry felt like a lonely outcast in the midst of a colorful garden, so Billy Bird tried to cheer him up.

One day, a little bird came hopping down the row close to Billy. The little bird saw Billy hanging down sadly on his branch. He hopped up to Billy and said in a very soft voice, "I am Billy Bird. Why do you look so sad?"

Billy Berry raised his eyes. "Why, Billy is my name, too. I am sad because I have no color and no one wants to be my friend. Everyone in this garden has a lovely color but me." Then two drops of dew rolled off the fat cheeks of Billy Berry.

Billy Bird was also rather drab, and had few friends, but he had resigned himself to his colorless life. His heart hurt for his new friend, Billy Berry. So he sought the wise counsel of Owl of the Forest. Owl whispered instructions to Billy Bird who flew back to the garden to share the good news with Billy Berry that a colorful surprise was coming.

Late that afternoon, it started to rain, and rain, and rain. Billy Berry drooped and became sad again. "I won't get my color today," he said.

Billy Bird just smiled and said, "Be patient. You will get your color soon."

When the shower was over, a rainbow appeared at the far end of the garden. It was so big it stretched from one side of the garden to the other. Suddenly, Billy Bird said, "Get ready for your color!" and with that, he flew straight toward the rainbow. On and on he flew toward the dazzling bright colors. Finally, he came to the red and flew past it to the orange, then on to the yellow and green. Just before indigo, there was the blue. Billy Bird flew straight through the blue until all the lovely, dripping color clung to his feathers. Down he went, straight to Billy Berry as fast as he could. All the flowers watched him come closer and closer. When he got to Billy Berry he shook his feathers and the blue came off and fell on his friend. Billy Berry laughed and laughed.

"Now I have color! This is the best color in the world. Thank you, thank you, Billy." As he turned to thank Billy, he got a second surprise. "Why, the color has stained you, too! Now you have a pretty color."

Billy Bird looked at himself. Yes, he was a very bright blue, too… Now the whole garden rejoiced and wanted to become friends. Even Petty Petunia smiled at Billy Berry.

Said Billy Berry, "I think I'll call you Billy Bluebird."

Said Billy Bird, "I think I'll call you Billy Blueberry."

They both laughed for joy.

Suddenly, a large shadow flew over the garden and they heard a wise voice say, "Whoooo ever helps a friend, helps themselves."

❧

Just like Billy Bird shook off his blue color onto Billy Berry, Mom did the same for her children. The ability to write was her "blue," and not a single child in her familial garden escaped receiving a portion of this colorful gift. This was the love letter she gave us.

Grammar and punctuation instruction, often in the form of verbal correction, was as much of our daily experience as milk with a meal. When I had a question about the meaning or spelling of a word, Mom had the answer: "Get the dictionary." Thick editions sat in different rooms for easy access. Poor grades in English were not an option.

Like my mother, I became a reader before I became a writer. I read sixty books in the second grade. I was proud that my consumption of prose also strengthened my vocabulary.

At the beginning of third grade, my teacher, Mrs. Urbanski, a young woman with big eyes and a beehive hairdo, scratched our new vocabulary on the blackboard. She asked the students who sat in my row to stand in front of our metal desks and recite a word to the class and spell it out loud. I was happy to be in the chosen row so I could show off my word prowess.

As the florescent lights hummed in the ceiling, the first student rose and read from the board, "Fohrt. F-O-R-T. Fohrt," then sat down.

"Thank you, Sharon," Mrs. Urbanski said. "Very good." Sharon beamed and was probably thankful for such an easy word.

My next classmate stood up and read, "Plan-it. P-L-A-N-E-T. Plan-it," then sat down.

"That's correct, Mary. Thank you." Mary also seemed pleased with herself.

My turn was next. I stood tall and summoned my most authoritative high-pitched voice to pronounce the third word on my teacher's list. "Ee-wee. E-W-E. Ee-wee."

Mrs. Urbanski chuckled and the room erupted in laughter. "No,

Kerry," my teacher informed me. "It's pronounced 'yoo.' I thought you were a country boy," she said. "A ewe is a female sheep."

Although I was embarrassed to my core, it didn't stop me from writing my first book that year. Now they're called graphic novels, but my comic book was in crayon and pencil, written on thick manila-colored paper. Influenced by Mom's frequent talk of UFOs, my book was about "flying saucers," which carried robots to Earth that shot red rays from their hands. These pages of my past, bound together with white paste, are my most cherished childhood items.

That same year, Mom and I conspired to send Mike and Pat, who were now away at the same college, a creative letter. We wrote short articles in a newspaper format with family news. Mike replied by creating a more polished version of what we sent. It was typed and formatted with bolded titles and bylines. Inspired by our capital city newspaper, Mike called his "newspaper" the *Stevens Star*.

Over the years, family members went to college and graduated. As grandkids arrived and the family spread out, Janet sought to keep us connected. She proposed the creation of a family magazine to be published and distributed at our annual reunions. Each extended family member, regardless of age, was expected to contribute an article. The littlest children drew pictures, but the others wrote about any topic. Some wrote about events over the past year, some on family history, while others addressed contemporary social issues. Sometimes a topic was chosen just to spark controversy among a family who was not of one mind. This magazine was dubbed the *Stevens Star*. The cover featured a six-pointed star—one point for each of us six kids. At the center of the star was a circle that depicted the union of our parents. Inspired by Mom, the *Stevens Star* was published continuously for thirty years.

The magazine gave me my first opportunity to write meaningful essays and to learn from others. I spent hours researching and writing to gain the respect of my literary-minded family members, which included Janet, an occasional professional writer and editor, and Pat, who writes a monthly article for an environmental engineering journal and has published over fifty professional papers.

"Why do I write all the time?" Pat said. "That's a trait which came from Mom. The skills to observe and extract information to write an interesting story...it's Mom who inspired me."

❧

Mom's writing was a gift of love she gave the community and her children. As she aged, her words even nourished her own heart, although other powerful forces threatened to steal her very heartbeat.

CHAPTER 28

Matters of the Heart

My flesh and my heart may fail, but God is the strength of my heart and my portion forever.

—Psalm 73:26

Dad sat alone on a hard, plastic chair in the waiting room, flipping through magazines without reading them. It was 7:00 a.m. and St. Joseph Hospital was just waking up. Nurses greeted each other down the hall and an orderly wheeled a squeaky gurney nearby. Although he and Mom were seventy-eight years old and had gotten up at 4:00 a.m. to be there, Dad was glad Mom's outpatient gall bladder surgery was scheduled early. He expected they'd both be home by noon and he'd still have time to mow the lawn.

Dad shifted his weight in the uncomfortable chair when he heard determined footsteps. He looked up and saw a man in scrubs with blue protective booties over his shoes. The man's face looked serious and tense.

"Mr. Stevens?" the man asked as he approached my father.

"Yes." Dad stood and shook the man's hand.

"I'm Dr. Mark. We removed your wife's gall bladder, but she won't wake up."

Dad's posture stiffened. "What? What do you mean?"

"Your wife's heart stopped, Mr. Stevens," said the doctor, "but we got it started again. But she's unconscious, so…"

"Is she dead?" Dad gasped.

Dr. Mark exhaled loudly, "I can't say for sure, Mr. Stevens. But we need to act quickly to find out what's wrong and hopefully bring her back for you. We need your permission to…"

"Do what you need to, Doctor," Dad interrupted in a shaky voice, staring at the floor. "Just do it…go ahead and do it…"

"Thank you, Mr. Stevens." Dr. Mark turned and walked quickly down the hall as Dad collapsed into the chair and buried his face in his hands.

❧

The story of Mom's health was not the story she had anticipated. She built walls of healthy living around herself, which she believed would protect her from illness and disease.

She was convinced that herbicides and pesticides hurt not only the environment, but also our bodies, so our family grew our own organic vegetables. She was adamant that green dandelion leaves and Lambs Quarter were a highly nutritious source of vitamins and minerals. While others killed these bitter weeds, Mom ate them. In the spring and summer of life, she drank unpasteurized whole milk and retrieved "mineral water" in one-gallon glass jugs from a regional spring. She washed down fistfuls of vitamins with that water, followed by pungent supplements such as desiccated liver and brewer's yeast tablets, all purported to improve her health. She avoided processed foods such as white sugar and flour and brushed her teeth with baking soda to avoid the fluoride added to commercial toothpaste. She admonished all who would listen not to go outside in cool weather with wet hair to avoid catching a cold. And when ailments arose, she turned to her chiropractor, as well as the natural remedies used in her childhood, eschewing modern medicines because of their side effects.

But like the fairy tale of "The Three Little Pigs," the materials she used to build her walls of healthy living failed to keep the wolf from entering her home. Too often, it seemed she'd used only sticks and straw, as a slow parade of maladies marched into her life.

❀

"It was on my fifteenth birthday that I noticed pain in my heart for the first time," Mom recalled years later. "No doubt that fall off the top of the slide in the early grades, and the blow to the front of my head when I accidentally dove into the floor of the swimming pool at McNaughton Park was beginning to catch up with me."

At the vibrant age of twenty-seven, less than three years after being married, and having given birth to Mike and Pat, Mom had a cyst on one of her ovaries removed. Her mother Effie came to live with her for months before Mom was fully recovered and able to care for her young family on her own again.

By her mid-thirties, still looking slim and capable, for unknown reasons Mom claimed she lacked the stamina being demanded of her as a farmer's wife with a growing family, writing:

> I made a colossal mistake of marrying a farmer, which requires such hard work. I do think it's the best way to raise a family, but my health takes constant renewing via chiropractic treatment and vitamins. But my energy still occurs in spurts. If I wash clothes very hard one day, I'm exhausted the next.

Mom entered menopause in her early forties and put on weight. Dad, who remained strong and fit, was not amused and frequently chastised her for eating too much and not getting enough exercise.

Folks who lived in the country got their exercise naturally through hard work. One day, Mom found herself in the middle of unwanted exercise. She believed it was caused by Dad's negligence. The event marked not only a turning point in her physical health, but it also hardened her heart toward my father.

It was a cloudy summer Saturday. Dad borrowed a small Ford tractor and sickle bar mower to cut down the tall canary grass that grew inside the fenced area of our three-acre homestead. My oldest brother's Guernsey cow and her calf, Hattie, lived inside the fenced area and the tall grass was too tough to eat. Dad needed to cut it down so new, tender grass could grow in its place. Wearing a plaid cotton shirt and ball cap, Dad opened the hand-built gate to the field and drove in the tractor. He dismounted to close the gate when Mom arrived in her workpants and sleeveless blouse. She had been weeding a nearby garden.

"Mick, you can't cut the grass with that sickle bar while the calf is hiding in it. You'll kill it or cut off its legs with that sharp blade."

Dad shook his head. "Berthella, I'm not going to cut off Hattie's legs. I'll see her."

"Then where is she? Can you see her now?" She stared straight at Dad.

"No, but I know she's out there, and I'll see her when I get close."

"Mick, you're going to cut off her legs. I just know it. At least go find her before you start cutting."

"I know what I'm doing. I'm not going to hurt her," he said as he removed his cap and ran his fingers through his hair.

Mom was not convinced and stayed inside the fenced area as Dad started cutting along the perimeter. Red-winged blackbirds lit from the grass and scolded Dad as their homes fell to the ground with the cut grass. At the far side of the field, Dad startled the calf hiding in the tall grass. It took off running straight for the sickle bar with its oscillating, sharp metal blade. Dad pushed in the clutch with his left foot and slammed on the brakes with his right, stopping the tractor. But the blade was powered by other means and continued to cut like monster scissors as Hattie ran straight into the teeth.

Although Mom couldn't see Hattie from the opposite side of the field, she knew what happened. She screamed and raised her arms in the air as she ran through the chest high grass to where Dad had stopped. She arrived heaving and saw the bottom four inches of one of Hattie's front legs severed and hanging by a tendon. Blood stained the calf's white hair. Hattie bucked and cried, running, falling, running, falling, with only three working legs and excruciating pain in the fourth.

"Mick, I told you so. Look what you did!" Mom shouted over the still-rumbling engine.

Mom took off to catch the injured calf. The tall grass and missing leg hampered the terrified Hattie long enough for Mom to catch up with it. At the right moment, Mom dove through the grass for Hattie's rear legs and thudded to the hard ground with a leg in each fist. The frightened animal had strength. She squealed and kicked her legs at Mom's head, freeing one leg from Mom's grip. Mom grabbed the remaining boney leg with both hands and clung tightly as Hattie continued to kick until Dad arrived and wrapped his arms around Hattie's front and rear legs, scooping the calf up in his arms and carried it away to be treated by a veterinarian. Mom lay on the rough ground in the middle of the trampled grass. She squeezed her eyes shut with each sharp pain piercing her chest.

Hattie survived and eventually learned to walk on three legs, but Mom struggled through life for quite some time afterward. Her pain continued, sometimes dull and constant, while other times spasmodic and debilitating. She never saw a medical doctor, but with the help of her chiropractor she diagnosed her condition as intercostal neuritis, pain caused by damage to the nerves between the rib bones. Mom needed frequent rest and described her condition this way:

I learned that everyone is led by a "two-horse team." One horse is the nervous system and the other is the glandular system. If one "horse" stumbles or falls, it throws off the other "horse." After going into early menopause, I had the accident with the calf, which gave me intercostal neuritis, which in turn, upset my glandular "horse," which was already diminished. I came close to death.

It wasn't obvious to others in our house that Mom came close to death. Based on her symptoms, and without the aid of the searchable Internet or a medical doctor, she often claimed she had the worst possible conditions. And when she spoke about such things as a "two-horse team," coupled with constant complaints of invisible issues, I think she seemed a little crazy to Dad.

Soon after the calf incident, Mom said she suffered a heart attack and was unable to leave her bed for many weeks. Janet was in high school and took on many of Mom's responsibilities: buying groceries, preparing our meals, and trying to keep the house in order. But Janet couldn't do everything. I was in first grade and learned to iron my own clothes, prepare my own school lunch, and get myself on the bus alone. Those weren't jobs I wanted, but I understood the need and became stronger and more independent because of the experience.

Mom felt neglected and struggled to find a sympathetic ear. We were a farm family that was expected to be sturdy, strong, and self-sufficient. Whether in sickness or in health, farmers were expected to work. My father believed if your body wasn't bleeding profusely or a bone wasn't sticking out, then things must not be too bad. A heart aching for no apparent reason was not cause for alarm or staying in bed. Dad's skepticism also crept into the children, causing some of us to wonder if Mom was "crying wolf" when no wolf existed.

Mom eventually recovered, but she attributed her heart attack to the incident with the calf. And since the calf incident was Dad's fault, so was her heart condition. Although her heart may have physically healed, it still harbored the disease of blame.

⁢

It was nearly fifteen years later, when Mom was in her late fifties, that Julie took her to the hospital for angina and she received her first prescription for nitroglycerin. She was also diagnosed with high blood pressure, but opted for natural remedies instead of prescription medicines, adding fish oil and garlic capsules to her regimen, and drinking hibiscus tea.

Mom's blood pressure continued to climb throughout her sixties, often hitting a dangerously high 210 over 160, twice the normal level. She had many "bad spells," but tried to avoid letting them slow her down. In 1990, at the age of seventy, while attending eight weekly presentations on famous gardens from all over the country, Mom discovered she couldn't live up to her aspirations.

"The slides were narrated by Fernwood Nature Center's chief naturalist," Mom said, "and we could ask questions at any time. I didn't go just to see the beautiful gardens, but to learn and share experiences with other gardeners. Did I ever get EXCITED! I was ready to come home and tear out all my gardens and start over, as I could now see how I'd made them wrong. But that is pure fantasy when my breathing is so difficult."

Tom was a chiropractor, a godsend to our mother. Whenever Mom had an episode of poor health, she'd consult Tom. One day, Tom sat at his desk in the back office, entering patient records when his phone rang.

"Hello," he said. He heard only a sigh but knew who it was.

"Hi. It's Mom."

"Hey, Mom. How are you?"

"Oh, okay, I guess. But I've been better. I'm having another spell."

"What's going on?"

"Well, I've got shortness of breath...and not much energy. I just don't feel right."

"Have you seen your doctor?"

"No, not really. I just don't know what to do."

"What about your blood pressure medicine? Are you taking it?"

"No. You know I'm afraid of what else that stuff may do to me."

"Mom, if you don't take it, you may be dead. Would that be better than the side effects?"

"Well, could you just come over to the house and give me an adjustment?"

"How 'bout you come over to the office tomorrow at 1:00. I'll take a short lunch and adjust you afterward. Okay?"

The calls became more frequent, and my brother dreaded them. "She was always releasing her burden onto me, asking 'what should I do?' She made me be her doctor and expected me to tell her what to do and how to do it. But then she didn't want to follow the advice, like taking her blood pressure medicine. It got to the point where I didn't want to hear from her anymore."

Finally, in one exasperating call, Tom had to share what was on his heart. Their relationship was at stake.

"Mom, I don't want to be your doctor. I just want to be your son," Tom said, earnestly. "This constant back and forth on your issues is getting in the way of our relationship…and honestly, it makes me not want to talk with you… But I do want to talk with you, because you're my mother. And I don't want to lose that."

The line was silent for a moment. "I see," Mom said, quietly. "And you know what? I agree with you. I understand… Does this mean I should find another chiropractor?"

"No, Mom, I can still give you chiropractic adjustments, but I want you to…I'd appreciate it if you turned to your medical doctor for assistance on your medical concerns. Just let me be your son."

And with that one conversation, Mom stopped treating my brother as her on-call doctor and their relationship flourished once again.

By the time she reached seventy-five, Mom had regularly scheduled appointments to visit Tom's office for free adjustments, which always made her feel better. The appointments also provided well-defined boundaries to discuss health issues. But one of Mom's appointments was like no other.

Mom waited for Tom, wearing only an open-back gown, as she sat on an adjustment table in an exam room. The window shade was drawn, which created an odd mix of light—both fluorescent and natural. Mom knew the routine. Tom would ask her to step on the scales and take her weight and height, then she'd lie on the table where he'd snap his reflex hammer in precise ways to return Mom's musculoskeletal system to its normal state.

"Hi, Mom," said Tom, as he entered the room in his white coat and glasses. He closed the door behind him. "How are you?"

"I'm fine...sort of."

"Sort of?"

"Well, do you want to know what breast cancer feels like?"

Tom's head shook involuntarily. "What are you talking about?"

"I've got breast cancer," she replied in a mix of light-hearted solemnity. "Or at least a tumor."

"Are you serious?"

"Yes. I just found out yesterday. Dad felt a lump on my right breast so I went to the doctor, like you've told me to do. The doctor thinks it's likely cancerous and needs to come out."

Tom took a step back. "Holy cow, Mom. I don't know what to say... How do you feel about it?"

Mom sighed and shrugged her shoulders. "Okay, I guess. What can I do about it? If it's cancer, it's cancer."

The room was silent as Mom stared at the floor and Tom stared blankly at Mom sitting alone on the exam table.

Suddenly, Mom lifted her head and looked straight into Tom's blue eyes and asked, "Do you want to know what breast cancer feels like?"

"What do you mean?" he asked, still trying to process her news.

"Have you ever felt a tumor before?"

"No."

"Would you like to feel my breast so you can feel what a tumor feels like? The experience may be helpful to you as a husband and a doctor."

Even faced with a potentially life-threatening disease, Mom couldn't stop being a teacher. She wanted some good to come from her misfortune. If she felt any unease at inviting her grown son to palpate her breast, she didn't show it. She gently grabbed my brother's hand and guided his fingers to the nearly-golf-ball size lump beneath her gown. Tom's trained fingers had never felt anything like it before. It was hard as a rock and had no "give" like nearly every other part of the human body he'd touched. On a professional level, it was exhilarating.

On a personal level, the implications of this unnatural lump took his breath away. His mother had cancer.

Mom's subsequent biopsy confirmed the doctor's suspicion. She was not ready to die and didn't dwell on that possible outcome. She remained reasonably upbeat and matter-of-fact about the experience, talking openly with anyone about her journey. There were no tears or lamentations that I saw. But I also lived more than a thousand miles away in Texas. Still in my thirties, I hadn't fully developed a sense of empathy, and I responded with an amount of detachment equal to Mom's matter-of-factness. When she went to the hospital for her mastectomy there was no "goodbye" or "I love you." I stayed in Texas awaiting the "all clear" call. When it came, I learned the cancer had not spread and she needed "only" radiation to bring death to the cancer that threatened her life.

Her sister, Joy, helped care for Mom after she returned home, as did Julie. Dad couldn't stomach emptying the surgical drain bulb, but he did begin to learn his way around the kitchen, helping to prepare his own meals. Mom elected not to have reconstructive surgery, and after the wound healed, she was fitted with a prosthesis.

The following summer, Mom and Dad made their annual trip to our Texas home, where Mom looked forward to swimming in our new pool. I hadn't seen them since the surgery and didn't know what to expect. When she arrived, she looked no different and seemed happy. But something changed when she put on her one-piece pink swimsuit suit and came out to the pool.

I stood shirtless in the shallow end as Mom grabbed the stainless-steel handrail and walked gingerly down the stairs into the clear blue water. I saw for the first time the empty space where her right breast once was. Her suit sagged and was partially open on that side, exposing her flat chest as she eased into the sparkling water.

"Ooh, this water's chilly, Kerry," she said as she stirred the water and squinted in the bright sun.

"I know. There's too much shade from the live oak trees. But you'll get used to it pretty quickly."

An uncomfortable silence flowed around us as I contemplated her missing breast.

"So, Mom, are you all healed up after your surgery?"

"Yes, I think so."

"Does it hurt?" I asked, moving my hands gently through the brisk water.

"No, not really. I still have to do my exercises to strengthen the muscles and keep them from tightening up. That's a little uncomfortable, but not painful."

It was painful for me, though, to see my mother like that. I wanted a deeper conversation but didn't know where to start. Because I lived so far away I had been isolated from much of the turmoil of the surgery.

"So what's it like to have only one breast?" I asked, clumsily.

"It hasn't really affected me, Kerry. And your dad doesn't seem to mind. Normally I wear my prosthesis, but I didn't want to get it wet in the pool. It was pretty expensive."

"Yeah, I noticed that, Mom."

"Does it look bad?" she asked, with raised eyebrows.

"No…I guess not. I've just never seen a woman with only one breast before. I'm still getting used to it."

The conversation paused again as we navigated this new territory and listened to a distant jet flying overhead.

"Well, it's healed up well," said Mom. "Do you want to see the scar?"

It was a bizarre, unexpected question—but so Mom. *Do I really want to see my mother's missing breast?* I wondered. That insatiable-curiosity part of my brain, the part which had been nurtured by my mother, proclaimed *heck yeah, I want to see something I've never seen before.*

As we stood in the waist deep water, my mother cupped one hand over her intact breast to hold the suit in place while she slipped the strap off the other shoulder, baring her flat chest to me as if she were a man. She showed me the large reddish scar the width of her breast and explained the procedure as if it had happened to someone else.

Hearing her story made my heart ache. She didn't dwell on the disease or the surgery, though; she was focused on the healing and the good things she still anticipated in her life.

"Mom, were you scared?" I finally asked, after she reassembled her swimsuit.

"No, I wasn't. When I die, I know I'm going to be resurrected. That's where I place my hope." Mom spoke slowly and confidently. "The Bible says God will wipe away all the tears and there will be no more death or sorrow.[1] I know that's my future. Although I'm not ready to die—I still have a lot stuff I want to do—when I'm gone, I know I'll live forever after the resurrection. So what's to be scared of? I do worry about Dad, though," she confided. "I don't know what he'd do without me."

I admired my Mom as we stood alone in the pool. She endured her cancer with such strength and shared her ordeal with me with such grace. She spit in the eye of death with assurance. Her actions were a remarkable indicator of her character. Although I found it inspiring, I didn't have the ability to express myself in word or deed.

⊙

As my mother recovered from her bout with cancer, her ever-present chest pains continued. She was diagnosed with gall bladder issues, which often mimic heart problems. That's when Dad took her to St. Joseph Hospital to have her gall bladder removed in the out-patient procedure. Although Dad expected they'd be home by noon and he could still mow the lawn that day, Dr. Mark's startling announcement that Mom's heart had stopped changed everything.

Is this how it ends? Dad must have thought, as his own heart raced. There was no family in the waiting room to comfort him, no one else to take charge while Dr. Mark fought to bring Mom back to life.

Dad found his way to a pay phone and asked the operator to call Tom's house. He spoke to my sister-in-law, Donna, who was a registered nurse. He was relieved to hear they would drop what they were doing and begin the hour and a half drive to the hospital. Between the two of them, they'd make sense of Mom's ordeal.

Dad returned to the waiting room where he could do nothing but wait. After what probably seemed like hours, Dr. Mark returned.

"Mr. Stevens, your wife is alive but on life support. Multiple arteries to her heart are blocked. In order save your wife, we need to perform bypass surgery immediately. You need to know the risk is higher for emergency coronary bypass surgeries like this, especially for older female patients who may be having a heart attack. Do we have your permission, Mr. Stevens?

"Doctor, is she still alive?"

"Yes, for now, Mr. Stevens. But I can't guarantee you she'll survive. I'm sorry."

"Is this open-heart surgery?"

"Yes, we have to open her chest to access her heart. Do we have your permission, Mr. Stevens?"

"Yes, I guess so," Dad muttered. "Do we have any other options?" he asked, searching Dr. Mark's eyes.

"I'm afraid not. There's a team of doctors and nurses standing by. Thank you, Mr. Stevens. We'll keep you updated."

When my brother and sister-in-law arrived, they learned three of her four arteries were nearly 100% blocked and Mom was undergoing quadruple bypass. They eased my father's burden by taking control of the situation and providing what comfort they could.

As she recovered in her hospital bed and was told what happened, Dad knew she was going to be okay when she turned her head toward him and said in a faint but firm voice, "I told you so. I had heart problems and nobody believed me."

It was a convicting statement of which most of us were guilty to some degree.

The ordeal also marked the catastrophic failure of Mom's "walls of healthy living." The wolf had burst through once again and nearly caused her demise. But, of course, Mom didn't see it that way. "Think about what my life would have been like if I hadn't taken care of myself all these years!" she boasted later.

✿

As Mom's physical heart healed, so did her emotional heart. In the year 2000, just two years after her near-death experience on the operating table and having her chest pried open, she wrote an article in the *Stevens Star*, recounting the highlights of the past year:

> It has been a fabulous year since the last year's issue of the *Stevens Star.* Last fall Pat took Dad and me to Belgium to visit with the members of the Stevens family who had not immigrated to the United States. It was a wonderful trip for an offspring and his parents.

She went on to describe the beautiful gardens, the delightful chicory-laced coffee, and a lovely sunrise she enjoyed on that trip. But her year wasn't over. Her next adventure was a trip with Tom, and his son, Matt.

> They took us to Pennsylvania to see the greatest design of Frank Lloyd Wright—The House on the Waterfall. It was lovely, of course, but also a bit bizarre when he designed the guest bedroom ceiling so low that the guests would unknowingly feel the need to go outside and appreciate nature… It was a nice day in the mountains, too.

She continued to share how great life had been through stories of attending a grandchild's orchestra performance, of visiting me in Texas, then having a party thrown for Dad and her by my sister, Janet, in Indianapolis. After that, it was off to Washington State to visit Pat, where "…the mountains were stunning and volcanoes were unbelievable." She concluded her article:

Yes, it has been a good year. Not only did Dad and I celebrate our respective 80th birthdays, but also our 55th wedding anniversary. I made pretty good gains after my operations and have set new goals and hunger for new things. Now that I'm 80 years old should I quit? My heart says "NO."

Indeed, her heart said "no," enticing Mom to embrace life anew. And just as she had done as a child, she allowed music to fill her aging soul.

CHAPTER 29

Music of the Years Gone By

What are the sounds of a soul? For Mom, her soul soared with the music that danced before her eyes, flowed beneath her fingers, and floated from her lips. For her entire life, from her *intro* to her *coda*, music was the sound of her soul.

Mom was immersed in music at an early age. A dozen community band members played free concerts of elegant classical pieces and lively Broadway hits and marches on a small white gazebo with wooden gingerbread trim. I can picture Mom and her younger sisters clasping hands and dancing to George Gershwin's "Rhapsody in Blue," or sitting on the cool grass listening quietly to the soft sounds of "Stardust" by Hoagy Carmichael.

Effie also brought music into their home. Despite their poverty from the Great Depression and divorce, Effie owned a ragged old piano that she painted in two different colors to hide exterior blemishes. But within the heart of the instrument, its strings still vibrated with sounds of life. Effie had minimal training and knew only one song by memory but wanted more for her children. Miraculously, she set aside enough money for occasional thirty-minute lessons, with the teacher giving each girl a ten-minute portion. Those lessons were the spark that set Mom's heart afire for the piano. By the time they were teenagers, the girls were accomplished pianists, playing together the "Sunshine Waltz" by H. P. Hopkins—a composition written for six hands on one piano.

Mom's love for music grew deeper with each passing year. She continued to teach herself after the lessons stopped and later learned the clarinet in high school. Music moved her like nothing else, as she described her feelings as a young adult.

To me, hearing beautiful, impressive music is almost like seeing a moving picture. Listening to a warm melodious song with my eyes closed, I can see moonlit waters lapping at marble steps in a lovely seashore garden in old Italy. Above, the stars seem as cut diamonds against blue velvet. The song ends and the scene fades.

Next comes a very rich and fiery composition. In this picture there are twirling skirts, stomping feet, and eyes and smiles that flash in sunny Spain as the village people dance in the square.

The music changes and I see a green forest. Two peasant lovers stand at the bottom of a pool of sunlight that streams through the top of a linden tree. They pour out their love to each other but no one is there to hear except a little brown thrush, his song ringing clearly and sweetly through the trees.

When Mom married and started her own family, she was determined to pass this gift of music to each child. Mike learned to play the trombone and was in the Purdue Marching Band in college. Pat animated the coronet and baritone horns. Janet's musical experiences seemed to be pressed from the same mold as Mom. She started piano lessons as a young child, later took voice lessons alongside Mom, and performed duets at Oak Grove Church. She then learned to play the organ, the flute, and the piccolo, while earning lead roles in high school musicals. She also performed with a Purdue concert band. Tom took piano lessons, and then expressed himself through the trombone, coronet, and French horn. While in high school, he also sang in the high school choir. Julie learned to play the piano and organ at a young age, and when she was older, sang at church. She also mastered the flute.

While my older siblings were demonstrating their musical prowess, I was busy proving to Mom that not all her children were like her. I was the sour note in the family composition.

On a Saturday morning in my mid-elementary years, I sat in my pajamas in our paneled family room watching cartoons. The smell of burned wood lingered in the fireplace from the previous night. Mom was tidying up the room around me. She paused as she approached my chair and then started a conversation rather nonchalantly.

"Kerry, I think it's time you start piano lessons."

"No, I don't wanna do that."

"You mean you don't *want to* do that. Why?" The tone in her voice changed slightly.

"Well, I've got other things to do."

"Kerry, I think you'll enjoy it. Music is fun. And it'll make you happy."

"I'm already happy. I'm happy just going to the ditch with Bryan."

"You won't be able to go to the ditch for the rest of your life. But you can enjoy piano for the rest of your life." The conversation started to feel like a lecture.

"How do you know I can't go to the ditch for the rest of my life? I just might. You don't know."

"Well, that's not really the point. There's so much more to music. And the piano is easy to learn. I think you'll like it."

"I don't think so," I said, adamantly.

"Well, I do. I've talked to Mrs. Brock, and you and Julie are going to start lessons next Wednesday, after school."

That was the end of the conversation.

When Wednesday came, I was at Mrs. Brock's house as Mom promised. It was a small, three-bedroom home with a cut stone façade, nestled in some rustling sycamore trees along the narrow highway 331, just two miles from our house.

With short, salt and pepper hair and wire-rimmed glasses, Mrs. Brock was a pleasant and proper woman. She sat on a chair just behind and to the left of the piano bench where I sat. I stared at the children on the cover of the lesson book she handed me. They looked remarkably like Dick and Jane from my First Grade Reader years earlier. These smiling music-loving children sat dutifully upright on the piano bench with their fingers arched perfectly over the keyboard as if their hands once held bubbles aloft, then froze permanently in that position. The musical notes printed inside the book were nearly the size of golf balls. I was certain even a blind man could spot them on the page. Maybe this was Mom's idea of fun, but it wasn't going to be mine.

As the afternoon sun streamed through the window, the torture began.

First, I learned middle C was located in the middle of the keyboard. Then I was taught how to play middle C with my right thumb, repeatedly pushing down on the hard, white key and releasing: *C—C—C—C—C*. I played middle C so many times I was ready for a *C-esta*. Then Mrs. Brock patiently instructed how to play middle C with my left thumb, which was remarkably similar: *C—C—C—C—C*. Not surprisingly, playing middle C with my left thumb was no more fun than playing it with the right.

"Okay, now we're going to mix it up," Mrs. Brock said with genuine glee. "You need to alternate playing middle C with your left and right thumbs."

As I played: *C (right)—C (left)—C (right)—C (left)—C (right)—C (left)*, my head rocked side to side like the clicking metronome, which sat on the piano lid above me, making me dizzy. For a young boy more comfortable making rafts to float down the ditch, wiring together an electric hot dog cooker, or chasing wild chickens into the corn fields, learning to play the piano was like learning to drink poison. I knew it would kill me sooner or later.

My family had no money for the music lessons any of us kids took, so Mom cleaned neighbors' homes or bartered with the teachers to pay for the instruction. In my case, Mom cleaned Mrs. Brock's home week after week during the hour Julie and I took our lessons.

After months of being trapped in Mrs. Brock's torture chamber every Wednesday afternoon with little progress to show, Mrs. Brock said, "Fuzz, let's see how you've progressed since last week." I looked out the window and saw dry sycamore leaves blowing across her lawn as she opened the book with the giant notes to "Mary Had a Little Lamb." "Play this," she said, nodding toward the poisonous page.

My shoulders slouched in defeat before I even started. I hadn't practiced this song all week.

"Sit up," she said. "You can't play slouched over like that. Sit up tall like you're proud of yourself."

I sucked in my stomach.

"No," she stated sternly, sitting more upright than before. "Pull your shoulders back like I've shown you." She grabbed my skinny shoulders from behind and forced them into position. "Now start."

I placed both thumbs on middle C, ready to embarrass myself.

"Fuzz," she interrupted. "Where does your left hand go for this song?" I stared at her blankly. Then she asked, "What's the first note you're going to play with the left hand?"

I studied the golf balls intently. "E?"

"That's correct. "

"But that's what I'm doing," I pleaded.

"No. You're left pinky needs to be on low C. Instead, you have your thumb on middle C. Try again."

I lined my hands up correctly, studied the giant notes, and began pressing the keys: *E—D—C—D—E—E—E*. I played haltingly with my right hand as my eyes bounced from the book to the keyboard and back again. The notes played by my left hand echoed after my right hand, as I struggled unsuccessfully to play them simultaneously. If the song were sung the way I played, it would have sounded like *Ma-Ma, ry-ry, had-had, a-a, lit-lit, tle-tle, lamb-lamb.*

"What is wrong, Fuzz? How many times have we practiced this? Now play it again, but play the notes of each hand at the same time, like it's written."

I began again: *E—D…*

"Stop," she nearly yelled. "Look at your hands." I stared down, but I already knew what was happening. They were shaking nervously. "Do you see how straight your fingers are? You're banging on the keys like a hammer. Now do it again, but correctly this time." I curved my hands like a spider, hoping one of them might bite Mrs. Brock, then started over.

Ma-Ma, ry-ry, had-had… Just then, she slapped her lap with a rolled-up music book as if she had seen the spiders I had imagined. Startled, my hands jerked from the keyboard.

"Berthella," Mrs. Brock shouted from the studio. "Would you come here, please?"

Mom popped into the room. "What's the matter?"

Without taking a breath, Mrs. Brock let it all out. "Your boy is not learning. He's no better than he was when we started lessons nearly a year and half ago. You're wasting your money, and I'm wasting my time. I no longer want him as a student."

Although I could have been insulted and angry, I was relieved by her words. Mrs. Brock told Mom what I had been trying to tell her from the beginning, that I was not a piano player and she couldn't make me be one.

Mrs. Brock was the key that unlocked me from my prison of bars and staves. Mom didn't argue with her. I assume it was difficult to argue with the obvious. So that was the end of my piano lessons. I had been right, and Mom was wrong.

❧

After all her children were grown and gone, Mom bought a new console piano for the living room. She also purchased a vibraphone and sang in a women's community choir to entertain civic groups and nursing homes in the region.

Like most people, Mom loved the music of her formative years. For her it was the 1920s, 30s, 40s, and 50s. Stacks of decades-old sheet music—mostly from garage sales, friends, and childhood—sat on floors and shelves, and in boxes around the house. The same is true for her vast collection of vinyl records. As she worked around the house or relaxed after church on Sunday afternoon, she often put a stack of 78s on the turntable and drifted into a happy place.

Music brought joy to Mom. But it was the piano she returned to year after year. Though she had stubby thick fingers with a thick nodule on a middle finger joint of her right hand, she had an amazing reach and dexterity. She'd often sit at the piano late at night, after others settled in for bed, and snap on a single light to illuminate the maze of black lines and dots. She'd tilt her head back to peer through bifocals, then begin to release the notes for an audience of stars.

Music spoke to her heart and soul. Her body relaxed, her face glowed, and she left her worries behind. When Mom's hands melded with the keys, you knew she was at peace. She was hearing, seeing, and feeling the vibrations of life in the beauty she created. As she played one of her lifetime favorite songs, "Stardust," the lyrics entranced her as much as the haunting melody of strings, surely evoking unspoken memories of the years gone by.

❧

Over time, I learned to appreciate the music of my youth. When I married and our only child, Elizabeth, came along, I was determined she would have piano lessons, too. But things were different for her than they were for me. One, I resisted the temptation to force her to learn (although she might disagree with that statement). More importantly, she demonstrated natural talent. So at four and one-half years old she began weekly lessons. One day a week I took Elizabeth to the piano teacher's house and watched her learn. The other six days I coached her at our piano, helping her enjoy the vibrations of its strings.

Because she was so young, Elizabeth first learned to play by ear. With her sharp mind and natural talent she blew past "Mary Had a Little Lamb" before Mary even knew she had a lamb. Well before the age when I was stumbling with that same young sheep, Elizabeth had mastered classical pieces from Beethoven and Vivaldi, playing pages of beautiful music with both hands, all from memory. She soon became proficient at reading music, as well.

Although I watched this evolution with my own eyes, it was still difficult to believe and to resist the tears that threatened to spill as I sat beside her on the bench. Her music was the most beautiful sound ever made in our home. When she played, she was happy. And when she was happy, I was happy.

As a child, I resisted Mom's efforts to inculcate me with the love of piano. But Elizabeth's playing reawakened in me what lay dormant for decades. As I coached her at home, I learned along with her. And I enjoyed it. I soon found myself sitting at the piano late at night, after she had gone to bed and the house was quiet, plunking out a song one note at a time with my index finger, as my foot rested on the "soft" pedal to not awaken her. Later, I began to put my fingers in the proper positions on the smooth keys and use all five digits on my right hand. Haltingly, recognizable tunes began to flow.

I finally got up the courage to start my own lessons with Elizabeth's teacher. After Elizabeth finished warming the bench, I sat at the same spot, with the same teacher, and learned my own music, although I needed more light to read it.

Each semester our teacher organized a recital for her students. I was not exempt, although I was a giant among them; some students' feet didn't even reach the floor from the piano bench. But this humbling experience birthed an idea. Mom and Dad lived in Indiana and I lived in Texas, and they planned to fly out for one of the recitals and to see me play. Rather than just watch me, I called Mom on the phone and asked if she wished to join me.

"You mean in a duet?" she said.

"Yes. Do you want to join me in the recital?"

Mom chuckled at the thought. She was in her eighties and her skills had waned. "What would we play?"

"We could pick whatever we want. My teacher won't mind."

"I've got some duets in my stacks of music," Mom said. Her voice gained energy.

"Well, I'm not that good, Mom. It can't be anything difficult."

"It's stuff from when I was a kid. I even have music for a trio… music that my sisters and I used to play." We both paused, thinking about what she had just said. Then Mom broke the silence.

"Hey, what if we played a trio? You, Elizabeth and me." The thought was voiced. I laughed out loud at what sounded like a ludicrous idea to a neophyte like me. "And I know just what song I want to play. I'm sure I still have it. It's called 'Sunshine Waltz.'"

After the call, Mom found "Sunshine Waltz," which was released in 1936, and sent me a photocopy. I was the least skilled of the three of us, but I decided I could handle this piece. We agreed who would play which parts—I would have the easier middle part—and began to practice separately. The piece was written for six hands on one piano, and I soon saw several problems. With Mom on one end, she would not be able to read the sheet music through her bifocals at the far side of the music stand. But we had an even bigger problem. Two adults and a child would not fit on a single piano bench. Fortunately, our piano teacher had a solution. She had a high quality electric keyboard she was willing to set next to her piano for the recital. That would allow two of us to sit at the piano and one at the electric keyboard, each with our own sheets of music.

Elizabeth and I practiced our parts, while Mom practiced at her house. As the day of the recital approached, we realized we needed to rehearse together. Mom and Dad were not due to arrive until the day of the recital, so we decided to rehearse over the phone.

"Hi, Mom," I spoke into the cordless handset on another call home. "Are you ready to practice?" Elizabeth and I were already sitting together in front of our piano.

"Yes, but how are we going to do this?"

"I'll set our handset on the music stand so you can hear our piano, and you do the same at your end," I said. "Hopefully we can hear each other."

"Okay," she replied as we each laid our phones into position.

"Can you hear me now?" I spoke in the direction of the prone mouthpiece.

"What?" I could barely hear her small voice.

"Can you hear me?"

"Yeah, I can now. I moved the phone a little closer."

"What? I didn't hear you," I shouted back.

Now Mom raised her voice and shouted back at her handset lying on her console. "I said, I can hear you now!"

"Okay. I'll count twice and then we'll start. Ready?"

"What?"

I shouted back, "I said I'll count to three, two times and then we'll start."

"Okay."

Elizabeth rolled her eyes as she waited for my cue. I spoke loudly with a waltz tempo and a melodic tone, "*One*, two, three. *One*, two three…"

What followed, sounded more like a sonic train wreck than a waltz, with each of the three parts mangled and piled on top the other. With the difficulty hearing, and the inability to sense each other's actions through sight, none of us started at the same time, played at the same pace, or consistently hit the correct notes. Within seconds, we all burst out laughing, unable to play any further. So we tried again. And again. And again, with the same results. The song never came together. It seemed this was a ludicrous idea after all.

Unbeknownst to me, Dad was sitting in the room near Mom and listened to the whole thing. He told me later that he was embarrassed for us before the recital even began. He saw no path to success for this calamitous trio. For him, it was like watching an episode of *The Three Stooges*. But he didn't intervene or share his reservations at the time. He let us children frolic.

When the day of reckoning arrived, Elizabeth and I sat together at the piano in front of rows of chairs set up in our teacher's living room. Mom took her seat at the adjacent electric keyboard. With our backs to the audience, I looked to my left at my daughter and to my right at my mother. I was the connection between the two. My mother loved piano and did her best to introduce it to me. In turn, I passed the gift onto my child. In a surprise blessing, Elizabeth then returned the gift to me tenfold in a joy for piano I had never known. As we sat there, I was poised to pass this gift back to my mother to complete the circle of love.

With a waltz tempo and a melodic tone, I whispered so only those two could hear me, "*One*, two, three. *One*, two, three…" and nodded as we began. Then a miracle happened. Beautiful music flowed from our instruments as if we were one set of hands. More than seventy years and a thousand miles had separated the oldest from the youngest, and where I had once turned my back on my mother's music, now it brought us together. We were complete. My mother and I were reconciled. And music filled our souls.

ℰ

After a couple of years of piano lessons, I stopped when my life got busier and my learning plateaued. Although my piano now sits forlornly in the corner, I have a retirement goal to return to this source of happiness. My mother was right, after all. Just as she did, I can enjoy the piano for the rest of my life and I intend to do so.

CHAPTER 30

Lonely Heart

LONELY! And what of that?
Some must be lonely; 'tis not given to all
To feel a heart responsive rise and fall,
To blend another life within its own:
Work can be done in loneliness. Work on.

DARK! Well, what of that?
Didst fondly dream the sun would never set?
Dost fear to lose thy way? Take courage yet!
Learn thou to walk by faith, and not by sight;
Thy steps will guided be, and guided right.

—Excerpted from "COURAGE! PRESS ON," by
Berthella Stevens

"Daddy, something's wrong with Mommy!" Janet cried as she tugged at his pant leg in the summer of 1956. Dad was guiding the rototiller through the garden. Although he couldn't hear her words, he could see the fear in his five-year-old daughter's eyes. He quickly turned off the noisy engine. As the smell of gasoline lingered in the air he asked, "What's the matter, Janet?"

"Daddy, something's wrong with Mommy!" she blurted again, twisting a blond pigtail between her fingers. "I don't know what to do."

"Where is she?"

"In the bathroom. She won't open the door."

Dad's long legs carried him quickly through the soft garden dirt, then across the grass toward the back steps. He could hear the wails even before he got to the farmhouse. He flung open the wooden screen door and leapt three stairs to the top of the steps and passed through the empty kitchen before the screen door banged closed behind him. Now Mom's deep sobs were louder and more painful as he rushed toward the bathroom and pushed open the door.

Mom sat sprawled in blood on the floor with her underwear around her ankles and her dress hiked high. She leaned against the side of the toilet, her hands cupped over the bowl, as her shuddering cries gripped my father. The blood on the floor, on her clothes, on her arms, was alarming.

He dropped to his knees beside her, "Berthella, what's the matter?" He was nearly shouting in her face as tears flooded her eyes, but still couldn't get her attention over her primal screams.

In the panic, he couldn't tell what happened but he knew she needed a doctor before things got worse.

Dad grabbed Mom under one arm to lift her as new beads of sweat formed on his brow. "Berthella, we need to get you to the hospital."

But the wails continued and Mom wouldn't budge. She was dead weight—unable or unwilling to stand.

Dad quickly positioned his body so he could partially lift her with his muscular shoulders. As he began to pull her up, a grisly mass slipped from her hands into the toilet and Mom screamed, "Noooo! I can't leave! I can't leave without my baby!"

Mom's hands dove into the water as she frantically fished out what Dad now saw was a tiny body, partially obscured in its placenta, still attached to the cord. Now he understood. Mom had been twenty weeks pregnant with their fifth child. And their lifeless baby was cradled in Mom's shaking hands.

CƷ

When I reflect on the arc of my mother's life, I see it bent toward loneliness.

It began with the father she never had, who left or was banished from the family, leaving Mom feeling vulnerable and scared as a child. There was no male presence to encourage her, to affirm her identity, or tell her she was loved. To know she had a father "out there, somewhere," who didn't care enough to be sure they had food and clothing, was almost too much to bear. Her entire life, Mom carried a deep sadness with her about her absent father, saying forlornly as an adult, "I don't know why Daddy left us."

Mom tried to escape this dark shadow by marrying my father, a stable family man. Although living on a farm had been Mom's dream since childhood, she encountered her Old Country in-laws who provided daily reminders that she didn't measure up as a proper housewife. And with her mother and sisters living at a distance, and no phone, Mom felt isolated. She hungered for personal conversation. Of course she had Dad, but he was usually working, and when he was at home he was not the kind of man to engage in intimate conversation. Mom persevered.

Then she lost the baby and plunged into an abyss she could barely crawl out of.

How it happened, no one knows. My older siblings, young and innocent at the time, don't remember. And my parents discussed little of the stillbirth with us kids. So I've portrayed how I picture it happening. But the painful effects were undeniable. Although Mom physically recovered from the tragedy, for months afterward, she lived in the shadow of death, unable to leave her bed. Her four living children were too young to assume her household responsibilities, so my father hired an Amish woman to care for our family when Mom's sisters or mother were unable to be there.

I don't think a mother ever stops loving a child, even one that had developed only twenty weeks in the womb. I know Mom never did. Although she eventually pulled herself from the darkness, the weight of that child's death always lay on her heart like a pall.

But as light began to return to her life, my parents' dream of owning the farm was stolen after fourteen years of my mother's "nonconformity" as an Old Country farm wife.

Mom certainly carried heavy burdens.

Later in life, as Mom's heart problems and other physical ailments emerged, many in the family were skeptical, withholding emotional support for her struggles. And as we children grew, we complained about burned meals, smelly kitchens, and clothes lost in the tangled laundry room.

In 1968, when I was ten and Mom was forty-eight, she wrote the poem "My Day," which began like this:

> *The beginning day weeps—*
> *Soggy and gray.*
> *I feel so cold,*
> *Baggy and saggy,*
> *Crabby, wrinkled and old.*
>
> *The work's not done.*
> *I slouch around the house,*
> *No pep, no joy.*
> *I'm a miserable louse.*

In retrospect, it's easy to see why she'd write such poetry. Mom felt put down all her life and struggled to lift herself up in the absence of others' praise or affirmation.

"Often through the years," Mom revealed in a paper hidden by time, "I suffered depressing thoughts of inadequacy and disappointment to my family. Even when the family started to mature and the extra time and effort I devoted to the children started to bear fruit and the hard work lessened, the idea that I should have been better still reared its ugly head."

Nonetheless, her children remained her life's priority, even as we became adults and moved away to Hawaii, to Texas, to Alabama, to Illinois, with some living elsewhere in Indiana. At a family reunion one year, she shared with us that for her, the worst time of the day was "any time I get lonesome and want to talk with my children—but usually can't."

It wasn't just her kids she missed. Mom also yearned for the supportive relationships of a church-home at Oak Grove. Her pointed insistence that only she possessed "The Truth" left her with emotional isolation and a bruised and lonely heart. It was difficult to keep friends.

☃

Late in the autumn season of Mom's life, she became enchanted with a new friend named Marilyn. They were similar in age and great bosom buddies. During my frequent phone conversations with Mom, I often heard stories about Marilyn and her going to a garden show, listening to an author speak about his book, or just riding together on a long drive for some errand Marilyn needed to do. They lived twenty miles apart, but that didn't seem to limit their relationship. When Mom spoke of Marilyn, her voice was light and airy, floating on a sea of joy. She'd never had a friend like that in my lifetime.

I traveled back to Indiana only once a year, and during the second year of Mom's and Marilyn's relationship, Mom invited me to go with her to visit Marilyn. So I got behind the wheel of Mom's beige Ford Focus and drove her to South Bend.

Mom and I followed the sidewalk under a canopy of walnut trees to Marilyn's modest ranch-style house and knocked on the door.

"Oh! What a surprise. I wasn't expecting you, Berthella," said Marilyn as she greeted us.

Marilyn's hair was dyed an unusual red chestnut and her hands quivered slightly as she clutched the door to hold herself steady.

"This is my son, Kerry, Marilyn. He's visiting all the way from Texas, and I just wanted you to meet him."

"Well, come in. Have a seat."

We walked down a hall to a musty family room paneled in dark wood while Marilyn fetched us glasses of too-sweet lemonade. She and Mom sat together almost shoulder-to-shoulder on a tattered gold couch, and I sat opposite them in a side chair watching quietly. Although Mom was heavier than Marilyn and wore glasses, they looked like two weathered peas in a pod.

Mom turned to Marilyn, "How have you been?"

"Oh, I've been fine. Can't complain."

"Well, I've been worried since I hadn't heard from you in a while." Mom lifted her left hand, spotted with age, and grasped Marilyn's right hand, which rested beside her on the couch. I never saw Mom hold another woman's hand before, and it thrilled my heart to see this companionship. Mom was so clearly very happy.

"My kids don't think I should be driving anymore, so they're always telling me I should stay home," replied Marilyn as she turned from Mom and looked in my direction.

"Oh, fiddlesticks. You drive fine. Don't let them tell you what to do."

"Well, they are my kids, Berthella," She said with resignation and maybe a touch of defensiveness as she returned her gaze toward Mom.

"Well, what about calling? You could still call me," Mom persisted, smiling.

"I suppose so…"

"Well what have you been doing?" Mom asked.

"Let's see… Last week I drove to Shipshewana to look at some antiques."

"Why didn't you call me? I would've loved to do that!"

"Oh, well, it was last-minute, I guess." Marilyn's eyes wandered the room as she spoke.

As I watched these delightful old ladies converse, each with a touch of rouge to color their paling faces, Mom squeezed Marilyn's hand more tightly. She was Mom's only close friend and had brought such needed joy late in life. Although their conversation seemed a bit socially unbalanced, I was happy that Mom had finally found a kindred spirit.

A few months later, as evening settled in around my home in Texas, I sat outside on my back patio cooling down after exercising and decided to call Mom just to check in.

"Hi, Mom. It's Kerry. How are you?" There was an unusually long pause before she answered.

"I'm okay, I guess," she said in a voice flattened by sadness.

"What wrong?"

"I hadn't heard much from Marilyn recently," she began haltingly. "And when I called her, a recording said her phone had been disconnected."

"What? I wonder how come?"

"That's what I wondered. I was actually somewhat alarmed, thinking something bad must've happened, but hoped it was only because she'd forgotten to pay her bill, or something like that." Mom's voice carried the weight of a broken heart. "So I got in the car and drove to her house to check on her. When I pulled in the driveway, I saw a 'For Sale' sign in the front yard."

Mom sounded like she was about to cry as she struggled to finish her story. I didn't interrupt.

"I could hardly believe it. She never said a word about wanting to move. So I knocked on her door to find out what was going on, and there was no answer. I walked around to the side of the house and peeked in the window… The place was empty."

"I'm sorry to hear that," I said, wondering how to soothe my mother's broken heart.

"So I walked through her yard to her neighbor's house and knocked on their door. The neighbor man told me her kids wanted her to move, but he didn't know where she'd gone."

There was silence between us except for muffled sniffles I could hear at Mom's end and chirping crickets at mine. The woman she thought was her best friend had left her without even saying goodbye.

Once again, Mom had tripped over the strength of her own personality. It was a chronic condition. But she found solace in writing
about this familiar challenge. This piece points to her loneliness and
the safe harbor of God's creation she sought during times of stormy
seas. Her friends might abandon her, but the trees would not.

I am most fortunate that I have a sink that looks out
over a small grove of trees; thirty trees occupy a space of
a little over a half acre. I get to watch the seasons come
and go, come and go. Is the repetition dull? Never. The
oft-repeated occurrences in my little grove are soothing
and stabilizing.

There is a healing balm for the wounded spirit when the
world has turned false. When I find that one whom I had always liked and respected from afar can only tolerate me and
be civil, or worse yet, cannot tolerate me and is very uncivil,
then I look at those trees. They don't turn their backs to me.
I can even go across the road to the grove and touch them.
They are there, anchored to the ground.

They do not have legs; they cannot walk away while I'm
talking. They do not have voices that berate me or recite
my faults. No, they are quiet, steadfast, and loyal. They
stay put... They are my friends, slowing the wind around
the house, giving shade on hot summer days and fruit in
season...

All this is part of the trees' promise to us: "We will stick by
you through heat and cold, through wind and rain, through
poverty and prosperity. We will never leave you or your children, or your children's children, through any will of our
own. We are your friends."

CʒƷ

It was a warm summer day in Indiana, perfect for our family reunion. I sat with some of my adult siblings, now with hair in shades of gray, at a long wooden table covered in yellow plastic in my brother's garage, away from Mom and the rest of the family. The large doors were open and flies buzzed around the paper plates stealing the last crumbs of cherry pie as we explored the social challenges our mother faced.

"On the surface, Mom's an outgoing, gregarious person who makes friends easily. She never met a stranger." Tom said. "She can strike up a conversation with all different kinds of people."

"Yeah, that's one reason she was successful writing 'The Party Line' years ago," I added. "Starting conversations with strangers is one of her hallmarks."

"But there's a difference between *making* friends and *keeping* friends," said Julie, who stared forlornly at the table for a moment. "Mom has no more friends. She doesn't seem to know how to *be* a friend. I've talked with her about things I'd see her do or say, but she can't seem to change her behavior… I know when she was a kid the sisters had to stick together and didn't get to develop friendships. So maybe that contributes. But Mom's critical side, the know-it-all side, ticks people off. She doesn't know when to stop talking, to stop trying to prove a point, to stop trying to convert someone to her beliefs… Not having friendships has been really hard on her."

"Clearly, she struggles with relationships," Janet said. "She isn't socially adept. I think she inherited that from Grandma Effie. She was raised to believe that she knew the answer to *everything*. Unfortunately, others find that off-putting and feel their opinions don't matter as much because 'Mom knows the truth' about whatever the topic is. That ate away at friendships she had… That makes me so sad," Janet said, looking away. "As nice as Mom is, and clever, and intelligent, she doesn't know how to maintain friendships."

"But I believe there's more to Mom's lonesomeness than just the fragmented relationships," Janet continued. "That period when she took anti-depressants was so nice. She was kinder to Dad and to others, and less crabby. I was so happy for her. I just wish she would have continued. They let her true feelings come out."

❧

While that family conversation brought no resolutions, the insights shared and the lens of time gave me clarity. Regardless of its cause, Mom had a lonely heart. Over the course of her life, she carried heavy burdens. She longed for a father she never had and a child who never lived. On the farm, she was isolated from the intimate conversations she had known with her sisters and mother and was broken by the theft of her dreams when she didn't measure up in the sight of her in-laws. When her growing family was living at home, she didn't receive the encouragement she needed; then, she spent her days missing us after we'd grown and left home. And try as she might, it was vinegar, not honey, she offered her friends.

As a child, I was completely unaware of anything I'd label as depression or loneliness. Mom was simply an enchanting person. Even as an adult, I had only an amorphous understanding of the challenges she faced, since I lived more than a thousand miles away. But as I've talked with family members and poured through Mom's written words, her loneliness has become real for me. I now feel her pain, with my own aches of empathy and regret.

But out of this dark cloud has emerged a stronger ray of light that shines on my mother. I see a woman who was stronger than I once believed. Who possessed more grit than I credited her for. And who deserves my admiration even more. Mom didn't let her loneliness define her. With courage and strength she fought her emotional battles and never gave up. She was a winner, believing the sun would always come out and chase away the clouds of despair.

CHAPTER 31

The Space Between Us

"This is the Lord's battle, and that so far as politics or social questions are concerned, you have no real solution. It is no part of your work to share in the struggle, for that it is the Lord's doing. Instead, you should press along the line of your own mission, proclaiming the heavenly kingdom at hand as the only remedy."

—Pastor Charles Taze Russell, adapted from
"The Divine Plan of the Ages," 1886

"Any religion that professes to be concerned with the souls of men and is not concerned with the slums that damn them, the economic conditions that strangle them, and the social conditions that cripple them is a dry-as-dust religion. Such a religion is the kind the Marxists like to see—an opiate of the people."

—Rev. Martin Luther King, Jr.,
"Stride Toward Freedom," 1958

"**Y**es, thank you… Thank you, Lord," my childhood preacher announced with quiet confidence from the oak pulpit. "If you accept Jesus in your heart this morning, just raise your hand… Yes, thank you for that."

I stood with my family in front of the worn wooden pew with my eyes closed and head bowed, holding my mother's right hand. Pastor Brown, a middle-aged man in glasses and a dark gray suit, continued his altar call in our simple Oak Grove Church, built to serve the area farmers.

"Yes…there. Thank you… Thank you, Lord." His voice spread like honey over the dozen families who worshipped in our tiny church surrounded by cornfields and country roads.

Although I had only recently started elementary school, I could do math. I stood there reverently in my pressed trousers and hand-me-down shirt, and silently counted each "yes" I heard, one for each person who presumably just accepted Jesus into his or her heart. There were nearly as many yeses as the thirty people in the sanctuary.

"If you want to be saved, just raise your hand. There's no need to speak or open your eyes," continued Pastor Brown as the organist played "Just as I Am" like a slow lullaby. If I hadn't been counting, it might've put me to sleep. "Just listen to the Lord and let Jesus into your heart… Yes, thank you."

I tilted my head to the side and squinted one eye open, hoping Mom's eyes remained tightly closed. Our church had no stained glass or air conditioning, and through the opened windows in the soft morning light I could see the white clapboard parsonage perched on a gentle rise. But what I really wanted to see was who was raising their hands. There were six of us in our family at church and we never raised our hands, so that only left two dozen of our neighbors.

"Yes… Thank you."

Darn, I missed that one, I thought as my opened eye scanned the room. I felt like I was hunting squirrels with a BB gun and one had just run behind a tree. As I waited for another, I wondered how we could have so many people who got "saved" during the altar calls. *Maybe it's the same people who keep getting saved over and over because it didn't work before, or maybe they just keep sinning and need do-overs.*

Just then, a fly buzzed my face and landed on my cheek. I raised my free hand and swatted him away.

"Yes! Thank you," said the preacher.

Oh my gosh, did I just get saved? The thought made me chuckle and Mom squeezed my hand, warning me to keep quiet.

ɞ

In the beginning, there was no space between my mother and me. My views about religion reflected hers, although Oak Grove Church formed the cornerstone of my understanding.

Our entire family attended Oak Grove Church. We never missed a Sunday, although we were usually late. That meant we often missed seeing the preacher signal the start of the worship service by ringing the steeple bell. It also meant we usually sat in the back row. In some ways, sitting in the back symbolized our somewhat detached relationship with Oak Grove. We never raised our hands to be saved and neither I nor my siblings were baptized, although Mom had been at a distant tent revival. We also never joined the church despite decades of regular attendance. That was because Mom refused to recite a traditional creed required for membership. Since she was our family's spiritual leader, none of us crossed through that gate into the fold of the church. Mom had been raised with the teachings of the late Pastor Russell who believed such creeds were symptoms of wrong beliefs.

Nonetheless, Oak Grove Church shaped the start of my spiritual journey. My elementary Sunday school teachers used clingy felt figures to show Moses coming down from Mt. Sinai with the Ten Commandments. They also set a paper boat afloat on a bubbling sea of vinegar and baking soda to tell the story of Jesus walking across the stormy water to his frightened disciples in the boat. And I was frequently reminded through kids' songs that Jesus loved little children like me.

My spiritual nurturing continued at home. Mom spent hours reading the Bible and took every opportunity to connect its contents with our lives. While watering her multi-colored plants she could launch into a retelling of the story of Joseph's coat of many colors. Or, a particularly rainy day could bring talk about the different levels on Noah's ark where all the animals lived.

But Mom's view of God was much bigger than Noah's ark. It encompassed all of Creation and the natural world. She saw God in the unfurling of a flower, in the butterflies that landed there, and the rainbows that crossed the sky. "God created the heavens and the earth," Mom often reminded me, and if I wanted proof that God existed I only needed to gaze into the star-studded sky.

On Christmas Eve in 1968, I wiped condensation from the cold window so I could do that. There was a crescent moon hanging in the western sky. Although I couldn't see anything unusual about the moon, I knew there was something remarkable going on because it was being broadcast on the television behind me. We had gathered as a family to glimpse a part of God's creation we'd never seen before.

I turned around and glanced at the TV. "Hurry, Mom! It's starting," I shouted upstairs in her direction. I plopped down beside Julie on the couch in our basement family room. Tom munched a bowl of salty popcorn while Janet sat apart from the others. Dad sat on the hearth poking a crackling fire. As Walter Cronkite recounted Apollo 8's journey to the moon, removing then replacing his dark-rimmed glasses as he spoke, I heard Mom's footsteps coming down the wooden stairs. I slid to the end of the couch so she had room.

"What did I miss?" she asked as she sat down beside me and I curled up with my head on her full-figured lap.

"He said this is their last orbit. They've finished all their scouting for a future landing site," I squealed. "Now we're looking at actual pictures of the moon through the window of their spacecraft!"

"Isn't that something!" Mom exclaimed, smiling. "God's handiwork right here on TV. Look at that!"

As the sun rose on the moon, casting long shadows across the craters, we saw a surface stark and gray, but beautiful. From his perch seventy miles above the moon's surface, Major William Anders pointed out the Sea of Triton, several thirty-mile-wide craters, and the Sea of Tranquility, a relatively smooth spot planned for the first landing.

"Wow. This is neat," was all I could say as my wide eyes remained glued to the screen.

Between beeps, NASA and the astronauts took turns speaking, and then without warning, Anders said, "For all the people on Earth, the crew of Apollo 8 has a message we would like to send you." He paused briefly, then began reading the story of Creation from the book of Genesis. "In the beginning God created the heaven and the earth. And the earth was without form, and void; and darkness was upon the face of the deep. And the Spirit of God moved upon the face of the waters. And God said, 'Let there be light': and there was light. And God saw the light, that it was good: and God divided the light from the darkness."[1]

All three astronauts were deeply religious men and took turns reading the Creation story, acknowledging the Creator of the very body that they orbited. Science, which had gotten them to the moon and often seemed at odds with God, now coexisted with God on national television while much of America celebrated the birth of God's son.

At the conclusion of the reading, Colonel Frank Borman added, "And from the crew of Apollo 8, we close with good night, good luck, a Merry Christmas, and God bless all of you—all of you on the good Earth."[2]

It was a breathtaking moment as our astronauts seemingly eyed the face of God and allowed us to share in the experience. I felt close to God and to my mother, and sensed hope for a bright future.

Unbeknownst to me as a child, it was a miraculous night all over the country. Many Americans felt beaten down as the year came to an end. Martin Luther King, Jr. and Bobby Kennedy had been assassinated, riots rooted in racism had burned across the land, and the Vietnam War sent home more boys in body bags than ever before. In the presidential election, the political party that escalated the war had been ousted in favor of the party that promised to end it. For many, society seemed to be ripping apart at its seams. We were a nation divided. But that Christmas Eve was special. For the first time, humans—Americans!—left the Earth and flew to the moon. And the occasion was marked by reflecting on the presence of God. Although we were separated as a people, the godly words and experiences of the astronauts united society on that Christmas Eve. It was a healing balm for the nation.

As I snuggled with Mom, I had no idea that evening would also symbolize my own spiritual journey—a journey where I launched into the darkness and pulled away from the *terra firma* of my mother's faith.

♋

High school marked the beginning of my spiritual separation, at least the visible part. In the preceding years, Mom's constant claims of possessing "The Truth," plus her unrelenting Bible lessons, served as wedges. Each unwanted and misplaced comment was like the strike of a hammer on the wedge, slowly splitting us spiritually apart. The cracks were small and unnoticed at first. But by the time I started high school, many of the bonds had been broken. But it was Oak Grove Church that caused me to rocket away.

One Sunday, Julie and I sat in the backseat of our boxy Ford on our way home from church. Dad drove while Mom sat beside him telling him something the preacher said that annoyed her. Although the windows were closed, I smelled recently spread cow manure from a nearby field as I mindlessly watched the trees pass by. I was fifteen years old with the mind of a budding engineer and the moody hormones of a teenager.

"How was Sunday school, Kerry?" Mom suddenly asked, waking me from my daydream.

"Eh, it was okay, I guess…but not really."

"Why is that?" she asked, turning to see my face.

I paused when the car hit a pothole and bounced. "It's not fun anymore… There's hardly anybody there I know or get along with… and nothing makes any sense."

"Oh? What doesn't make sense?" Mom turned back around and looked straight through the front windshield.

I scoffed, "Like the story of Noah's Ark. You know how many species of animals there are, Mom? You know there's no way they all could fit in that one little boat…and with all their food. And somehow the polar bears got there from the Artic and didn't die. Stuff like that doesn't make any sense."

"I see," said Mom.

"And do ya know how much water it would've taken to cover the *entire* earth and all the mountains? There isn't enough water on the planet to do that… So I brought that up to Doug this morning. He's supposed to be my Sunday school teacher, but he couldn't explain it." Then I added mockingly, "He just said, 'God works in mysterious ways.'"

"Not everybody thinks like you do, Kerry. He might never have thought about that before."

"Okay, fine. Then why am I going to Sunday school if I'm not learning anything? And, Mom, you know there's only four of us in the whole Sunday school class. And I'm not friends with any of them."

Silence lingered in the air, and then she asked, "So what do you want to do, Kerry?"

I didn't have to think very long for that answer. "I don't want to go to church any more. I've had enough."

Dark shadows moved over the car as we passed beneath overhanging trees while Mom still stared out the front windshield. "Okay. That's fine," she finally said.

My body jolted in disbelief. *What? You're going to let me NOT go to church anymore? Just like that, with no argument? Am I still dreaming?*

❦

Although I stopped attending church, I still saw myself as a "good kid." I didn't drink, smoke, or swear and believed I never would. But through new friendships I made in high school, I stepped onto a slippery slope and lost my balance. I started smoking sweet-flavored cigars and quickly moved on to illegal substances. The first beer I swore I'd never drink led to copious amounts of liquor, which attracted unseemly behavior like a magnet. And the honesty in which I was grounded was replaced by thievery and manipulation. Because college lay ahead, I worked summers in a sweltering motorhome factory where I learned to curse with the best of them.

During all this, I had unbridled freedom at home and kept my secret life hidden from Mom. On many weekends when I arrived home in the wee hours, she'd be sitting alone in the living room with a single light on in the quiet house. As she heard the car drive in, she'd often pop up from her comfortable chair and attempt to greet me at the door in her cotton nightgown.

"Where have you been, Kerry?" she'd ask calmly, as if she were truly interested.

I stood in the dimly-lit hallway, unable to get by her. "Hanging out."

"Who were you with?" she queried, as she stepped in a bit too close for my comfort. She seemed to be checking my eyes and smelling my body, searching for signs of danger.

"Just Dave and them."

She asked all the questions a responsible parent would ask, but with a tone that wasn't pushy or accusatory.

Then I turned my body sideways and slipped by her without stopping, slinking down the dark wooden stairs to my bedroom in the basement.

In college, there was no need to hide my new self, which continued to expand. When I graduated with an engineering degree and took a job a thousand miles away in Tucson, Arizona, the excellent salary removed the last limit on my behavior. By the time I was twenty-five, I had violated nearly every commandment on God's Top Ten List, plus a few others that God apparently hadn't considered. I had separated myself from the religion of my youth, the teachings of my mother, and filled the void with the shadows of immoral and illegal behavior. My spiritual rocket spun into the darkness of deep space.

If my mother had known the truth of my life, she surely would have considered me "lost." And maybe she did feel that way. And maybe she silently prayed for me every day. But I didn't know if she did because we didn't talk about important things. Out of necessity on my part, our conversations remained on the surface, avoiding the large and increasing numbers of craters that scarred my life. I shared only a sanitized version of who I had become.

Janet had some sense of the life I was leading, and she expressed fear that I would get myself killed. I shrugged off her comment, even as problems mounted, and it became more difficult for me to deny I had lost my way.

❦

Because of limited career opportunities in Tucson, after a few years I requested a transfer to Austin, Texas, where my employer was starting a promising new mission. Although I had many friends in Arizona, I hadn't put down roots, so when the transfer was approved, I moved alone.

I sat in an aisle seat in nice slacks and white shirt on the flight to my new home. My skinny legs were long, and I stretched them out into the aisle. The seat next to me was empty, but a man a few years older than me stared out his window from the far seat as we began our ascent. After we reached cruising altitude, I received a cold Coke from the flight attendant and removed my seat belt, settling in for the 900-mile flight.

The steady whir of the jet engines was relaxing as I thought about my transition. It felt odd to be moving to a new city without taking tools with me. As an engineer, my primary tool was my brain. *If Dad moved from one city to another, an entire van of saws, hammers, and drills would have to go with him. And farmers can't just move their barns, silos, and herds of cows. They're stuck where they are,* I thought. *What freedom I have.*

I glanced out the window, past the face of the man who still stared at the clouds. The sun was high in the sky and reflected off the leading edge of the silver wing.

You know, it's almost like I'm starting over, I pondered. *In Austin I won't know a single soul. I'm leaving my entire adult life behind me in Tucson.*

I sighed when I thought about what was getting further away with each minute in flight. Yes, I'd had a lot of fun in my life. But there was a part of me—a rather large, heavy part—which no longer fit so well. I thought about the car accidents, the words of the counselor and the judge, the promiscuity, my abused body, the arrests, the broken relationships, and all the places I spent my time and money. It weighed me down. My face flushed when I thought about the pain that I incurred and caused others. *What's happening?* I thought. As I reflected on those unseemly aspects of the life I was leaving behind, I realized that ugly side of me could be washed away. I was moving to a new place, with new friends, and new work. A place where no one knew my past. I blinked back tears as I realized for the first time I had a stunning opportunity.

I felt the urge to fasten my seat belt to keep from floating away, unencumbered by the gravity of transgression. I was escaping the inertia that had pulled me into a life of darkness that I no longer wanted. In that moment, I did not sense God in my life, but it was certainly a godly moment of amazing grace. I had been given the gift of a new beginning and I intended to open it when I arrived in Austin.

Suddenly, the pilot interrupted my thoughts. "Ladies and gentlemen," I heard through the speaker above my head. "We're about to begin our descent into Austin. The flight attendants will be coming through the aisles to pick up your empty cups. Please fasten your seatbelts."

No, I thought, *I'm not beginning my descent into Austin. My descent began in high school, continued through college, and ended in darkness in Tucson. When I land in Austin, I'm beginning my ascent into something new and unknown.*

⊗

As I settled into my new home, I was careful how I spent my time and chose my friends. I also became a teetotaler once more. Although I sometimes wandered from this chosen path, I never changed direction. When I met Gloria and we discussed marriage, we affirmed a desire for God's presence in our relationship, as we both had in childhood, and committed to defining it together. We began by sitting together on a chaise lounge on Sunday mornings in our new house, reading the Bible out loud from cover to cover. It was a pleasant time, but tough to draw meaning from obscure or violent stories, the lists of names and numbers, and the repeated stories that were told differently each time they appeared.

After our daughter Elizabeth was born, we recognized that our Sunday morning Bible study wasn't going to give Elizabeth the spiritual foundation we envisioned. So we went to church. We shopped around and settled on the United Methodist Church, which was theologically "half way between this and that." Methodism did not believe in a literal interpretation of the Bible but felt its adherents should use all their God-given faculties to interpret the God-inspired text. Although Scripture was given primacy, Methodists were encouraged to also consider tradition, experiences, and reason. They weren't expected to "check their brain at the door," but to bring questions and doubt for exploration and personal growth. As an intellectual, that appealed to me.

When I dropped Elizabeth off at her new Sunday school class, it felt like a missed opportunity for me. Because I spent so many hours at work, and three-year-old Elizabeth went to bed early and still napped midday, we didn't have much time together. I learned her class needed another teacher, so I volunteered. I knew little about young children and nothing about teaching Sunday school, but the curriculum was provided. *What could go wrong?*

Early in my teaching tenure, I spent hours preparing for a lesson on how to pray. I sat on the floor in my home-office and pulled apart stickers, cut out paper hands and strips of paper, and glued and stapled things together for the little hands that were still learning such things.

My lesson plan was typed neatly and I made a big poster with the Bible verse expressed in words and pictures.

On Sunday morning, I got to class early to set up. The small room smelled of Play-Doh and was just wide enough for a long kid-sized table and kid-sized chairs. I set plastic tubs of crayons on the table and measured Goldfish snacks onto mini-plates in front of each chair. Although my mother never taught me how to pray, my lesson would teach Elizabeth and her class how to do so. After I finished setting up, I offered a silent prayer for God to use me to reach the children.

The room was soon filled with ten rambunctious three- and four-year-olds. I got on my knees to greet each one by name and helped them to the table as their parents left for other activities. I felt more energy in the room than normal, and the children laughed and shouted louder than usual as they adjusted to each other's presence. Just as I was ready to start the lesson, a mother and child arrived at the door who I didn't recognize.

"Hi, I'm Kerry, the Sunday school teacher. How are you?" I extended my hand to the mother and lowered my six-foot frame to greet her daughter.

"Hi, Kerry. My name is Barb and this is my daughter, Megan. Is it okay if I sit in the back of the class to observe? This is our first time visiting your church."

"Sure, of course. Have a seat."

I found a place for Megan and moved to the front of the room to begin the lesson, now a few minutes late.

"Good morning, everyone! How are you today?" I asked with my kid-friendliest voice.

None of the kids responded. They were too busy laughing and picking on one another. Then someone spilled their plate of Goldfish crackers on the floor and started crying, which prompted another child to cry even though nothing happened to her. I quickly consoled one child and picked up the crackers, then hobbled on my bony knees to attend to the second crier.

Things settled down a bit, and I returned to my lesson to explain that prayer was just talking to God.

"Hey, God!" shouted one giggly child. "I'm talking to you. Can you hear me?"

"Yes, God can hear you," I interjected. "But you don't need to shout to be heard. Let's use our inside voices." Then, other children began shouting as I tried to refocus the class. After I returned to my lesson plan, an argument broke out, followed by two tubs of crayons scattered across the floor. Soon the entire class was riotous with shouting and laughter, making it difficult to hear anything. Stickers were peeled off and stuck on clothing instead of paper, and the set of praying hands I had meticulously cut out for each child were crumpled up and thrown across the room. Then someone passed gas filling the room with a foul smell and eleven screams of "Eww!"

At the far end of the class, Barb, the visiting mother, sat quietly and expressionless. I knew her poker face was simply an act of kindness for my failed teaching.

When class was over, I was devastated and nearly in tears. Not only had I not made it through the lesson, but chaos had reigned throughout. The kids obviously learned nothing, and I probably scared away a new family from our church. I felt this was an important lesson at which I had unequivocally failed. I failed the kids and failed God and returned home in a state of depression.

After lunch, I sat alone on my recliner in the family room, trying to read the newspaper while my failed Sunday school lesson played over and over in my mind. Gloria and Elizabeth retreated upstairs to stay out of my moody way. When the phone rang, I forced myself to get up and answer it.

"Hi, Kerry, this is Susan. Is Elizabeth able to come over and play with Ashley?" Susan's family lived in our neighborhood and had recently been visiting our church. Four-year-old Ashley was in the Sunday school class I'd taught that day. Although Susan's voice sounded happy and light, I dreaded to hear what Ashley must have said to her mom about our class.

"Hi, Susan. Yeah, Elizabeth is here," I said, struggling to resurrect my happy voice. "Want me to walk her over to your house?"

"No, that's okay. Ashley and I will walk over to your place and pick her up."

"Sounds good. We'll see you in a few minutes."

"Oh, Kerry," Susan said as I was eager to hang up the phone. "There's one other thing." I shook my head and dreaded what was coming next. I didn't want to hear it.

"I want to thank you for teaching Ashley how to pray today during Sunday school," Susan told me. "That was something Phil and I wanted to talk with Ashley about but we didn't know what to say or how to have the conversation. She came home from your class and said she wanted to pray before we ate lunch, to thank God for our meal... Her words nearly took my breath away. So we talked for a few minutes about what she learned in your class, and for the first time we prayed together as a family. It was a very moving experience for Phil and me... and I just want to thank you."

I thanked Susan and hung up the phone as quickly as I could before the tears burst from my eyes. Although I had seen myself as a failure, God seemed to use that opportunity in even more powerful ways than I ever imagined. It lifted my spirits to realize the class was effective after all. But it transformed my heart to recognize that in the midst of what I perceived as failures, I had been in the presence of God. It was a powerful lesson for me, the teacher.

∝

During that time, my mother was thrilled that I had returned to attending church, and the space between us seemed to shrink a little. But she wasn't enamored that I'd joined a "mainline" denomination. The teachings of Pastor Russell, whom Mom greatly admired and followed, were "anti-establishment." Russell's followers were instructed to stay away from denominational instruction because the denominations didn't understand or follow the Bible correctly. So when Mom learned

I was teaching Elizabeth's Sunday school class, she was concerned I might be leading little children astray, prompting a package and the following letter to arrive:

Dear Kerry,

These green books were sent to me by the leader of our Bible study group when I asked for something I could send to you since you have the responsibility of teaching a Sunday school class (and maybe more classes later, since you're good at it). You'll need to know what's in the Bible and where to find it so that you don't get stuck in "traditional" or denominational teaching. Of course these books don't come close to containing all that is in the Bible but it's the best start.

The big book, called "The Divine Plan of the Ages," is the first in a series of six, written by Charles Russell. I've found he is the most published author on the Bible since Apostle Paul, and certainly the most beloved since congregations all over the world voted for him to be their pastor.

Pastor Russell said that "Truth-seekers should empty their vessels of the muddy waters of tradition and fill them at the fountain of truth." So if you have any questions—just ask. These writings to most people are as rich as fruitcake—not nutty, you understand.

The Divine Plan of the Ages was the second most important religious book in Mom's life, after the Bible. Written by Pastor Russell more than one hundred years earlier, it contained "The Truth" about God's plan for humanity, and Mom wielded its insights like a club throughout her life.

Although Mom and I were now both people of faith, her unwavering adherence to the unorthodox Pastor Russell and her unsolicited advice continued to split us apart, as they had during my adolescence.

Not only was her dusty, long-forgotten book not fit for three-year-olds, it wasn't even fit for adults. She had one thing right, though, in her letter to me. A fruitcake was an appropriate analogy. *The Divine Plan of the Ages* was indeed nutty, and too heavy to digest. It went the way of all fruitcakes, into the trash.

But there was another book I read which altered the trajectory of my life as much as Pastor Russell's changed Mom's.

Strength to Love is a collection of some of Rev. Martin Luther King Jr.'s sermons. Originally published in 1963, it reflects a fusion of Christian teachings with a social consciousness on issues of race and injustice in America. It's a theology he described as being concerned "with the whole man, not only his soul but his body, not only his spiritual well-being, but his material well-being."[3] King's wife, Coretta, wrote that the book "best explains the central element of Martin Luther King, Jr.'s philosophy of nonviolence: His belief in a divine, loving presence that binds all life."[4]

King's sermons spoke to my mind and to my heart. His insights were profound and his language poetic. I had to read slowly and deliberately as each paragraph felt like a fine dessert that tantalized my taste buds. King wrote of the need for Christians to have a tough mind and a tender heart,[5] while loving our enemies and being a good neighbor. And he characterized love as an action and not just an emotion.

In one chapter, King struck at the heart of my mother's belief that only she possessed "The Truth," writing:

> Life at its best is a creative synthesis of opposites in fruitful harmony. The philosopher Hegel said that truth is found neither in the thesis nor the antithesis, but in an emergent synthesis, which reconciles the two.[6]

When it came to the Bible and God's plan for humanity, Mom saw a world of right and wrong. She was always right and I (and nearly everyone else) was wrong. There was no reconciliation of views. But King allowed me to imagine a synthesis of gray between the black and white of my mother's world.

As I devoured King's book, his words struck me like lightning, clearing away the clouds that hung over traditional religious debates. His sermons contained deep insights, informing readers that "science investigates, religion interprets... The two are not rivals," then challenging them to "learn that to expect God to do everything while we do nothing is not faith, but superstition."[7]

Paragraph after paragraph broke my heart and fed my soul. His beautiful writing centered on God, showed me that being a Christian wasn't just about right beliefs but also about right actions. It was about doing the things that Christ did, not just about believing the things Christ said. King brought together my mind and heart in a rightful cause to act with my hands and feet.

My zealous reaction to King's words was similar to my mother's reaction to Pastor Russell's. Both of us were shaped and animated by what we read. But the worldviews we read from these two Christian leaders couldn't be more different. One instructed his followers to not engage in social issues because that was God's work to do, while the other implored his followers to engage because that was how God carried out God's work. Mom's journey traveled in one direction while mine took me in the other, increasing the space between us.

CB

Strength to Love left me hungry for more faith wisdom, and the desire to understand the racial and economic divide in which I lived. I poured over more of King's works and words. When I finished, I yearned to be like this intelligent man-of-the-cloth, this man of peace and courage, this man of deep thought and deep action. Although he, too, made grave mistakes, he modeled Jesus' teachings as he strove to be perfected into God's call on his life.

To appreciate King and the struggles of African-Americans more deeply, I planned a week-long family vacation to visit the most well-known sites of civil unrest in the South. Gloria, eight-year-old Elizabeth, and I visited the tiny town of Selma, Alabama, walked across the Edmund Pettus Bridge, and spoke with two people who had been a part of that bloody Sunday. We went to Montgomery, Alabama and drove past King's former home and church, and the spot where Rosa Parks was arrested. We visited the streets of Birmingham, where Bull Connor lashed out with dogs and fire hoses on children and civil rights activists, and where four little girls were brutally murdered with a bomb in the Sixteenth Street Baptist Church. And we crossed the spot near Anniston, Alabama, where a Greyhound bus carrying Freedom Riders was attacked and burned. It was a heart-wrenching trip. But I wouldn't trade it for anything because it made the suffering and struggle for justice real and personal. It carved away the mythology of the era, leaving bare the naked struggle of the oppressed, and those who had the strength to fight evil with love.

But more important to me than reliving these historical events, was experiencing the source of King's vision and strength. Above all else, Rev. King was a man of faith. So on Sunday morning, *before* we began our week-long Civil Rights tour, the three of us attended a worship service at Ebenezer Baptist Church in Atlanta This congregation was the congregation that King led, as did his father before him. It was here we needed to be grounded to prepare for the struggles we would relive in the week ahead.

Since King's death, the congregation moved to a new building across the street from the original church, and we sat in the back and admired the sweeping architecture, the stunning elevated baptismal pool, and large colorful hats of the women. Then, after being energized by gospel-style music, a preacher in a black suit and tie came to the pulpit. He was a tall man and one of King's cohorts from the 1960s, returning to Ebenezer to celebrate King's work. When I planned the trip, I was unaware it coincided with this special Sunday. I also didn't know that Coretta Scott King still attended church there. And because it was a special Sunday, the three King children were also sitting in the congregation. The preacher stood up at the paneled pulpit and recounted the work that he and Martin engaged in, their struggles and their triumphs, and how the presence of God guided their work. He spoke directly to King's children by name as he lifted up their father. And he preached in that familiar cadence of Southern black preachers. When I closed my eyes, I could hear King speaking—speaking to the congregation as an oracle of God's word—speaking to me, calling me to a life of faith in action.

After the service, Gloria and Elizabeth approached Mrs. King and asked for a picture. She graciously obliged. Today, that photo of Coretta Scott King, standing with her arm around eight-year-old Elizabeth, is one of my most cherished photos. Her embrace by the transformative power of love in America stands in sharp contrast to my own childhood experiences.

☙

As Elizabeth advanced to an older Sunday school class each year, I followed her as her teacher, gaining more insight and knowledge. I deeply researched and studied my lessons as if I were going to teach adults, then distilled the messages in a way that honored the curiosity, intellect, and playfulness of kids. Where Mom had used *The Divine Plan of the Ages* and a concordance as her Bible study aides, I used a highly-regarded study Bible with modern scholarly analysis and commentary and accessed the nearly infinite resources of the Internet.

As I matured in my faith, I recognized the Jesus whom King had spoken about. Jesus wasn't just a kind man who loved children and sought souls for eternal life. His heart broke for those suffering on the margins of society. He stated at the outset of his ministry that he had come for the poor, the prisoners, the blind, and the oppressed.[8] And he went on to tell his followers that whenever they fed the hungry, clothed the naked, cared for the sick, and visited the prisoners they were also serving him.[9] In the parable of the Good Samaritan, Jesus challenged his followers to go against the norm and cross social boundaries to address the needs of those hurting. He summarized the entirety of God's law in two simple commands: Love God and love your neighbors.[10]

Although Jesus promised he'd prepare a future place in Heaven for his followers,[11] he was also a rebel who opposed authority and challenged normal standards of behavior in order to transform the world in which he presently lived.

This was the man whom Dr. Martin Luther King and I both worshipped, and the man into whose life I was baptized as an adult.

King once said that most people are like thermometers that register the temperature of majority opinion, and not thermostats that change the temperature of society.[12] As a follower of Jesus, I wanted to be a thermostat for the transformation of the world.

With a fire burning in my soul, I experienced multiple "awakenings" to the issues in the world and how the love of God, expressed through my actions, might serve as a thermostat. Over time, I led adult ministries at our church and in other faith-based nonprofits focused on environmental stewardship, poverty in a developing nation, and racial healing in our community, as well as teaching Sunday school for twenty years.

While my mother focused on life *after* death, I concentrated on those wondering about life *before* death. I believed Jesus came to teach us how to live and love, not just how to be ready for death.

Although Mom and I possessed different worldviews when it came to faith, we shared a unique kinship because I was the only "churched" child in our family. That provided an important outlet for her to talk about this foundational component of her life. Once a week or so we'd chat on the phone for nearly an hour, and invariably the conversation turned to matters of faith and became monologues, as she revealed some arcane insight she'd gotten from a recent Bible study group, or the hope she retained for the greatness of the coming resurrection.

While we seldom agreed, we seldom argued. There was a time in my life when I had violated nearly all of the Ten Commandments, but when I accepted the gift of the new beginning, I renewed my commitment to honor my mother and father. In my mind, that meant remaining respectful and not arguing or pointing out what I saw as fallacies in her fruitcake. I usually just listened—or more accurately, tuned her out. I didn't try to understand who she was or why she believed what she believed. I just went silent. Although it felt rude to ignore such an elemental part of her being, that seemed prudent as a way to preserve family ties and avoid conflict. I saw no bridge across the divide.

಄

"Gracious God," began my preacher in his warm and inviting voice to all of us gathered in the sanctuary on Christmas Eve with our heads bowed, "we give you thanks on this holy night, that through your son's birth your love has broken through the barriers that separate us. That you have connected Heaven to Earth and you have brought eternity into our souls and love into our hearts. So we give you thanks for this gift of love that you place in our arms, whose name is Jesus Christ. And we ask that your love would draw our hearts close to each other as we draw closer to you. We ask this in the name of the infant born this night. Amen."

I lifted my head and opened my eyes. The altar area in front of me was draped with delicate green garlands. Large white candles burned on the altar table on each side of an opened Bible; and tall spruce trees, adorned with tiny white lights, stood at the sides of the room.

"You may be seated," instructed the pastor.

As I sat down on the cushioned pew, I looked to my right and saw smiles on the faces of Gloria and Elizabeth, a budding young lady with dark eyes and hair. As a family, we had never missed Christmas Eve service. Celebrating the birth of the man who led my life was the highlight of my year.

I turned my head and looked to my left. I saw the reason this Christmas was even more special. There, listening intently to the preacher recite the Christmas story from the book of Luke, sat my mother and father. This was the first Christmas they'd spent in Texas, a miracle since Dad didn't like to leave his house in the winter. But they'd made an exception, partly because they believed with their advancing age and decreasing mobility, this trip may be the last time they could travel to see me.

I looked at Mom, who sat beside me, and saw deep creases radiating from the edges of her eyes. The flickering light from the altar candles reflected in her glasses. The rouge on her cheeks, which sagged with the weight of years gone by, accented the lovely fuchsia dress she wore. I silently thanked God for the opportunity for us to be together on this special night.

"Would you please stand, as you're able, for our next song?" invited the music leader, as he raised his arms.

I grabbed a thick blue hymnal from the back of the pew in front of me and opened it to page 234 and offered it to Mom. "O Come All Ye Faithful" was a familiar tune and both of us knew the words by heart. But we stood side-by-side, each holding half the book, connected by the words we sang and the sounds of the organ that reverberated in the room.

O come, all ye faithful,
Joyful and triumphant,
O come ye, O come ye, to Bethlehem.

As we lifted our joyful voices, the words I'd heard so many times took on new meaning. Mom and I were the "faithful" who had come together as adults for the first time to celebrate the birth of Jesus. I felt closer to her as I slipped the hymnal back into its holder at the end of the song.

Mom's hands rested in her lap as she watched children in the front of the church prepare to light candles. I reached over and gently laid my open hand on top of hers. Without looking at me, she simply rotated her palm to mine and we clasped our hands together. Though age had robbed the suppleness of her skin, her hand felt strong.

At the front of the church, a child began the story of the Advent candles placed in a wreath, which symbolized the meaning of Christmas.

"The first candle," the young boy announced, "is the candle of Hope." As he spoke, a young girl struggled with a long candle lighter to reach one of the four candles in the circle of greenery.

As I held Mom's hand, I thought about the meaning of hope. *Mom and I both believe that the love of God expressed through Jesus brings hope to a hurting world. Though Mom is focused on life after death, and I'm focused on life before death, it's the same hope.*

"The second candle," the boy said "is the candle of Peace." As he spoke, the girl lifted her lighter to ignite the wick on the adjacent candle.

Mom and I both hold peace in our hearts, I thought. *Though she longs for a future world renewed like the Garden of Eden where pain and fighting will be no more, and I yearn for an earthly world of nonviolence, it's the same peace.*

The young boy at the front glanced at the paper in his hands and read out loud, "The third candle is the candle of Joy." Now the girl moved to the other side of the wreath to reach the third candle with her lighter. But I was lost in reflection.

Clearly, Mom and I both hold joy in our souls. She finds it in Creation around her: in the stars, the flowers, the rainbows, and butterflies. And so do I! It's the same joy!

My heart quickened and my face warmed as I began to recognize the ties that bound us together. Lost in my thoughts, the children had become invisible but their words were enlightening.

"The fourth candle is the candle of Love."

Mom and I both hold love in our hearts. We both love God. While I express God's love through the transformation of the world, and Mom expresses God's love in her reminders of God's Word, it's the same love.

Symbolically located at the center of the four candles that encircled it, was the last candle called the Christ Candle. It represents the source of hope, peace, joy, and love. As the wick from this final candle caught fire, my heart was aflame, as well. *Mom and I are both followers of Jesus,* I realized. *Although she follows him straight to the resurrection and eternal life, and I follow him to serve those on the margins of society along the way, he's the same Jesus.*

Salty tears slipped down my face and onto my lap as I felt the empty space between us become filled with the presence of Christ. *We are both children of God. That's the truth.*

"As we come to the close of our service tonight," said the pastor as he stood near the Advent wreath, "I'll light one candle using the flame of the Christ Candle. In turn, that one candle will light another. Using the unlit candles at your pew, we'll continue lighting candles in this way until we each hold the light of Christ in our hands."

The incandescent lights in the sanctuary were turned off and the organist began to play "Silent Night," as one by one, candles began to brighten the dark room.

"Let us sing," exclaimed the pastor with outstretched arms.

> *Silent night, holy night,*
> *All is calm, all is bright*
> *Round yon virgin mother and child.*
> *Holy Infant, so tender and mild,*
> *Sleep in heavenly peace,*
> *Sleep in heavenly peace.*

As the familiar music washed over me, I reflected on the deep meaning of the evening. Although the night had been calm and peaceful, it was also a night of joyful reconciliation of mother and child.

Just then, Mom turned to me with her newly-lighted candle in her hands. I tipped the wick of my unlit candle into her flame, as she symbolically passed the light of Christ to me, just as she had done when I was a child. But as I gazed at Mom's face, bathed in the soft yellow glow of her candle, this time I understood. This time, the light swept away the darkness that once filled the space between us.

> *Silent night, holy night,*
> *Son of God, love's pure light;*
> *Radiant beams from thy holy face*
> *With the dawn of redeeming grace,*
> *Jesus, Lord, at thy birth,*
> *Jesus, Lord, at thy birth.*

WINTER

Winter Prelude

W inter is the season of loss. Slowly, darkness swallows the steady companionship of light, and gardens of colorful adventures fade away. Rainbows of vivid thoughts grow dim in this season of my mother's journey.

Though winter consumes, it also gives back. Quiet moments of reflection reveal what once was unseen, bringing clarity to life's treasures and healing to life's wounds. Above all, winter is the time to dream of the coming of spring, when lifelessness becomes life once again.

Yes, winter is the last season of this love letter, but it is not the end. My love for my mother lives on.

CHAPTER 32

As Time Goes By

Where does time go, when time goes by?
Does it hang in star-glistened chains
From somewhere quite high?

    Can it be heard? Is there a sound?
    Is it hidden in the wind?
    Will it ever be found?

        Does it wait in cupped petals so sweet
        Where nectar lies fragrant
        And bees sup from wells deep?

Oh, I know where it might be—
Perhaps in the salt smell
In from the sea.

        Where, oh, where has all our time gone?
        Could we find just a bit of it
        In the lark's trill at dawn?

    Has our Maker spiraled it up in a shell

*Of Golden Tomorrows
When all shall be well?*

*Shall He run it all backwards, unhidden from view,
For the blessing of creation
When all things are made new?*

—"Where Does Time Go?" by Berthella Stevens,
inspired by Revelations 21:1, 5 and Acts 3:21

As the rhythm of winter settled into Mom's life, she was not fallow as a field blanketed with snow. She was not destined for quiet days in the rocking chair. She aged with grace through her eighties, continuing to pursue her interests from earlier seasons in her life. But winter was not always kind. Like an unstoppable river racing to the sea, time took its toll.

ᬠ

The things Mom loved as a child, she loved as an adult. Raspberries, swimming, flowers, and writing were several of the spices that brought flavor to her life. But as a senior adult, helping hands were offered so she could continue to taste the fullness of life.

Mom first picked wild raspberries on her grandparents' farm. But now, with increasing shortness of breath and less stability in her gait, it was a challenge to reach patches of these delectable fruits. My nephew, Theodore, came up with a clever idea.

"I helped Grandma and Grandpa climb into our minivan," Theodore shared with me as we sat at his kitchen table one afternoon, "and we drove a thousand feet across my washboard field to the edge of a little woods where the black raspberries grew. It was a pretty bumpy ride. I drove right up to the berry patch and opened the door. Then Grandma and Grandpa sat on the edge inside the van and picked to their hearts' content!" With bright eyes and a smile, he added, "They didn't have to deal with tall grass or tripping on rocks. When they finished, they had a pretty nice bowl of sweet raspberries, which we brought back to the house and put on ice cream."

Throughout her life, Mom enjoyed swimming in the bracing rivers and lakes, and that didn't change when she aged. But those less predictable bodies of water were replaced by more placid venues.

"It was quite a chore for her to get her bathing suit on, with her stiff muscles and joints," Mike told me. "But she'd do it, and then climb into the warm water of my pool. She'd grab one of those long, floating noodles and paddle out into the deep end. I always cringed, thinking, *man, we're going to have a disaster here soon. She's going to slip off one of those little things and sink.* But nothing ever happened."

Her pretty gardens still brought her joy, too; although the natural forces of entropy—a gradual decline of order, marked by weeds and wildness—slowly took over the beauty that had once dominated the spaces. But that didn't stop her from caring for these things she loved. After the sun set and the heat of day passed, Mom picked her way carefully over the unlit stone walkways and stooped beneath low-hanging branches of a crabapple tree, dragging her garden hose to sprinkle her beloved flowers.

These simple experiences defined Mom, exercising her body and settling her soul. With the written word, she also stimulated her mind, sharing her past and present for our family's enjoyment.

In the *Stevens Star*, she regaled us with stories of visiting the 1932 Chicago World's Fair, of vacations she took to visit family members, and explained the origins of her fascination with blue glass. As she aged, she enlisted her children to type up the stories she dictated.

In one story about a memory of her grandparents' farm she wrote, "The brain is a wonderful thing. It has the power to bring joy into lives by revealing comforting memories of days gone by... Our brains are a marvelous creation. And as our bodies begin to wear down with our age, our brains can remain active, allowing us to relive those most pleasant times in our past."

Mom's mind fueled her life. It never tired of new adventures. There was always something else she wanted to see, visit, or explore.

She was frustrated, however, with the tension she experienced between her brain, which felt thirty-five years young, and her body, which couldn't keep up.

While Mom was aware of this struggle, I began to notice her brain was slowing, as well. It was subtle at first, as I observed on a trip back to Indiana.

There, Mom and I rocked slowly on her porch swing one evening, after she finished watering her plants. Lightning bugs flashed for mates in the yard, as the clink of the overhead chain kept time with our conversation. Mom had recently celebrated a birthday, and I asked how she felt turning that age.

"I feel great," she said, grasping the chain with one hand. "I love every birthday."

"Really? Why is that?"

"Because birthdays sure beat the alternative!" she quipped, chuckling at her own reference to death. That was Mom, always "quick on the draw."

"I don't worry too much about getting old," she continued as she gazed at the flirting fireflies. "Things could be worse."

"Yeah, I suppose you're right," I replied without making eye contact, soaking in the peaceful evening in the country.

"It's like that famous actress," Mom quickly interjected, turning toward me. "Oh, what's her name? Uh…rats, I don't remember now. But her name's not important, I guess… Anyway, she refused to accept the aging process and went to a doctor to have her skin tightened. They made her skin so tight, however, that whenever she sat down, her mouth flew open!"

I looked at Mom and laughed along with her. Still, it was uncharacteristic for her to stumble on the names and not have every fact at her fingertips. Unfortunately, this rather benign level of forgetfulness grew like a slow cancer with the passage of time and deteriorating health.

CB

Mom's high blood pressure never let up as winter winds blew through her life. When she finally relented to staying on medicine to reduce it, she often forgot to take it, resulting in emergency trips to the hospital with blood pressure readings in the deadly 300s. With such high pressure on her heart for many years, her muscle of life was wearing out, losing its ability to pump all the blood her body needed.

Doctors diagnosed Mom with congestive heart failure, which meant her heart and blood flow were no longer strong enough to remove the fluids that naturally built up, causing her lungs to become congested. That was the cause of the shortness of breath she often experienced, since she no longer got a lung-full of air. It also explained the tightness she felt in her chest and the increasing need for rest after only a moderate amount of activity.

The degraded blood flow created other issues, as well. Without adequate blood streaming to her brain she was hit with "mini strokes," which were temporarily debilitating but left no permanent damage. And sadly, it seemed this long-term diminished blood flow to her brain also brought dementia.

Mom didn't have Alzheimer's, but her cognitive abilities degraded. Her short-term memory wavered and paranoia filled in the voids. When she misplaced personal items in the house, she believed a relative was repeatedly breaking in and stealing her things. And her life-long connection with one of her sisters frayed as Mom became fixated over a years-ago transgression she believed had been committed.

For most of their lives, Mom and her two younger sisters, Dorothy and Joy, were bosom buddies, steadfast as the "three sisters" stars in the belt of the constellation of Orion. As young women, they always appeared in photographs together, posing in bathing suits, or at band concerts, usually arranged in birth order. They had suffered together as children of the Depression, raised their own children together as adults, and assisted each other during times of need as they aged. But when Mom's dementia produced cutting accusations against Dorothy, it severed the ties that had bound them together.

Mom didn't hide the fact that this lifelong relationship was broken. She talked about it constantly. It dominated conversations as she repeatedly tore down her sister to anyone who would listen. She and Dorothy had long passed the point of resolving the issue themselves, as Mom's acid tongue and Dorothy's reluctance to compromise fueled the flames that burned through the relationship they once cherished.

Their feud was particularly hard on me. My aunts had always been a part of my life. But it hurt even more to see Mom in anguish in the last season of her life. She had lost all of her friends, and now she was losing a lifelong relationship with her sister. Mom needed more support, not less, and I felt compelled to act. I flew home to try and reconcile Mom with her sister.

Mom and I sat together in her living room while Dad was working outside on some project. It was morning and the sun's rays slanted through the front door and across the hallway, warming the aqua carpet at our feet. Mom sat in her overstuffed white chair with an arm cover missing, revealing some sort of grime. A small table, buried in blue glass, seashells, and stacks of magazines separated us.

I sighed, reticent but driven to engage. "Tell me what's going on with you and Dorothy, Mom."

Her plump arms rested on the chair's high arms and she looked straight at me. "I've told you before. She has things which belong to me."

"What things?" Until now, everything I knew I'd learned over imperfect phone calls. I needed the facts.

"She has my grandmother Ella May's doll, which I played with as a child. It wears a cute, blue pinafore… And she has Grandma's dress, too."

"So why do you think these things belong to you?"

"Before Mama died, she said I should get these things, which had belonged to her mother. But when Dorothy divvied up the estate, she kept those things for herself, knowing full well they belonged to me." Mom's eyes left my face as she turned and seemed to look away deep into her thoughts.

I uncrossed my legs and leaned forward in my chair. "Mom, that would have been…more than twenty years ago. Why are you just now making an issue about this?"

"About what?" she asked, as she turned back toward me.

"About those things. They're just *things*," I blurted, allowing my frustration to show.

"What things are you talking about?" Mom asked as she blinked and cocked her head to one side.

I shook my head in disbelief. "The doll and the dress, Mom!"

"I know! Dorothy stole them from me. She's such a thief. Just nasty... Can you believe it?"

Although I was frustrated, I now had enough information to begin my "shuttle diplomacy." I jumped into my rental car and drove twenty miles to Dorothy's house.

Dorothy greeted me at the door in her usual house dress, then hesitantly ushered me into her dimly lit family room. She looked healthy and fit, but the house was cluttered and smelled of cats and the food they ate.

"Dorothy, Mom is upset because she believes you have your Grandma Blyly's doll and dress, which Mom believes she was supposed to get."

"That's not *true!*" Dorothy said with a high-pitched emphasis on the last word. "Mama didn't give those things to your mom. We all agreed on who got what when Mama died. We all got different things."

"What did my Mom get?"

"I don't remember," she replied, shaking her head. "That was more than twenty years ago! Then out of the blue your Mom accuses me of cheating her and stealing stuff from her. Ha! Who does she think she is? She's been so rude and mean to me."

"Dorothy, you know Mom has dementia. I think that's why this has come up. Something has triggered this misunderstanding. I think that's what it is—and she can't let go of it. It's consuming her."

"Well, that's not my fault, Kerry," she said, clutching the arms of her chair and gazing out the window, shaded by an overgrown lilac bush.

"I recognize that. But is it worth severing the relationship with your sister over this?"

"I'm not the one who caused this problem!" she retorted, turning back toward me. "I actually tried to be nice, at first. But she wouldn't let up."

I pleaded with my voice and eyes. "I know. But are you willing to help solve it?"

"No. I'm not giving anything to your mom." She stiffened in her chair as if she'd turned to stone.

I was unsure how to proceed. I silently rubbed my temple for a few moments as a Persian kitty slipped past my chair and rubbed my leg with her back, letting out a soft cry for attention.

"Dorothy," I began again, "would you mind showing me the things?"

"Why?" Her eyes narrowed at my question.

"I just want to see them. To see what this is all about. It just breaks my heart that you and Mom won't talk to each other anymore. And Mom's in the winter of her life. Who knows how much time she has left, Dorothy? Do you want to leave this world with one of the most important relationships in your life—at least in my mom's life—broken? I don't... She needs you now. Now is not the time to throw it all away over children's toys."

The dam had burst and a jumble of words tumbled out. I fought back tears. I just couldn't understand how these two wizened women could throw away a relationship more than eighty years old over a doll that neither of them would ever play with. Inside, I knew it wasn't really about the doll. It was about the emotional connection it represented between Mom and her kindred spirit grandmother, Ella May. But it was still difficult to fathom.

"Well," Dorothy said, staring at her empty hands, "the things are downstairs in a back room. We can go look at them, if you want."

Dorothy's basement, with piles and stacks of things on the floor and on tables, reminded me of a canceled rummage sale. In a musty back room, she opened and closed boxes, then removed and replaced dusty items from shelves as she searched unsuccessfully for the doll.

"Oh. Now I remember," she said, turning to me as she leaned on a stack of boxes. "I gave the doll to Dawn. She said she was going to have it refurbished. She really liked it, so I gave it to her so she'd have something from her great-grandmother."

"So she's not going to want to give it back to Mom, I suppose?"

Dorothy's eyebrows rose. "No, of course not. And there's no 'giving back' because it never belonged to your mother."

"Okay, so what about the dress? Can I please see it?"

Dorothy opened another door into a large cluttered dark closet and pulled a dangling string to turn on the light. Soon she emerged with three simple dresses on black wire hangers and held each one high for my inspection.

"Look at this gray one," she said as she turned it around to show me the back. "See that big hole which looks like it was burned?" Dorothy was grinning now. "Mama was wearing this dress when she turned her back to a fireplace to warm her backside and her dress caught on fire! The men in the room had to smack her behind to put out the flames. I can't imagine how embarrassed she was to not only catch her dress on fire, but to have those men touching her private parts."

I laughed at the story of my grandmother but was confused. I was expecting to see the dress worn by my great grandmother, Ella May, not my grandmother, whom the sisters referred to as "Mama."

"So where's the dark blue dress with the white polka dots?" I asked.

Dorothy frowned. "What dress is that? I don't remember Mama having a dress like that."

"It's not a dress your mom wore. It's the one Ella May wore in every single picture I've ever seen of her. She apparently had just one dress. That's the one Mom wants."

"I've never had that dress. I don't think Mama ever did, either." She stared upward, searching her memory. "These dresses all belonged to Mama," she finally said, motioning toward the small wardrobe that hung from her other hand.

I thanked Dorothy and took off, eager to share with Mom what I'd learned. As I suspected, there was a misunderstanding.

Misunderstandings can be corrected, I thought, giving me a glimmer of hope for my mother trapped in a prison of animosity.

ᢀ

The grandfather clock chimed three times as Mom and I sat down in the same chairs for another session. This time the sun was hot, coming in through the large, west-facing picture window. Mom slumped in her chair with her shoulders pulled forward. She seemed tired.

"Where have you been?" she asked.

"Mom, I went to talk with Dorothy," I reminded her.

"Oh, that's right... So, what did she say? The same things she probably told me, I assume," she said, waving one hand dismissively in air.

I explained to Mom that the doll was well taken care of and would eventually be preserved in a glass case. And that Dorothy did not have Ella May's dress.

"She's lying. That's just like her." Mom's shoulders stiffened as she sat upright in the chair.

"Mom! That's your sister," I nearly barked. "You've never talked like that about her before. Why are you doing this? I know this hurts you, but it's also hurting me to see you like this. This is not the mother I grew up with... And to see you throw away such an important relationship near the end of your own life...that just really hurts. I can't stand to watch this happen." I looked away as I fought back tears for a second time that day.

I knew it was Mom's dementia speaking to me, but it was difficult to separate her from her disease. Although her mind was tiring and approaching its fill, I sensed my words had an impact, softening her resolve. Her entire body relaxed into her chair as she stared into space.

"Isn't it a good thing, Mom, the doll is going to be preserved for decades? What would you do with it anyway? It would sit on a shelf until someone else had to clean it off after you're gone... and then who knows what would happen to it? You know no one else in the family is clamoring for it. So isn't it good that someone loves it and will care for it for years to come?"

Mom sat quietly during my lecture, then I sat quietly awaiting a response. Either her brain was tiring and slowly shutting down, or she was seriously contemplating what I said.

"Yes, you're probably right, Kerry. That's probably best for the doll," she finally said.

I closed my eyes as her words brought such relief from angst and encouragement to press on. "And Dorothy doesn't even have your grandmother's blue dress with the white polka dots," I reminded her, scooting forward in my seat. "Since she doesn't have it, are you able to let go of that demon, Mom? To let bygones be bygones?"

Her reply was swift. "Then I should at least get Mama's dresses!"

"Mom, what will you do with them if she gave them to you?" I pleaded.

"That's just what I want," she said, adamantly. "If I can't get the doll or my grandmother's dress, then I should get Mama's."

"So if Dorothy agrees to give your mother's old dresses to you, then you'll forget this whole affair and reconcile with your sister?"

The moment of truth had arrived. Mom thought about it for quite a while, then with apparent earnestness, she turned to me and simply replied "yes." Then her gaze drifted to her weedy gardens outside the window.

I smiled. Although Dorothy didn't indicate she would give up those dresses, at least now there was a potential pathway to reconciliation. "Mom, you don't know how happy this makes me. I'll go back to Dorothy's house and tell her you'll forget about the doll and you're willing to make amends if she's willing to give you your mother's dresses."

"What are you talking about?" Mom's head snapped back in my direction. "I never said that."

I blinked several times before responding. "Yes, you did. You just said it."

"No, I did not! Dorothy stole my grandmother's doll and dress from me, and I want them back. She's a nasty thief, and I won't speak with her again unless she gives me what she's stolen!"

"Mom, just one minute ago, that's what you told me!" I sat up in my chair.

Mom crossed her arms loosely. "I never did, Kerry. I don't know what you're talking about."

I was demoralized. Every inch of ground I had gained in the conversation was wiped out in a blink of my mother's eyes, or more accurately, in a break within a synapse of my mother's brain. *Why did I try to reason with someone whose mental faculties are impaired? Why would reason ever trump a problem born of disease?*

I was unable to walk away and let one of Mom's last relationships wither and die. The next morning, while Mom was still fresh, we went back to the living room and sat in the same chairs for a third time. I started the previous conversation all over again, as if it had never occurred. Fortunately, Mom came to the same reasonable conclusion she had before the break in her synapse. So I returned to Dorothy's with the proposal, hoping her heart had softened, too.

Three hours later, it was with great satisfaction I returned to Mom's house with trophies held high. I had all three decades-old dresses, including the one with the back burned off. As Mom rested on the cool fabric of the couch in the living room, she scanned my prizes and smiled.

CB

Although the wall had been removed between Dorothy and my mom, the relationship was not yet mended. I thought if I could recreate an experience from their past, maybe that would be enough for them to reconnect.

As children, they loved free band concerts in the park, one of the few sources of entertainment the impoverished family could afford. I was tickled when I discovered that in two days, in their childhood hometown of Elkhart, a free concert in the park was scheduled. I talked with Mom, and then called both my aunts. All agreed they would attend. That was a major accomplishment in itself.

During the outdoor concert, the sisters, all octogenarians, sat side-by-side, smiling, and seemed to enjoy the reunion as the brass instruments played and the air cooled after the summer sunset. Mom and Dorothy talked amicably, but I never heard an apology, which would have been unlike Mom, anyway. But at least they were back together. After the concert, before each sister went her separate way, I asked if I could take a photo of the three of them.

"Sure," they said, automatically lining up in birth order. They sat on a low rock ledge in their pretty, but practical, outfits.

I smiled as I remembered one of my favorite pictures of them. In the old photo, they were young, vibrant, and attractive women posing in swimsuits on a sandy shore, turned just so, with shoulders interlaced behind the next sister, looking seductively into the camera. But as I looked through the viewfinder to take the new photo, I saw the movement of time in their lives. Sitting on the ledge before me, were three women with creases of grief and grace in their faces. Although sixty years had gone by since their original photo in the sand, they were the same three sisters, as steadfast as those in Orion's belt.

After I snapped the picture, the middle sister, Joy, stood up, leaving a gap between Dorothy and Mom. I saw Mom lean over and gently pat Dorothy's hand. Then Dorothy returned the gesture with a gentle squeeze on my mother's leathery hand. They had reconciled. Mom was freed.

⊱

As Mom's congestive heart failure worsened, she found it increasingly difficult to breathe and do physically productive things. Her progressive dementia also made it difficult to do cognitively productive things. That's when Dad realized he had to step up.

He assumed responsibility for seeing that Mom took her daily medications on time and began to learn his way around the kitchen, dressed in a flannel shirt and boots like he was working in the garage. Meals weren't elaborate, but he kept them from starving. Janet, and

Tom's wife, Donna, also prepared meals and frequently delivered them to Mom and Dad, driving multiple hours round trip.

Things seemed to be running well until Mom's blood pressure spiked and she ended up in the emergency room. Dad forgot to give Mom her medicine, and Mom forgot that Dad forgot. This happened frequently, indicating Dad's abilities might be diminishing, as well. That became obvious to me on my next trip home to Indiana.

As I often did on my visits, I volunteered to work on any projects that Mom or Dad wanted me to do. It was the least I could do—given the much larger tasks my nearby siblings took on to care for our parents. On this trip, Dad expressed the desire to have their porch light turn on and off automatically so he didn't need to remember to do it every day. Could I do that, he asked?

"Sure. That's easy enough," I responded, standing in the hallway on linoleum nearly as old as me.

"How would you do it?" he asked. I thought he was testing me; to be sure I wouldn't do something stupid. He knew I had basic skills in electrical wiring, so I thought it odd he felt the need to test me. But I responded in the familiar shorthand of two knowledgeable people.

"Well, you've got power running inside the lamppost which comes from this switch," I said, pointing to the hard, plastic switch on the wall beside us. "So I'd just tap into that line in the post and install a dusk-to-dawn switch. Then you just flip on the switch inside the house and don't touch it again."

"How would you do that?" he asked again, removing his cap and scratching his head.

I was perplexed by his nearly identical question since electrical projects didn't get much simpler than that one. *Maybe he isn't testing me,* I thought.

"Let's go outside and take a look," I suggested. Dad stepped carefully out the door and we ambled across the patio as the aluminum storm door banged shut behind us. Standing in front of the light, I repeated my instructions with a little more detail, unsure whether I was proving myself to him or educating him.

"There's a power line running inside this lamppost," I said, pointing to the black, five-foot metal pole in front of us, which sported a jasmine vine. "See this outlet on the side? I'd pop out this outlet to get to the wire, then install the dusk-to-dawn switch in its place."

Dad stooped down and studied the post and the outlet. "So what would make the light turn on and off automatically so I don't have to do it every day?"

I struggled to find the words for the seemingly obvious answer. "The dusk-to-dawn switch. When the sun comes up, the switch will turn itself off and the electricity will stop flowing to the light. At night, the switch will open itself and let electricity flow to the light, turning it on."

"Hmm…okay," he said, sounding a bit skeptical.

It was a stunning moment for me. My father had wired more houses in his career as a homebuilder than I could count. Earlier in his life, he knew the building codes and had the tools to bring electricity to the most complicated homes. My brothers and he had hammered every nail in his own home, strung every electrical wire, and laid every brick. Dad even installed the lamppost that stood in front of us. But in that moment on the patio, he was stumped about how to put a single switch, in a single power line, for a single light. I knew my father physically stood beside me, but his essence was slipping away. Speechless, I swallowed hard, hoping Dad didn't hear the sounds of my breaking heart.

∞

Not long after my disquieting visits home, there was talk in the family about whether Mom and Dad could continue to live independently. Although several siblings worked tirelessly to support our parents, from my distant vantage point I was concerned my parents' desires might be overridden. My dad had long said he wanted to die in his own home, and neither he nor Mom relished the idea of leaving the place they had created with their own hands. I wasn't involved in their day-to-day care like other siblings, but I believed honoring my parents included allowing them to make their own choices. I got on the phone in a series of calls to see what I could do from afar.

Dad said everything would be okay if he could just remember to give Mom her medicine. So I researched a number of electronic pill boxes with multiple programmable reminders and discussed them with Tom. He and Donna provided most of the care for our aging parents. He was opposed, saying it was too complicated for them to use. I countered that Tom could set the timers, then fill up the pill box once a week. Although we were on the phone, I could see him shaking his head "no." So that idea died.

Later, in a surprise response over the phone, Dad asked for help with their meals to ease the reliance on the family.

"How about Meals-on-Wheels?" I asked him.

"No, that's for old people. I don't want to do that."

So I looked around and found another food delivery service for seniors who agreed to bring frozen dishes from a nearby town every two weeks.

Surprisingly, Dad agreed to this deal, and I was thrilled that this could help them retain an independent life without burdening my siblings. But soon there were complaints about the quality and cost of the food, and Dad stopped the service.

As time went by, I asked Dad, "Are you ready to consider an assisted living facility?"

"You can look around," he said.

I was surprised, but happy this might be another viable option for them. I eagerly researched all the senior living places in the region and sent the information to Dad. He decided against pursuing that and said he and Mom would simply make it work, living in the home they built. Although it wasn't clear to me he made the best decision, I was happy they were happy.

But my happiness was short-lived when I got another call from Tom. I was sitting in front of my computer in my upstairs office preparing the following week's Sunday school lesson when the phone rang.

"Kerry, I know you mean well," Tom began, "but the things you're doing aren't helping. Mom and Dad can't live by themselves anymore."

I swiveled nervously in my chair. "When I'm visiting, I'm the only one who's actually living with them, Tom, and watching their behavior. I think if you just…"

Tom interrupted, "Look, the problems are bigger than any of us can manage. One more missed medication and Mom could be dead. I don't think you want that. And the junk is just piling up inside the house because neither can keep it clean. Mom can't even go up and down the stairs anymore because she's out of breath." I held my tongue as he continued, "So, Donna and I go over to try to clean up the place, and Mom gets angry at us for throwing away all her papers. And then nobody wants to talk to each other."

"Well, what about a cleaning service? We can just hire a maid," I proposed, staring blankly at my computer screen as I imagined the inside of my parents' cluttered home.

"And do what? Have someone else throw away her stuff, which will still make Mom mad?"

"The maid could at least wash the dishes," I retorted.

"It's not that simple. Dad can't keep up the outside, so I have to go over there and mow his grass or fix things when they break. So Donna and/or I are driving over there at least once or twice a week, sometimes more, to help them. That's a three-hour drive, round trip. If we spend two or three hours working on something while we're there… that's half a day. Donna and I both work. We've got our own place to take care of, and our family. We can't keep doing this."

"Oh, so this is about you?" I challenged. There was a pause in our conversation as I had second thoughts about what I'd said, and Tom contemplated his response.

"On a practical level, it is, 'cause there's nobody else around to do it. But it's not just that. Last week, in the middle of a cold snap—in the single digits—Dad called and said their furnace went out and he couldn't fix it. I told him to pack a few things and I'd be over to pick them up and they could stay with us until I could fix the furnace. Then I dropped what I was doing and went out on the icy roads to get them. When I got there, Dad was walking around the house with a blowtorch to heat the rooms! It was an open flame, Kerry, a big ol' flame blowing out of the nozzle and he was carrying it around like it was a flashlight… He could have easily caught the drapes on fire, stacks of newspapers, anything! And then the house would have burned down with them inside. That's not how I want our parents to die."

The conversation was boiling with emotion. We both were concerned about the welfare of Mom and Dad, but we had come from different places and taken different roads to get there. We sat in silence, allowing the heat of the moment to pass, as the wisdom in Tom's heartfelt words began to reveal itself.

I sighed, and then broke the lull. "So where would they live if they didn't live at home?"

"They could live with us," Tom offered. "Donna and I are both very happy to do that for them…knowing that our place will be the last place they'll ever live."

It was hard to imagine my parents being uprooted from their creation as they approached the end of their lives. And it was difficult to hear "the last place they'll ever live." Until now, their deaths had always been an abstract thought. But somehow, with this move, their inevitable deaths became real for me.

A chill raced through my body. "I see," was all I could utter.

"Donna is already involved in Mom's medical issues, and since she's a nurse, it's just a natural fit for her to take over Mom's care," Tom continued.

Obviously, he's already thought through all of this, I thought. "Where would they sleep? You know Mom can't climb stairs," I asked, quietly.

"We've already decided that we'd give them our master bedroom on the ground floor, and Donna and I would move to the guest room upstairs… And we'd bring over some of their things, like their chairs, so they feel at home... No one wants to see them die in an accident at home, Kerry, or be confined in a nursing home. We're willing—actually, we're happy—to have them live with us."

I closed my eyes and rubbed the middle of my forehead. I didn't like what I was hearing, but I understood it was probably the best solution. "Have you discussed this with them?"

"Yes."

"And?"

"Mom is okay with it. Dad is...umm, he understands."

"Tom, you know Dad always said he wanted to die in his own bed, in his own home."

Now Tom let out a long sigh, "I know. But...it's not gonna happen... I think he'll come around as time goes by."

CHAPTER 33

Saying Goodbye

Dad cried twice in his life. The first time was when he was born and the doctor spanked his heinie. The second time was when he stood in front of his mother's casket forty-three years later. I wasn't around the first time he cried, but I was there for the second. It wasn't a sobbing bawl with a river of tears; he stood stalwart and silent, as a couple of drops rolled down his cheeks before he quickly wiped them away with the front of his hand. Dad wasn't the kind of man who cried. At least that's what I thought, until time took its toll.

☙

Growing up, I knew how to spell affection but didn't know how to show it. It was seldom modeled. I don't remember ever seeing my parents kiss or hug each other. I only recall seeing them hold hands when my father was trying to hurry my mother along by pulling her. And if he put his arm around her, it was usually for a posed picture. My mother kissed my boo-boos when I was small, and she rocked me at night until I attended kindergarten and I announced I was too old to be rocked. After that, there were no hugs, no kisses, and there was never an "I love you." Whenever we departed each other's presence, it was marked with a wave of a hand or a simple "bye." As a family, we weren't opposed to affection—it just didn't exist. Although I never asked anyone else in our community, maybe that's just how things were with rural Midwestern folks.

When I married, I joined a Southern Hispanic family glued together by affection. Everyone hugged hello when they arrived and hugged again when they said goodbye. And men hugged men. Not just timid side hugs, but chest-to-chest bear hugs. Holding hands wasn't just for parents and young children when they crossed the street. Men played guitar and sang love songs, and my mother-in-law and at least one brother-in-law told me they loved me. They helped me learn the proper way to say goodbye—with a hug.

When I returned to Indiana and greeted siblings and parents with hugs, I was met with surprise and reservation, even suspicion. It seemed as if I spoke a new language, and they weren't quite sure they understood it. My sisters were more receptive, and at least one had already broken out of our affection-free zone. My brothers? Not so much. Hugs were stiff and reserved—as if I had a communicable disease they might catch if we truly embraced.

My mother quickly adapted to my hugs, embracing me fully and long. I could feel my essence being sucked out and absorbed by Mom, as if I brought cool, fresh water to her parched soul. She didn't want to let go.

Hugging my father was like hugging a board. He was stiff, flat, and didn't hug back. I felt no emotion or closeness coming from our embraces. His hugs felt more like tolerance than love. But that was the way he was raised. He didn't hug, and I believed he didn't cry.

❧

My brother, Tom, an outdoorsman at heart and a chiropractor by day, had forty acres of land in the country. Tom's wooded grounds hid morel mushrooms in spring, kept aloft red-tailed hawks, and cradled a pond brimming with bullfrogs. It was a peaceful place, not unlike my parents' smaller homestead, an hour and half away. It was here my parents moved when they said goodbye to their own homestead of forty-seven years.

The first several months after the move were challenging for Dad. Still fit, but heavier around the middle, unusual waves of emotion threatened to overtake him. He silently fought back with pursed lips, closed eyes, and a quivering chin. But whatever triggered the tremor was more powerful. Rusty valves were pried open and salty droplets of grief rolled down his leathery cheeks.

I don't know why Dad cried. He never shared the reason. Perhaps he missed his hand-built home, the earthy gardens he tilled, or the nesting bluebirds. Perhaps it was the rippling waters on the heart-shaped pond he dug, the slippery fish he caught, or the rhythmic creak of the churning windmill. Or maybe it hurt to face the truth that he would not die in his own bed, in his own home. Tom and his wife, Donna, provided comfort with kind words or a quick hug when they witnessed Dad's infrequent moments of anguish.

Tom was stocky and clean-shaven, while Donna's pleasant smile was framed by shoulder-length hair. Both were in their late fifties and graying when Mom and Dad moved into their two-story country home with white pillars on a wide front porch that overlooked an expansive green yard. Inside their home, the kitchen, family room, and eating areas were on the first floor, along with a spacious master suite, which they vacated for Mom and Dad. They brought one of Mom's chairs from the old house and placed it in a corner next to a dresser.

Mom and Dad lacked nothing and received excellent care. Donna prepared their meals, washed their clothes, and cleaned their bedroom. Because of diminished mobility, Mom often needed extra help with dressing, showering, and using the bathroom. While Donna worked during the day, her daughter, Katie, came over to assist. Katie's rambunctious toddler, Taylan, usually accompanied her.

"I really enjoyed getting to know Grandma on a more personal level," Katie told me as we reminisced at her kitchen table. "She and Taylan would have races all over the house. He would ride his fire-truck-red tricycle and Grandma raced him in her wheelchair. She was so funny."

That fun side of Mom's personality never waned.

Although she used a wheelchair, she wasn't confined to it. Still overweight and struggling to peer through the proper place in her tri-focal glasses, Mom could shuffle shorter distances. One day, Tom and his family returned from his daughter, Allison's, graduation. Allison and her boyfriend walked ahead of Mom up the plywood wheelchair ramp Tom built to the back door. The boyfriend wore his pants in a way that most males in the area did not, pulled down with his underwear-clad butt clearly visible. Mischief overcame Mom as she watched the young man enter the house. She turned around to see who was behind her, and seeing only Tom and Donna, Mom pulled her pants down to her thighs, exposing her pink underwear as she slowly swung her backside side-to-side to emphasize her imitation as she ambled up the ramp. Tom and Donna burst out laughing and grabbed the railing to steady themselves.

Mom retained her core personality traits, like her humor, but time seemed to run backwards for her, as she became increasingly in touch with her past and less connected with her present. "She might have forgotten what she had for breakfast," said Katie, "but she could remember stories of her childhood like they had just happened." She spoke frequently of her absent-from-life father in glowing terms, remarking what a good daddy he had been to her, although that wasn't the way she portrayed him for most of her life.

One day, Julie and her son Clay came to visit Mom. They greeted her in her bedroom as she sat in her lounge chair pairing socks Donna had washed. Clay was a teenager, growing like a weed, tall and thin, with Stevens-blond hair.

"Hi, Mom. How are you?" asked Julie, brightening the already-sunny room.

Mom looked up from her lap of fuzzy socks and smiled. "What a nice surprise! I'm fine. How are you?"

"Good. So do you know who this is?" Julie asked, motioning toward Clay.

"Of course! That's your son."

"Do you know his name?" Julie persisted.

"Well, if you don't know his name, I'm not going to tell you," Mom said with a wry smile.

Whether she didn't remember her grandson's name or was just being sassy wasn't clear. But it was a witty response, nonetheless.

⅓

Mom's slow disconnect from the present had a positive side. She didn't dwell on the recent changes in her life, like leaving their home and no longer driving. She voluntarily said goodbye to her car and didn't look back. Dad, on the other hand, didn't want to give up his keys, although his driving frightened Tom.

Tom shared his concern with me in a phone call.

"The other day, I was driving behind Dad as he drove his truck from their house to our house," Tom told me. "At one point, we were going through a 40-mph speed zone on the highway which had a separate lane for the slow Amish buggies. Anyway, Dad continued driving 60 mph, in the buggy lane, quickly closing in on a horse and buggy. I said 'Holy cow! He's going to hit 'em!' Then at the last minute, he pulled back into his lane, barely missing 'em."

"Oh, geez," I replied, shaking my head. "Well, when I was home last, before they moved to your house, I rode with him on some errand into Bremen. He told me where we were going, but then passed the turnoff. I didn't think too much about it, figurin' he must have decided to do something else beforehand. But after we'd gone about a mile past the street, and completely left town, he suddenly said, 'Where am I?'"

"He got lost in Bremen?"

"Well, it took him awhile to get his bearings, but he figured it out and turned around and made it to the place he was going."

"I don't think he should be driving anymore," said Tom, firmly. "I'm going to take him to the optometrist. I just don't think he can see very well."

"That seems like a wise move... Before he hurts someone."

After our call, Tom scheduled the appointment. It was a thorough exam, with the doctor looking for signs of problems associated with old age. After the examination, the doctor sat on a tall stool in front of a counter, studying the results on her laptop. Dad remained in the gray exam chair while Tom sat quietly in the corner.

Suddenly, the doctor whirled the stool away from the counter and faced Dad. She pushed the overhead instrument cluster out of the way and dropped a pen into the pocket of her white lab coat.

"Mr. Stevens," began the doctor, "your eyesight's not bad for a ninety-year-old."

"Well, I'm not quite ninety, Doc," said my father with a straight face. "My birthday is in a couple of weeks... And my wife's ninetieth birthday is pretty soon, too."

"Well, happy early-birthday to both of you, then! That's quite an accomplishment."

"I think a bigger accomplishment may be I'll soon have been married sixty-five years," Dad added, as a faint smile emerged.

"Is that so?"

"Yeah, our anniversary is about the same time as my birthday... It's hard to believe that in two weeks I'll have been married that long... I've been lucky; I haven't had too many health problems, either."

"Well, that's what I want to discuss with you, Mr. Stevens," said the doctor, eager to take back the conversation. "Although your eyesight's not *bad* for a ninety-year-old, it's not very good."

"Oh? What did you find? I've had problems with cataracts over the years."

"Yes, your cataracts are back. Have you noticed cloudiness?"

Dad nodded. "Yes, but it's mainly in my right eye, so I just close it and use my left eye when I really have to see something."

"If it was just cataracts, we could probably do something about that," the doctor said, looking straight at Dad. "But I see other issues, as well."

"Really?" Dad asked, but didn't sound surprised.

"I'm afraid so. Your central vision is deteriorating, which is not uncommon when we age. The central vision is especially important for driving."

"Well, I'm driving okay, Doc. I try to stay on the side roads and drive slowly, just to be safe."

"Mr. Stevens, based on my exam, I don't think you should get behind the wheel anymore. Your vision has deteriorated too much. It just isn't safe."

Dad let out a short cough as if he were choking. "What? Doc, I've got to drive. If I can't drive anymore, it'll kill me."

"Mr. Stevens, *not driving* won't kill you. But *driving* may… I think it's time you gave your keys to your son," said the doctor as she turned around and faced my brother.

Dad just sighed and his shoulders slumped. He wasn't the type of person who argued with authority. He didn't want to say goodbye to driving, but he reluctantly agreed.

For the next several days, Dad was sullen and withdrawn. On Tuesday, five days after the appointment, it was warm and muggy and had rained off and on, keeping Dad inside most of the day. Late in the afternoon, he wandered into their bedroom and saw Mom lying on top of their white bedspread, taking a nap. Although Dad never lay down to nap in the middle of the day, he did so that day. He removed his shoes and lay down behind Mom, who was sleeping partly on her side.

Then, the man who seldom showed affection snuggled up tight, spooning my mother. He draped one arm across her waist and he laid his head gently on her shoulder, then closed his eyes and slumbered. Together like lovebirds, they embraced like they had sixty-five years earlier on their honeymoon, when they nestled in a hammock strung between sturdy trees, as sunbeams burned through the shade of the woods. Perhaps that was Dad's dream.

❦

Donna knocked and the bedroom door squeaked as she opened it. "Mom, Dad. It's time for supper. Are you ready to eat?" Although they were her in-laws, Donna treated them like her own blood, addressing them with the same names used by their children. She had returned from work and prepared supper. The smell of pan-fried pork chops filled the air.

She took two steps into her former bedroom to get closer. "Mom, Dad, are you hungry?"

"Huh?" Mom grunted, as she opened her eyes. "I must have fallen asleep… And look who joined me!" she said with a broad sleepy smile when she felt Dad's embrace. "Wonders never cease! Mick, wake up. It's time for supper."

Mom gently shook Dad's warm hairy arm, which still hugged her waist. "What?" Dad murmured.

"Mick, it's time for supper. We need to get up."

By the time Mom and Dad arrived and took their seats, supper was waiting on the heavy oak table. Walls of windows surrounded them. Dad watched the setting sun but said nothing. Mom was talkative, refreshed, and happy from her nap and the loving hug she'd received while she slept.

"Where's Tom?" asked Mom.

"He had to run some errands. He'll eat later," Donna said.

"Ooh. Those mashed potatoes look good. Are those fresh from your garden?" asked Mom.

Donna rearranged the bowls to make more room as she talked. "No, it's too early for potatoes, Mom. It's only the first of June. But Tom planted the new ones already. Here, try this broccoli," she said, passing a glass bowl heaped with steaming green heads to Mom. "*This* is from our garden. We got it in early this year. It's fresh off the stalk. Dad, do you want a pork chop?"

Donna picked up the platter of pork chops to hand to Dad. He didn't respond. He stared straight ahead, seemingly lost in thought. Then Donna saw what she had seen only a few times before. Dad's chin quivered and his lips were pursed tightly shut. His shoulders drooped.

She knew tears were likely to follow, as Dad fought back another wave of emotion.

"Dad? Are you okay?"

Donna pushed her chair back, scraping the tiled floor, and walked over to comfort Dad as his eyes closed and his head dropped to his chest as if he had fallen asleep.

Donna shook his shoulders. "Dad, are you okay?" She got no response, and instinctively checked his pulse in his neck as she had for so many patients she nursed.

"What's the matter with Mick?" Mom asked. "He didn't fall asleep at the table, did he? He just woke up from a nap."

Donna twisted her necklace as she spoke. "Mom, stay right there. Don't move. I'll be right back."

She rushed to the next room out of earshot of Mom and dialed three digits on her phone.

"What's your emergency?" asked the voice on the other end.

C∞

Tom saw a call coming in on his cell phone from Donna as he walked to his truck after finishing his errands. "Hey, what's up?"

"Tom, your Dad passed out during supper, and he's being transported to the hospital now. The EMTs started CPR on him at the house since he's never had any heart problems before."

"So his heart stopped?"

"Yes."

"Did they revive him?" His voice was higher pitched as he clutched his phone tightly.

"Not yet. He didn't respond."

"Is he dead?"

There was silence on the line as Tom pressed the phone against his ear, standing alone in the rain-soaked parking lot.

"Is he dead, Donna?"

"Tom, you just need to get to the hospital. I told them you were coming. As soon as I get Mom ready, we'll meet you there. Fortunately, she didn't see them performing CPR."

"Donna, you're a registered nurse! Is my dad dead?" Tom could feel his body tingling.

"Tom, I'm sorry. He wasn't breathing and his heart was stopped when he left here. Please, just hurry."

∽

Tom wasn't far from the hospital when he got Donna's call, so he arrived before the ambulance. He was waiting under the brick portico just outside the door of the ER when he overheard an ER attendant tell a doctor that a patient was inbound with a full cardiac arrest.

Tom heard the siren wailing before he saw the white van, bristling with flashing red lights, turn the corner. The ER doctor, dressed in blue scrubs, hurried through the sliding glass door to meet the ambulance as it pulled under the portico. Tom hurried to the ambulance, as well, prompting the doctor to ask, "Are you Tom?"

"I am."

The ambulance driver leapt from the vehicle and ran to the back and opened the door with the metallic clank of a bank vault. Tom saw Dad lying on the gurney flanked by walls of gadgets, as an attendant performed CPR.

Still trying to engage Tom, the ER doctor interrupted Tom's thoughts. "Are you this patient's son?"

Tom's eyes never left my father as he answered, "Yes."

"Do you have medical power of attorney?"

"I do."

The EMT pulled the gurney from the rear of the ambulance and extended and locked the legs with a click, allowing Tom to see Dad's ashen face. Tom's first career had been as a mortician. He recognized death.

Tom turned to the EMT pumping on Dad's chest and asked, "How long has it been since he's breathed?"

"At least twenty-five minutes, sir," the technician responded, briefly looking up from his task of saving my father's life.

"Doesn't that mean he's dead?" asked Tom, almost as a declaration.

"Yes sir… I'm sorry."

"Then stop the CPR."

"If they stop," interjected the ER doctor, "that means your father will never come back. Do you understand?"

"I do," said Tom, staring at our lifeless father.

ᘓ

Dad was laid in a bed in a room near the ER, normally used for recovery after surgery. It wasn't medically required, but was done as an act of kindness by the hospital since they knew Mom was on her way. The curtains had been drawn over the glass windows and the lights turned off. An empty IV pole stood in one corner. Only Tom waited inside, oblivious to the smell of antiseptic and the cacophony of voices in the hall of doctors, nurses, and patients who still had breath.

Then familiar voices got Tom's attention when he heard Mom shuffling down the hall with Donna, coming toward the room. He stepped into the doorway to greet Mom.

"What's wrong with Mick, Tom? Is he going to be okay?" Mom asked, with a wrinkled brow.

Tom sighed, holding back his own tears. He was still running on adrenaline.

"Mom," Tom said, touching her arm, "Dad is dead."

Mom caught her breath as if she'd seen a ghost, and Tom grabbed her arm to steady her. "He's dead? How did he die?"

"His heart stopped. Just like that," Tom said, snapping his fingers. "And he was gone."

Even in the midst of the noise of the ER, silence covered my family. Finally, Mom asked, "Is he in here?" She motioned around Tom into the room.

"Yes…he is," Tom said, and stepped aside.

Mom walked slowly and respectfully across the dimly lit room to say goodbye. Although my dad lay only feet away from her, the distance must have seemed like miles. Tom and Donna wrapped their arms around each other and waited near the door as Mom hesitantly approached the bed.

Mom knew the man lying before her was her husband. She knew he was dead. But because of her mental illness, she spent more time living in the past and less in the present, providing an emotional buffer to this tragedy.

She took a deep breath and let it out as she looked into Dad's face. She studied his torso, clad in familiar flannel and work pants, remembering his hug just an hour before. As if in slow motion, she extended one hand and gently slipped it under one of Dad's, lifting it softly away from his body. It was already cool to her touch. She laid her other hand over the top of Dad's, and tightly squeezed her hands together as if she were extracting his last bit of life and love.

Then Mom gently returned Dad's lifeless hand to his side and looked longingly into his ashen face once more and said, "I should have given you more sex."

CHAPTER 34

Legacy of Jewels

"Good morning, Mom. How are you?" I stood in the doorway of my mother's bedroom at my brother's house. She sat on the edge of her bed, fiddling with her watch. Donna had helped Mom dress for the day in comfortable slacks and a blouse, adorned with a blue and green butterfly pin.

Dad passed away several months earlier, and since then, Mom's health declined rapidly. Tom alerted me it was time to come visit her. When I arrived in Indiana, the once-green grass was crunchy and brown; the trees were bare. Winter was in the air.

"Oh! What a surprise!" Mom said, raising both hands in the air. "When did you arrive?" Her face lit up as she spoke.

"I came yesterday, Mom."

"Oh, I didn't even know you were coming. But I'm glad you're here."

I chose not to remind her that we had already spent the afternoon and evening together the day before.

"How are you feeling today?" I asked as I walked across the room and sat down beside her on the cotton bedspread. I smelled a lavender cachet on her nightstand, which must have made the journey from her chest of drawers at my childhood home.

With congestive heart failure, Mom's lungs were slowly filling with fluid because her heart was too weak to pull it out. With decreasing lung capacity, she needed more frequent breaths, often interrupting her sentences. Her medication temporarily drained some of the excess fluid from her system, but its effectiveness was limited, partly due to its side effect of kidney damage. Each day was a delicate balancing act between medication and congestion. We all knew the congestion would eventually fill her lungs, and that day was getting closer. There was nothing we could do to stop it.

"I'm still breathing, aren't I?" she responded wryly with a faint smile. "And I've had my breakfast and I…wait, did I have my breakfast?" Mom's eyes narrowed.

"Yes, Donna said you ate earlier. Sorry I missed it. With the time change, my body is still an hour behind."

"Well, I'm sure it was good. Donna's a good cook, you know…" Mom paused for a breath, and I heard a faint gurgle. "She takes good care of me. I'm so thankful for her…and for Tom. I don't know what we would have done." She turned and looked out the window behind her nightstand. The morning light softened the wrinkles in her face.

Although Mom's mental faculties wavered, and now mostly dwelled in the past, this morning she seemed bright and alert, with relative clarity of thought. I was thankful to spend the day with the mother who'd raised me, and not one I didn't recognize.

"Are you ready to get started on your earrings?" I asked.

"What are we doing with my earrings?"

"We're going to organize them. Yesterday you complained that all your earrings got mixed up during your move, and you had a hard time finding a matched pair."

"Oh, yes! Good! I'm glad you're going to help me," she said between labored breaths. "I've got dozens and dozens of earrings but nothing to wear… Doesn't that sound just like a woman?" We both smiled at her humorous intended sexism.

Donna knocked on the partially open bedroom door, then stepped in, dressed in jeans for housecleaning.

"How's it going in here?" she asked.

"We're getting ready to organize her earrings," I said.

"What do you need?"

"Well, I think we can just use that beige table in the corner. If you have an extra chair for me, we'll just spread the earrings on the table and sort them until we find all the pairs."

Donna left to get a chair, and I steadied Mom into her wheelchair, then pushed her across the carpet to the table. On top was a small black cabinet with a dozen clear, plastic bins, each holding a jumble of earrings.

Donna returned with a cushioned dining room chair. "If you need anything else, just holler," she said, leaving Mom and me alone in the room.

"Okay, thanks," I replied.

I sat across from Mom at the modest-sized table. There appeared to be hundreds of lonely earrings sitting in the bins, hoping to be reunited with their mates.

I looked at Mom. "Well, where do you want to start?"

She sighed, not sure what to do next, then frowned as she thought about the enormity of the task. So I volunteered a plan.

"How 'bout we just dump them all on the table and spread them out and start looking for doubles?" I suggested, waving my right hand over the bare table surface.

Mom's face lit up again. "Okay. That sounds fine."

Soon the table was a kaleidoscope of jewelry accumulated over Mom's entire life. It looked like a rainbow exploded. Our job was to bring order to the colorful chaos.

Mom's eyes immediately spotted a clip-on earring with a square, faceted emerald-green stone, which she delicately picked up as her eyes searched for its companion. Meanwhile, I looked for a specific pair of bright turquoise earrings. It had been many years since I had last seen them, but my memory remained vivid.

"Huh!" I said as my eyes quickly latched on to one. "I found it!"

"You've got a match already?" Mom asked as she searched the table for the emerald green partner.

"No, not yet. But I found one I was looking for."

Within seconds, I spotted its missing twin. Each of the earrings consisted of a quarter-sized cluster of tiny, rough turquoise stones. They looked rugged, yet elegant, and had a clip on their backs.

"Mom, do you recognize these?" I said, holding them out for inspection.

"Oh, I love those earrings," she said. "They're such a pretty shade of blue... But I haven't worn them in years. I wonder where they've been?"

"When I was five, I watched you getting ready to go to town. You had on a nice dress. As I watched, you looked into the mirror, trying on one piece of jewelry, then another, finally settling on a matching set of earrings and a necklace. I thought you looked so pretty."

Mom looked up. "That's a sweet thing to say, Kerry."

"So I asked you, 'Can I wear some jewelry, too?'"

"What did I say?"

"You hesitated a bit, then tested my resolve, asking, 'Are you sure that's what you want to do?'"

"Oohh! Now I remember! You insisted that you wanted to wear my jewelry, so I let you do it... I remember now!" Her eyes were large and bright.

"Yep. So you took your jewelry box down from the chest of drawers and let me look at each piece. I turned over each pair of earrings in my hands, wondering which ones would let me be as pretty as you. And I finally settled on this pair of clip-on turquoise earrings," I said, opening my hand again in front of Mom.

"So you remember what happened after that, right?" Mom asked.

"I do."

"You also put on the matching beads," Mom said before stopping for a breath. "...I wonder what happened to those? Anyway...we went to town and parked on Plymouth Street, and you got out of the car...and I held your hand as we walked down the sidewalk to go to the store."

I laughed as I remembered what came next.

Mom continued telling me her version of events. "I saw a well-dressed man walking toward us on the sidewalk… And sure enough, he glanced down at you and frowned…then glanced up at me and pursed his lips, then back down to you…as he walked past… I felt your little hand grip mine more tightly…but I didn't say anything.

"I remember feeling that something wasn't right," I added. "But I didn't know exactly what. So I asked if we could go back to the car, and I took everything off and put it under the backseat."

We each had a broad, silent smile as we warmly remembered that moment shared by just the two of us nearly five decades past.

"Why did you let me do that, Mom?"

"Do what?"

"Wear women's jewelry to town."

"What should I have done? That's what you wanted to do. That's who you were." She looked down into the trove of trinkets for the friend she sought, as she continued to talk. "What else would I have done?"

"Were you embarrassed?"

"No. I wasn't embarrassed… It was certainly unusual, but isn't that what… Oh, look what I found, Kerry. I found it!" Mom held up a gorgeous pair of earrings with translucent stones the color of spring. "This is the first piece of jewelry your dad ever gave me…after my wedding ring."

A sense of sadness settled over her as the emerald-green stones transported her further back in time. Her face relaxed and the corners of her mouth drooped as she stared at the paired earrings in her hands. After Dad's death, she searched for ways to remain connected, wearing his flannel shirts and wedding ring. And now, as we sat together, looking for companions for lonesome earrings, the very first match she made reunited her with her spouse.

"What was the occasion?"

"It was when Mike was born."

"Those look like real emeralds. Are they?"

"Well, they're real to me! But I don't think they are… Most of this stuff is just costume jewelry… A lot of it came from the Avon lady… But these are my jewels, nonetheless." She squeezed the pair tightly in her hand before giving them to me.

I placed both the turquoise and the emerald pairs gingerly into an empty bin.

"So why did Dad give you emerald earrings?"

"That's Mike's birthstone. He was born in May… Of course, that's my birthstone, too."

The moment passed as I listened to my brother's grandfather clock chime the top of the hour in the next room. Mom and I silently scanned the scattered earrings, seeking to reunite more pairs. I picked up a post earring shaped like a delicate gold leaf. A cluster of iridescent pink and blue stones shimmered in the center of the hammered metal leaf as I moved the earring back and forth in the soft morning light. It had been a frosty night, and now-melted dew still clung to the corners of the window glass beside us.

Mom seemed deep in thought as her hands rested together in her lap and she stared absentmindedly at her treasures on the table.

"You know, Mike is the most like your dad," she said without looking up. "He's as solid and honest as they come… He loved the farm as much as Mick… It's no surprise he chose to live in the country on his own small farm…and plant that forest of trees…and collect all those tractors!" She smiled at the memories of her firstborn. "And…he was a good Ag teacher, too! I don't know why he stopped doing that… But you know what?"

"Nope. What?"

"Most of all, I think he's a great father to his four boys… Both he and Suzanne did well… Those boys turned out to be fine men. One of them is a teacher, too! You know, I always thought I could've been a teacher."

"I found it!" I blurted when I saw the shiny golden leaf from the jumble of jewelry. They rattled together in my hand as I placed the pair in a bin.

"I'd better get looking," Mom said as her hand floated over the table. She selected a single French wire adornment with a dangling diamond-shape, faced with swirls of blues and the sheen of mother-of-pearl.

"You kids have really turned out well," Mom said as she browsed the table for the companion of the earring in her hand. "When Mike and Pat were growing up…they were two peas in a pod."

As Mom contemplated her children, I picked out my next gem and began to search for its lookalike. It was a post earring with a smooth, deep-blue ball, faced with a delicate pink flower and miniature green leaves, dangling from a tiny gold bead.

"Pat is so smart!" Mom shared without prompting. "And he's got such smart kids, too! All four of them… Some of them are engineers, I think."

"Yeah, Jennifer and Sarah are both engineers," I said. "You know, when Pat got his first engineering degree that inspired me to do the same when I went to college."

"You two had an unusual connection for a while… Pat was always so curious and mischievous…and you guys did stuff together you probably shouldn't have."

I smiled, but remained silent, thinking of more than one well-known story that involved Pat and me and the police.

"I found it! I found another match." I held my hand open so Mom could see the pair of vibrant blue earrings with the sparkling pink flowers.

"Good for you," she said. "How many have you found so far?"

"Just two pairs."

"How many have I found?"

"Just one. But it was an important one. It was the emeralds Dad gave you."

"I did? Where are they?"

"I put them in the bin for safe-keeping."

Mom nodded, apparently satisfied. Then she said, "Those you just found with the pink flowers…are really pretty. I think Janet would like those."

"No, Mom. It's *Jyoti*."

"What's Jyoti?"

"Janet changed her name to Jyoti a long time ago."

"Why did she do that?" she asked, looking over the top of her glasses. "Janet was a perfectly good name… I named her myself."

"Jyoti means 'divine light' in India. She…" Mom had known Jyoti's history, of course, but to re-explain the long story of my sister's connection with the Indian culture and her name change seemed unnecessary, so I let it drop.

"Regardless," Mom said, "those earrings you found remind me of her… She loves flowers so much…and she's so gregarious. She's a people-person… And colors! Boy, does she like color in her life… She was always a free spirit…and kind of rebelled against normalcy." Mom sighed as she stared blankly at the puzzle of separated partners on the table. "You know, I think of all the kids, Janet is most like me… And she raised those two girls all by herself…like Mama did for us after Daddy left… And her two girls turned out to be beautiful young women… All you kids have just turned out so well… I don't how it happened, but you did."

"Hey, look what I found!" Mom cried with new energy. In one hand she held the dangling diamond shape with swirls of blue, and in the other hand was its twin. "Ta-da! How many have I matched now?"

"That's two for you and two for me. But we're not competing, Mom."

Just then, Donna knocked on the door and stepped just inside the bedroom. She wore a jacket and held car keys in one hand.

"I'm getting ready to run some errands. Mom, do you need anything?"

Mom slowly turned her stiff body in Donna's direction, but still couldn't see her. "Nothing that I can think of," she responded.

"Okay. Kerry, if something comes up, just give me a call. I won't be far away," Donna said.

"Okay. Thanks," I replied. "We're just sitting here exploring life."

Donna chuckled, turned, and disappeared.

As I looked at the table scattered with Mom's jewelry, I realized how true my offhand comment to Donna had been. Each of Mom's earrings had been purchased and worn in different seasons of her life. Over the years, she lovingly touched each one, deciding what to wear based on how she felt or looked that day. Each earring brought joy to her life and made her feel special. And now I was reliving those seasons with her, holding in my hands what she once held in hers, listening to the beauty her jewels brought to mind.

Mom interrupted my daydream. "Are you still looking?"

"Yes," I replied, picking up an unusual earring that caught my eye. "Look at this one. It's made of bone."

I showed Mom the French wire earring with a loop of small white bone pieces dangling from it. She tilted her head back slightly to get a better look through her trifocal glasses.

"No, that's not bone, Kerry…that's tiny bits of shell… Coral, I think."

"Oh. Well, it looks like bone."

"I don't remember where I got that one… But I thought of Tom just now…when I saw it."

"Tom? What does he have to do with coral earrings?"

"Nothing… But you said it looked like bone, and that's Tom."

"Because he's a chiropractor?"

"Of course! He's done such good for the world…fixing people up, helping them get well… If you don't have your health…" she said, slowly shaking her head, "…you just don't have life… Tom brings back life. He's certainly done that for me… I don't know what I would've done without him… And Donna, too, of course… They've made our lives more comfortable as we prepare to die."

Mom turned and looked out the window at a red cardinal sitting on the bird feeder and sighed. We both knew her winter was drawing to a close. Her words about dying weighed heavy on my heart. I felt thankful to just linger peacefully in my mother's presence. I didn't want it to end.

Mom turned back to me. "How many kids does Tom have?"

"Four: Matt, Katie, Allison, and Nick."

"That's right," she said, nodding. "And we now have two chiropractors in the family...since Matt graduated... And Katie comes over to visit with me most days...and brings her little boy with her... This family has certainly given me life."

I realized I had been sitting still just listening to Mom speak and hadn't looked for the mate to the white coral in my hands. Mom had also been lost in her reflections of gratitude, but soon turned back to the search for pairs. I saw her pick up a single earring that looked like a petite Christmas wreath. Instead of greenery, the wreath was woven with gold. Instead of holly berries, spiraling rows of turquoise, ruby, and emerald colored stones adorned its surface. I remembered her frequently wearing those when I was a child because the colors complemented so many of her outfits. But I had my own match to find, so I kept looking.

"I found another pair! Here's the other coral earring," I said, holding up the jagged pair between two fingers.

Mom smiled without looking up from the spread of earrings before us.

I grabbed another orphan to find its companion. "Have you heard from Julie lately?" I asked after a bit.

"No. I don't think so...I don't know where they're at," Mom said, shaking her head while she searched.

"Donna said she and her boys were just here last weekend."

"Oh, well, then maybe they were... Sometimes I forget... Julie's got smart boys, though. I always knew she'd have smart kids... I always told her that. She's got smart kids... All you kids are so smart... I don't know how you got that way," she said with a smile that looked like a wink.

"I don't know either, Mom. I guess we're just lucky," I replied, hoping she heard the irony in my voice.

"It wasn't her fault, you know."

I looked up. "Fault about what?"

"You know. With Dad," she said, returning my gaze. "She didn't think Mick loved her...because he seldom paid attention to her... But that's not true... He did love her. He just didn't know how... And there were other things...but it wasn't her fault. He loved her."

I let out a long sigh but was otherwise silent. Mom's eyes seemed to study the table again as she spoke slowly. "It always hurt me when she...shared those feelings with me... She has such a tender heart... I know what it's like to grow up without a father... But there wasn't much I could do... And you know, Dad didn't show much affection to me either...when you kids were growing up... But Julie was there for me... I could tell her about anything as she got older...and she'd listen... I know she didn't always appreciate me calling her...when I felt so lonely... But I didn't know what else to do... She helped me get through some dark times... I hope she knows that."

"Have you told her, Mom?"

"Told her what?"

"How much you appreciate what she did for you?"

"Who?"

"Julie!"

"I don't know. Maybe...I don't know."

Mom looked down at the scattered earrings, still absentmindedly searching for the duplicate "wreath" while I picked up a large bamboo hoop. Within seconds, I found its tan counterpart, put them in a bin, and picked out another, shaped like a curved feather. Inside the dark brown curvature, the spine and delicate feather-like fingers were made of gold, with a translucent aquamarine stone mounted at the top. With its distinct size and shape, I quickly found its lookalike and set it inside a bin.

"Mom, how are you coming along with that wreath? Do you need some help?"

"What wreath?"

"The one in your hand. You're looking for its mate. Do you need some help?"

"Oh. Sure you can help me... I didn't know that's what I was looking for," she said, glancing at the lonesome earring in her hand.

I surveyed the table for the wreath's double instead of picking up a new earring for my own search. But I was troubled. Mom had spoken about all her kids but me. I wanted to hear what she thought of me, but I was reluctant to ask.

"Oh, look, Mom. I found it." I gently took the one from Mom's hand and placed the two together side-by-side in a bin, then grabbed another at random.

"Mom, do you want to keep looking, or are you getting tired?"

"Sure. Which one should I look for?"

"Can you help me find this one?" I held out the one I had just picked up. It was a snap-on earring with a cluster of small discs of mother-of-pearl. Depending on the angle, the disks shimmered blue, pink, green, or just white.

As we searched together, my heart ached to hear what Mom might have to say about me. *After all, this may be the last face-to-face conversation we'll ever have,* I thought. I finally summoned the courage to ask her what was on my mind.

"Mom, what about me? What do you think about when you think about me?"

Mom sighed again and took in as much breath as the fluid in her lungs allowed. Her shoulders drooped. I could tell she was getting tired and wondered if I should have pushed her.

She looked into my eyes and said, "Well, you're a go-getter… You've always been that way. And you're smart… All you kids are smart… I don't know how it turned out that way… I thought you were going to be our valedictorian…I always wanted in the family." Mom's voice started to sound a bit gravely.

"Well, I came pretty close, Mom."

"I know… I'm not disappointed in you… And you're going to change the world. I just know it… And your daughter…she's a crackerjack… She's already changing the world…bringing all those water wells to Africa… She's just like you, you know."

I sat quietly, soaking in her words, holding back tears as she continued.

"And when you get tired of being an engineer…you know what I think you're going to do?" Mom's gaze never left my face.

"No," I murmured.

"I think you're going to be…a teacher…or writer."

"Well, I've been teaching Sunday school for nearly fifteen years."

"I know! And you're good at it! You have a gift… I also think you have a gift for writing… Maybe you'll write a book someday."

"Yeah…maybe. What would I write about?"

"Well, I don't know… But it will be about something you love… And when you do, it'll be a good one… I'll buy the first copy."

"You got a deal, Mom. I might even sign it for you," I said with a smile, as I turned and wiped away a tear.

"I miss you, Kerry… You live so far away," she said as she glanced out the window. "I don't get to see you often enough." Mom sighed again and cleared her throat. She was struggling to breathe.

"There is something I regret, though," Mom said, turning back toward me.

"What's that?"

"I don't think I told you kids enough…that I loved you."

"Mom, you *never* told me that you loved me… Well, I take that back. You told me once, years ago when you were taking antidepressants."

"Well, I'm sorry about that… That's one of my regrets," she said softly, looking at her hands resting in her lap.

"But you *showed* me you loved me, Mom. Many times," I said, as tears welled up again in my eyes.

"I did? When did I do that?"

I sat up in my chair. "Well, when I was seven years old and you let me bake that pie by myself for the first time."

"I didn't *let* you do that… You just did it while I was on the phone."

"And when you woke me up in the middle of the night to see the Northern Lights."

"I woke anyone who would get up."

"But you made it feel like it was just for you and me. But when you made me take piano lessons," I chuckled, "that didn't feel like love at the time. But it does now."

Mom sat listening and didn't respond, as I continued.

"And you know what else? Best of all, you let me be me, when I was growing up. You let me be the boy God made me to be; then challenged me to be just a little bit better. That's a pretty big love, Mom."

A few tears rolled down my cheeks, and I sniffled as I stared out the window at the naked trees. I felt Mom's winter drawing to a close.

"Mom, what do you think your legacy will be?" I asked, after I wiped my face and turned back toward her.

She didn't hesitate to answer, as if she'd thought about that question her entire life.

"My legacy is you, Kerry," she replied, gesturing toward me with one hand. "And all your brothers and sisters... My family is my legacy... Some people leave a treasure chest...filled with diamonds... But you are my jewels... And I'm so proud of what each of you has become...and your children... I can leave this world knowing I've done my job... But you know what? My legacy is in the *past*... I'm looking forward to the *future*... That will be a glorious time when I can...glimpse the face of God... That is my hope and that is my future."

CHAPTER 35

Spring Awaits

In the bulb there is a flower; in the seed, an apple tree;
In cocoons, a hidden promise: butterflies will soon be free!
In the cold and snow of winter there's a spring that waits to be,
Unrevealed until its season, something God alone can see.

There's a song in every silence, seeking word and melody;
There's a dawn in every darkness, bringing hope to you and me.
From the past will come the future; what it holds, a mystery,
Unrevealed until its season, something God alone can see.

In our end is our beginning; in our time, infinity;
In our doubt there is believing; in our life, eternity,
In our death, a resurrection; at the last, a victory,
Unrevealed until its season, something God alone can see.

—"Hymn of Promise." Words & music: Natalie Sleeth,
© 1986 Hope Publishing Company, Carol Stream, IL
60188. All rights reserved. Used by permission.

B ands of snow slithered across the highway like snakes, fleeing the bitter cold in one drift only to be entombed by another. As I drove, they reminded me of the anguish I could not escape. It was midday, but a deep gray descended like a pall around us. Wind buffeted the car as I clicked the headlights between high and low beams, hoping one would illuminate more of the road and less of the blinding snow.

"Gloria, could you turn on the radio and see if you can find a weather forecast?" I asked.

Before we left our home in Texas and flew to Indiana, the weatherman predicted "The Blizzard of the Century" would hit the Northern Indiana region of my childhood. But we had no choice. We had to be in Bremen by 4:00 p.m. for the visitation.

"Ice has started to accumulate at the airport," the Indianapolis weatherman reported on the radio station Gloria found, "and some flights are being canceled. Hundreds of flights were canceled in Chicago earlier today as this massive storm comes in from the west."

Our plane arrived in Indianapolis only an hour before, just as the storm hit. We now journeyed up Highway 421 in a rental car. While ice brought Indianapolis to a stop, our enemy was snow as we drove one hundred forty miles north to Bremen and the center of the storm.

"Northern Indiana is already experiencing heavy snowfall, with a forecast of up to a foot this afternoon and evening," continued the weatherman. "Winds have picked up and are forecast to reach 50 to 60 miles per hour. Widespread snowdrifts of two to five feet are expected, with deeper drifts in some locations. Temperatures will remain below freezing through Wednesday."

It was Tuesday, February 1—the dead of winter. Unaccustomed to such winter driving, my knuckles stiffened from my firm grip on the wheel. I released my right hand and flexed my fingers as I reached down to shut off the radio. Gloria turned to face me, silently searching for emotional clues.

"Dad, is it going to be okay?" Elizabeth asked from the backseat. I could hear the child-like fear in her voice although she was a senior in high school.

"I think so. The road looks worse than it is. It's not slippery and we'll be at the funeral home before it gets too bad… I just don't know what it's going to be like, though, for other folks coming to the visitation tonight." I cleared my throat. "I guess we'll see."

Although my outward demeanor may have reassured Elizabeth, inside my heart and mind were in a sorrowful dance with my mother's death. As my family and I rode together in silence, I'm certain we all contemplated what it meant to lose a grandmother, a mother-in-law, and the North Star in my life.

Propelled by an insatiable desire to learn, experience, and share new things, Mom outlived the expectations of many. But at ninety years of age, she teetered between the life she loved and the life she longed for. So the recent call I received from Tom was not a surprise. As I drove toward the funeral home, our conversation replayed in my mind.

It was Friday night, and Gloria and I had just finished watching a movie at home when his call came in.

"Donna and I had been out for the evening, Mike and Suzanne had come to visit Mom while we were out," Tom said, pausing. "Shortly after they left, we got a call from Katie. 'Something's not right with Grandma,' she told us. 'You need to come home.' When we arrived, Mom was restless and distressed. 'I can't breathe,' she told us. So we got her out of bed and helped her over to her chair in the family room where she could sit upright…but that didn't help much. 'I can't breathe. I can't breathe,' she repeated with a strained whisper… Her lungs were filling up with fluid, as we knew they would. Unfortunately, there was nothing we could do about it any longer… We took her blood pressure. It was sixty over thirty," he said, as his voice cracked. "It was almost as if she waited until she visited one last time with her firstborn, and then couldn't hang on any longer."

I let out a long sigh and flipped my headlights from low to high beams several more times, as if that might erase the memory of that conversation. It didn't help.

"The hospice doctor had given us a prescription to ease Mom's anxiety when the time came," Tom said, "so we gave her a dose, and it calmed her down for a little while, and she stopped complaining about not being able to breathe… But then she announced, 'I'm dying.'"

Tears welled up in my eyes as I imagined my mother knowing her death was imminent, wondering how she felt. *Was she frightened?* I blinked to clear my vision as I struggled to see through the increasingly heavy snow and wiped a couple of tears from my cheek. The only sound was the hum of the tires and the occasional "whoosh" when they hit deeper snow.

"She said, 'I'm dying, I'm dying,' and became re-agitated... So I got one of her CDs we brought from her house and put it in the player. It was slow and peaceful—beautiful piano music, one of her favorites... That seemed to calm her some, and then her blood pressure dropped to forty over thirty, and she told us one last time...'I'm dying.'"

"Donna and I just sat there with Mom...one of us on each side...and held her hands as we said goodbye and she slipped away."

I inhaled and pursed my lips tightly, unsuccessfully fighting tears. Gloria noticed when I wiped my face once more.

"You okay, Kerry?" she asked as she placed a hand on my right thigh. "I'd offer to drive, but I don't think I can do it in this weather. I've never driven in snow."

"Can you give me a tissue, please? I'll be fine," I sighed.

The snowfall was getting heavier and the empty white fields looked like a moonscape. I turned on the wipers. I shook my head and tried to knock loose the thoughts of Mom's death. I tried to replace them with thoughts of what lay ahead. Living in Texas, so far away from Mom and Dad, always limited my ability to help them. That caused those who lived nearby to shoulder most of the responsibility, which always weighed on my conscience. So it was an honor when I was asked to prepare an obituary for the newspaper, plan Mom's service with the Oak Grove preacher, and deliver the eulogy. I was able to do those things from afar before we left home, while my siblings handled other responsibilities of death. *But how is this blizzard going to affect tomorrow's service?* I wondered.

Writing the obituary was not particularly difficult. I just copied the format from my father's, whom we buried eight months prior, and changed the personal details to fit my mother. But the eulogy was an altogether different challenge.

With my eyes on the snow-covered road, my mind reexamined the struggles I had encountered over the past three days. *How do I describe the fullness of my mother's life? How do I identify what's important to share? What can I say to let others know, really know, this person I loved? How do I tell her story in a way that honors her, and is meaningful for those left behind?* And to make it more challenging, I had five siblings who each had their own ideas about what should be included. Although I was privileged to eulogize my mother, it also felt like a task where I was guaranteed to fall short. I reminded myself that what's said after a person dies is not nearly as important as the life already lived. There was nothing I could say that would change the goodness that Mom brought to so many others…and me. *My eulogy will merely be the period at the end of the sentence of her life.*

As we got closer to Bremen, we encountered fewer and fewer sets of headlights. Snow was now accumulating on the edges of the windshield, beyond the reach of the wipers. But the anxiety of driving was quickly being buried by the trepidation of seeing Mom lying in her casket.

There was a part of me that felt all this might not be true; that it hadn't happened; that she wasn't really dead. But I knew when I saw her lifeless body in the casket that I would no longer be able to deny the truth. I would have to let go of this fifty-year relationship with the mother I loved and grasp a new life without her in it. I knew I needed to face the truth and see my mother one last time.

As we pulled into Mishler Funeral Home, my heart raced and tears welled up in my eyes once more. I shifted in my seat to regain my emotional center. The mostly-empty parking lot was covered in snow, hiding the painted lines. The only cars I saw belonged to my siblings, and I followed their snow tracks to find a place to park.

With the angst of driving now gone, the anxiety of seeing my mother, lifeless in a coffin, was crushing. I had been imagining this moment for miles. There was no turning back. Knots twisted in my stomach, threatening to break through.

"I'm going in," I announced to no one in particular, as I flung open my door and stepped from the car without waiting for Gloria and

Elizabeth. Gusts of ice-cold wind shocked my uncovered head, sending chills through my body and nearly knocking me off my feet as I picked my way through the drifting snow to the funeral home's front doors. My mother was somewhere inside, waiting for me.

Fighting the wind, I pulled the cold handle of a large white door and entered the calmness within.

There was a small room on the left and at the end of that room I saw my mother, just thirty feet away, surrounded by flowers. Though there were clusters of family standing around talking, I was pulled past them by the gravity of death, rushing to say goodbye to my mother. Within seconds, I bent over her casket, clasped one of her hands with mine and slipped my other under her shoulder in an awkward hug.

Hot, salty tears fell to her bosom, leaving stains of sorrow on her blouse.

My chest shuddered. I took a deep breath and stood upright, looking at Mom lying peacefully in her lace-lined casket. I stared into her bespectacled face, which seemed asleep in sweet dreams. She wore a cream-colored blouse festooned with patterns of orange, yellow, and pink flowers, and strands of green leaves. The white pearl buttons on her blouse matched her pearl earrings and necklace. Tears flowed freely when I realized how her colorful outfit was so appropriate for the colorful life she led.

I slipped both of my hands under both of Mom's and squeezed them tightly, as I lowered my head and closed my wet eyes. Mom's hands were dry, stiff and cool, but as I clung tightly, I sensed the presence of the life they once brought. My mind flooded with memories.

Mom, yours are the hands that cuddled me late at night when we discovered the mouse, which sang only for us. These hands cradled our beloved rooster, Blackie White Feather, and stroked the feathered cheeks of Baby, our owl. Your hands erased the pain of my aching head through tender massage of my feet and pointed out my new friends in the sky. And these same hands threw apple cores and banana peels in a fun-filled fight... Mom, your hands also brought you joy as they floated beautifully over the ivory keys, nourishing your soul with song, then flew furiously across your Underwood releasing your soul to the typed word. And yours are the same hands, Mom, I grasped on Christmas Eve as we shared a moment of hope in the Christ we worshipped.

I took a deep breath and let it out slowly as I opened my eyes and raised my head. I felt changed, somehow. While holding Mom's hands, life replaced death. I released my grip and gently laid her hands across her waist once more, then dried my eyes. Yes, Mom was asleep in death. It was true. But I felt peace.

I sighed deeply once more, and then turned around to see what had only been a blur when I entered the space. The modest windowless room was softly lit. Mom's casket was at one end, with a backdrop of pastel draperies. The sweet fragrance of flowers lingered in the air. Pictures sat on small tables on the periphery, accompanied by Mom's wedding dress, and other personal possessions. I walked around the room and hugged family members as visitors began to arrive.

A few folks from Oak Grove Church showed up, followed by friends of my siblings who lived nearby, then neighbors. They brought expressions of condolence, memories of Mom, and regular updates on the blizzard. There were reports of neighbors who were already socked in by drifting snow and couldn't get down their long lanes. Another neighbor reported sliding off the road into the ditch and being rescued by a Good Samaritan on his tractor.

Mrs. Bellman, my fourth-grade teacher and neighbor approached me as I stood receiving greeters.

"Kerry, I'm so sorry for your loss," she began, reaching to grasp my hands. She had a pleasant face with ample laugh lines. "Your mom was a good person and an even better mother."

"Thank you, Mrs. Bellman. I appreciate your kind words."

"So what are you doing now? Where are you living?"

As I shared a brief update of my life, I noticed Tom approach and waited patiently until Mrs. Bellman left.

"The storm's getting worse, Kerry," Tom said with trepidation. "Before long, even the highways will probably be shut down."

"I believe it. It was scary driving up here."

"And it's forecast to continue through the night. There's no way we're going to be able to hold Mom's service tomorrow," he added.

"What would we do then?"

"We think we should have the service tonight."

"Can we do that?"

"You're the one who planned it. That's a question for you."

"Well, the preacher won't be able to get down the country roads to get here."

"I can get him in my truck," said Tom. "It's four-wheel drive with a snowplow on front."

"Well...I've got my eulogy and CD with music sitting in the car. So I guess we could... What about chairs and stuff?"

"Mishler's said they can set up the room right away."

"Okay. Then let's do it."

By the time the service began, only the hardiest of souls remained. It was mostly family, with a handful of neighbors and friends. An elegant oak and brass podium was set up next to Mom's casket, and Rev. Skaggs stood there in his black suit and greeted the gathering. He told us he'd only been Mom's pastor for ten years and recounted a few memories. He then lifted a prayer of thanksgiving for our mother's life.

When he finished, Rev. Skaggs invited others to share a reflection. Jyoti and Tom stood and shared enlightening stories, as did several cousins. After everyone took their seats, the CD that I'd brought for the service began to play. I sat in silence with everyone else, with my head bowed as the melodic voice of a female soloist pierced the air.

Amazing grace! How sweet the sound
That saved a wretch like me!
I once was lost, but now am found;
Was blind, but now I see.

The singer's voice was haunting, clear, and angelic. I felt as if she sang just to me, telling my story of redemption. "Amazing Grace" was my favorite song, and I chose it for Mom's service partly for that reason. As the next verse began, a deep solitary piano accompanied the soloist, emphasizing the emotions of the words.

Through many dangers, toils and snares,
I have already come;
'Tis grace hath brought me safe thus far,
And grace will lead me home.

This was one of Mom's favorite songs, too. She took comfort in such music. It settled her soul. She had overcome so much in her life, propelled by the promise of the resurrection. God's amazing grace had blessed both of us, first by opening my eyes, then by leading Mom home. This was now *our* song.

When the music stopped, it was time for my eulogy. I believed that when I finished, my mother's story would be over. I prayed it would honor her and comfort those who grieved. I opened my eyes, took a deep breath, and stepped to the podium. I smiled at the folks in the room who chose to be there in the midst of a storm. Then I looked down at my notes and began to share with them the mother that only my siblings and I knew.

"In times such as these," I said, raising one hand, "we often contemplate God's amazing grace as we turn to our Creator—for comfort for the grieving, and for thankfulness for the life that we honor. By design, we all must leave this life, of course. In Ecclesiastes 3, we learn:

There is a time for everything, and a season for every activity
under the heavens:
A time to sow and a time to reap,
A time to tear down and a time to build,
A time to be born and a time to die.

"In death, some of us are blessed with a quick and painless passing, as my father experienced this past June. But some, like my mother, diminish more slowly, seemingly turning back time as they change from an independent adult to a more child-like state, dependent again on others for care. Although this can be an agonizing period, it seems somehow quite natural, as the parent first cares for the children, guiding them gently into adulthood, and then the roles reverse as the children guide their parent back to her future.

"As my mother aged, time and disease took its toll on both her body and mind. But as she entered the winter season of her life, she was blessed—indeed we all were blessed that she had my brother, Tom, his wife, Donna, and their adult daughter, Katie, to care for her. Tom and Donna took my mother into their home, gave up their own bed, and saw to her constant needs—from bathing, dressing, eating, seeing to her medical care, and staying up with her through troubled nights. Serving our mother's needs around the clock, Donna has been a true saint as she carried out most of this responsibility. For many months, her and my brother's lives took an uncharted path, as Mom enjoyed the comforts of family and hearth, and the circle of life was completed."

I paused and looked up from my notes and gazed at Tom and Donna, sitting in the front row. "On behalf of the entire family, we'd like to thank each of you, and especially sister Donna, for this tremendous gift you gave Mom and the rest of us."

I sensed both relief and grief in Tom's face, his eyes glistening with tears.

"But as we mourn the passing of our mother, grandmother, sister, aunt, and friend, let us also reflect on, and be thankful for, the many blessings she brought us."

I explained to the small gathering how Mom's childhood experiences left indelible imprints on her life, especially her love of nature, which sprang from her time on her grandparents' farm.

"With an eye for beauty, she grew colorful gardens of fragrant flowers around our home. From roses to lilies, flowers were ever-present. Even the winters found towering red amaryllis growing indoors. She crafted a flowing rock garden down a gentle slope behind our house, pretty enough to inspire my sister to get married there."

I looked up from my notes at Jyoti, sitting just feet away. The memory of Mom's beautiful flowers, so much like her own, brought a broad smile to her face.

"Bold colors symbolized Mom's life," I continued, "bursting forth in collections of blue glass, Flamingo Red walls, and dozens of festive earrings."

I shared how Mom's respect for God's creation extended to the animal kingdom, with stories of Blackie White Feather, Baby, and an unusual assortment of rats, rabbits, and ducks. And how she was often ahead of her time, advocating for healthier food and drink for our family.

"Long before Perrier and Evian, our mother was a fan of bottled spring water. Of course, it didn't come from the store. It was fetched directly from a spring and put into one-gallon glass jugs and hauled home. This water, affectionately known as 'mineral water,' was supposed to have a multitude of health benefits, although the rest of us felt we were too good to drink it. Little did we know, we could have become filthy rich if we had thought about selling it. But back then, who thought anyone would pay good money for something you could get free from the tap?

"Mom could see the future and wasn't afraid to pursue it. As pioneers frequently are—she was sometimes ridiculed for not being like everyone else—especially by us kids. Although she may have embarrassed *us* at times, we were a great source of pride for *her*. She breathed into us a certain intellect and an inquisitive nature, believing we all grew up to be responsible adults—although that remains open for debate."

Soft laughter jostled around the room. I paused and noticed Mike and Pat chuckling, joy in their smiles.

I looked back at my notes and went on to share tales of scientific experiments she tolerated, Northern Lights she revealed, and her devil-may-care attitude, which brought warm memories of a garbage fight inside our home.

"One time, Mom asked my sister, Julie, why she chose to hang out and go shopping with her, even though Julie was a teenager. Mom remarked that teenagers are not supposed to like their parents. But because of Mom's playful spirit, Julie said she'd rather be with Mom than with her own friends. As her children, we were richly blessed by our mother and have much for which to be thankful."

I looked up at Julie on the end of the front row. Though her heart still grieved, I could see tears of gratitude in her eyes, as she nodded enthusiastically. Then I took a deep breath and looked around the room before giving voice to the reason we were there.

"Mom loved music, especially from stringed instruments, and found pleasure in playing piano for most of her life. This past Friday, Mom died quietly doing what she enjoyed—listening to beautiful piano music.

"She was also a lover of the written word, treasuring books, newspapers, and magazines. As a result, she was a living reference library—the first Google before we had the Internet. She had a rich vocabulary with a strong grasp of grammar and didn't hesitate to correct a speaker's word use. Until just a few years ago, she continued to correct my use of 'I' when I should have said 'me.'

"But writing held a special place in Mom's heart. She wrote lovely poetry, prayers, memories, and adventurous fictional short stories— works of art created for the enjoyment of writing. A few of her titles were: 'New Zealand My Beloved,' 'Winter Dawn,' and 'Survival!'. Here is a sample of one her poems called 'The Chickadee.' It starts like this:

> *The cheeky, chirring chickadee*
> *Is as cheerful as he can be.*
> *He darts, he dips*
> *And grabs his seed.*
> *He gives me lip*
> *Though I fill his need.*

I smiled as I described her tale closest to my heart. "And my favorite story is called 'The Night the Mouse Sang'. It chronicles a magical moment when I was snuggled with my mother in our darkened house, rocking in a chair at one a.m., being serenaded by a melodious mouse."

"As a prolific writer, one of Mom's lifelong aspirations was to publish a book. Although a niece recently packaged one of Mom's stories to resemble a published work, bringing her great pleasure near the end of life, Mom's dream remains unfulfilled."

I paused and looked earnestly into the eyes of the small group of neighbors and family who honored our mother. Though a storm raged outside, I sensed peace in the room. The ending of Mom's story was just moments away, but it also marked the beginning of an even greater tale—her sequel of hope.

"My mother descended from a long line of preachers, extending to her father. Spiritual faith was the foundation of her life. Pursuing Biblical truth was in her blood. That truth inspired her to look forward to the resurrection, God's ultimate amazing grace.

"Today, her winter season of life has ended, but she awaits the new spring, with the renewing of life and relationships, when Christ breaks the bonds of death and she touches the face of God.

"Amen."

Acknowledgments

I t's said it takes a village to raise a child, and I believe it. It also takes a village to write a book. At least in my case. Some writers are blessed with beautiful prose that easily flows from their minds to the pages. That's not me. I work hard to bring interesting thoughts to print; I can't do it alone. This book would not have been birthed without the support of many people.

My daughter Elizabeth meticulously transcribed Mom's two hundred "The Party Line" interviews from forty-year-old, difficult-to-read articles lifted from *The Bremen Enquirer*. After my parents died and my siblings did all the hard work of cleaning out our parents' home and preparing it for sale, they dutifully set aside Mom's other writings for me.

When it came time to write, I joined the San Gabriel Writers League to learn where to start. There, Janet Kilgore agreed to mentor me without even being asked, and supported me in many ways throughout the entire process. We discussed the craft of writing and the tools and techniques, and she pointed me toward the Writers' League of Texas. I took many of their classes, including one that planted the seed for the book's structure.

I interviewed many family members to gather their memories, including siblings Mike, Pat, Jyoti, Tom, and Julie, plus some of their children, including Theodore, Benjamin, Zachary, Sarah, Matt, and Katie. My Aunt Joy and cousins Debby and Dawn also provided valuable insight, as did childhood neighbors Ruth, Burt, and Bryan Manges, and my parents' last pastor at Oak Grove Church, Kevin Skaggs.

My wife, Gloria, patiently waited as I sat alone writing in my home office for more than two years. Then these early readers critiqued what I wrote, offering invaluable advice: Kris Beavers, Howard Hatfield, Catherine Castoro, Teresa Bitner, Don Guerrant, Janet Kilgore, Jyoti Rae, plus family members whose lives appear in the book.

Mindy Reed, Danylle Salinas, and Danielle Acee from The Authors' Assistant, smoothed out the rough spots of my manuscript, turning it into a more appealing story with their skilled editing and interior design. Jane Dixon Smith, from JD Smith Design, captured the emotional meaning of my mother's life to create a beautiful cover.

Each of these people left an indelible impression on me and the book you've read. I am forever grateful for the gifts they, and others, shared so I could honor the mother I love. To all I say, "Thank you! And my mother thanks you. May your own journeys be so richly blessed."

Notes

If you enjoyed reading *Forever Herself,* please consider leaving a review on Amazon, Goodreads, or another readers' site.

A variety of book club discussion questions are available for free download at www.kerrylstevens.com.

SPRING

Chapter 2: Stolen Dreams

[1]Proverbs 27:17

[2]The Auctioneers Chant: http://rmfarm.tripod.com/chant.html

Chapter 3: Broken Promises

[1]http://www.elkhartcountyhistory.org/exhibits/online/; http://www.amishcountry.org/explore-the-area/area-history/; http://www.u-s-history.com/pages/h2267.html; https://en.wikipedia.org/wiki/Elkhart,_Indiana

[2]Matthew 6:34a NRSV

Chapter 4: Heaven's Borderland

[1]The hymn derives from the King James Version of Isaiah 62:4; "Thou shalt no more be termed Forsaken; neither shall thy land any more be termed Desolate; but thou shalt be called Hephzibah and thy land Beulah; for the LORD delighteth in thee, and thy land shall be married."

Chapter 5: In the Beginning

[1]http://www.ohiohistorycentral.org/w/Charles_Osborn; http://ncpedia.org/biography/osborn-charles; http://www.porterhistory.org/2016/10/charles-osborn-father-of-abolitionists.html

[2]http://pastorRussell.blogspot.com/2009/07/pastor-Russell.html; Circulation from http://www.bible411.com/publishers-forward/; "About the Author": https://www.amazon.com/Divine-Plan-Ages-Charles-Russell/dp/0972824308/ref=sr_1_1?s=books&ie=UTF8&qid=1484759428&sr=1-1; https://en.wikipedia.org/wiki/Charles_Taze_Russell; Broad information taken from *The Divine Plan for the Ages*, by Pastor Taze Russell

[3]Isaiah 30:26 KJV

SUMMER

Chapter 7: Freedom Unlocked

[1]https://en.wikipedia.org/wiki/Potawatomi_Trail_of_Death; *South Bend Tribune*, "Michiana" magazine, "All about Bremen", Sept. 28, 1986

Chapter 12: D is for Didactic

[1]Exodus 20:12, paraphrased

Chapter 15: Crisis and Credibility

[1]https://en.wikipedia.org/wiki/Polio_vaccine; http://www.history.com/news/8-things-you-may-not-know-about-jonas-salk-and-the-polio-vaccine
[2]https://en.wikipedia.org/wiki/History_of_chiropractic
[3]http://www.npr.org/sections/health-shots/2012/10/16/162670836/wiping-out-polio-how-the-u-s-snuffed-out-a-killer; https://www.cdc.gov/features/poliofacts/
[4]https://en.wikipedia.org/wiki/Elizabeth_Kenny
[5]Ibid

Chapter 16: Au Naturel

[1]John 9:1-12

FALL

Chapter 20: Riding Through the Rainbow

[1]"Riding Through the Rainbow" was originally published in *Forever Learning Institute Sun*, South Bend, IN, circa 1985

Chapter 22: Spreading Wings

[1]Prayer adapted from p. 39 of "Release My Grip." © 2017 Group Publishing, Inc. Used by permission. All rights reserved. No unauthorized use or duplication permitted.

Chapter 23: Belt of Truth

[1]Broad information taken from *The Divine Plan of the Ages*, by Pastor Taze Russell

Chapter 24: Mirror of Prejudice

[1]"Letter from the Birmingham Jail," https://www.goodreads.com/book/show/203899.Letter_from_the_Birmingham_Jail

Chapter 26: Greed to Grace

[1]2 Corinthians 9:7

[2]From everyone to whom much has been given, much will be required; and from the one to whom much has been entrusted, even more will be demanded. —Luke 12:48b, NRSV

[3]John Newton: https://en.wikipedia.org/wiki/John_Newton

Chapter 28: Matters of the Heart

[1]Revelation 21:4

Chapter 31: The Space Between Us

[1]Genesis 1:1-4, KJV

[2]YouTube: https://www.youtube.com/watch?v=1aIf0G2PtHo&t=421s

[3]Martin Luther King, Jr. and the Global Freedom Struggle: http://kingencyclopedia.stanford.edu/encyclopedia/encyclopedia/enc_strength_to_love_1963/; http://kingencyclopedia.stanford.edu/encyclopedia/encyclopedia/enc_social_gospel/index.html

[4]"Strength to Love" by Martin Luther King, Jr.

[5]"Be ye therefore wise as serpents and harmless as doves."—Matthew 10:16 KJV

[6]*Strength to Love*, by Martin Luther King, Jr

[7]Ibid

[8]Luke 4:14-21

[9]Matthew 25:35-40

[10]Luke 10:25-37

[11]John 14:2-3

[12]Martin Luther King, Jr., "Letter from Birmingham City Jail"

Made in the USA
Middletown, DE
25 January 2019